UNDERSTANDING
WOMEN'S MAGAZINES

Understanding Women's Magazines investigates the changing landscape of women's magazines. Anna Gough-Yates focuses on the successes, failures and shifting fortunes of a number of magazines including *Elle*, *Marie Claire*, *Cosmopolitan*, *Frank*, *New Woman* and *Red* and considers the dramatic developments that have taken place in women's magazine publishing in the last two decades.

Understanding Women's Magazines examines the transformation in the production, advertising and marketing practices of women's magazines. Arguing that these changes were driven by political and economic shifts, commercial cultures and the need to get closer to the reader, the book shows how this has led to an increased focus on consumer lifestyles and attempts by publishers to identify and target a 'New Woman'.

Anna Gough-Yates is Lecturer in the Sociology of Culture and Communication at Brunel University. She is co-editor with Bill Osgerby of *Action TV: Tough Guys, Smooth Operators and Foxy Chicks*, published by Routledge in 2001.

UNDERSTANDING WOMEN'S MAGAZINES

Publishing, markets and readerships

Anna Gough-Yates

Routledge
Taylor & Francis Group

LONDON AND NEW YORK

First published 2003
by Routledge
11 New Fetter Lane, London EC4P 4EE

Simultaneously published in the USA and Canada
by Routledge
29 West 35th Street, New York, NY 10001

Routledge is an imprint of the Taylor & Francis Group

© 2003 Anna Gough-Yates

Typeset in Times by
BOOK NOW Ltd
Printed and bound in Great Britain by
TJ International Ltd, Padstow, Cornwall

British Library Cataloguing in Publication Data
A catalogue record for this book is available from the British Library

Library of Congress Cataloging in Publication Data
Gough-Yates, Anna, 1968–
Understanding women's magazines : publishing, markets and readerships /
Anna Gough-Yates.
p. cm.
Includes bibliographical references and index.
1. Women's periodicals, English–Great Britain–History–20th century. I. Title.

PN5124.W6 G68 2003
051′.082′09410904–dc 21   2002028356

ISBN 0-415-21638-9 (hbk)
ISBN 0-415-21639-7 (pbk)

FOR MY GRANDMA, TEHIAY,
WITH LOVE

CONTENTS

FIGURES

ACKNOWLEDGEMENTS

This book could not have been written without a great deal of help and support from other people. I am grateful for the time and suggestions offered by those working within the women's magazine industry at the start of this project. In particular, I would like to acknowledge the assistance of Karen Clayman and Becky Gee, Jenny Barnett, Victoria Harwood and Mandi Norwood who all offered insights into the business of women's magazines. Many librarians were also important in helping me to track down research material for this project. I would particularly like to convey my gratitude to Helen Evans and Andy Forbes of the Mountbatten Library at Southampton Institute who were always helpful in locating research material, David Doughan and Penny Martin at the Fawcett Library, and the Open Library at the Open University.

I have been fortunate to receive sound advice about this study both in its form as a doctoral thesis and as a book. Acknowledgements are particularly due to Ann Gray who was a superb supervisor for this study in its doctoral form. Jo Van Every and Michael Green also offered significant support and ideas in the (now, regrettably, former) Department of Sociology and Cultural Studies at the University of Birmingham. Acknowledgements are also due to Janice Winship who offered useful comments on this project as a thesis. I would also like to thank Rebecca Barden and Christopher Cudmore at Routledge for taking an interest in this book from its inception, as well as the anonymous readers of an early draft who provided many helpful comments and suggestions.

Special thanks for support are due to current colleagues in the Department of Human Sciences at Brunel University, and in the Arts Faculty and Region 13 of the Open University. Thanks for support are also due to former colleagues in the Department of Cultural Studies at the University of East London. I would also like to thank my friends and family for encouraging me to write, and to take time off from writing – especially Charlotte Bush; Debbi Collis and Glyn Fielding; Kate Denston, Derek, Charlie (and the indefatigable Popeye); and Kevin, Vicki, Josh and Sam Gough-Yates. Above all, I would like to convey my gratitude to Bill Osgerby who has shared ideas, friendship and nachos throughout the life of this book.

The author and publisher would like to thank the following for permission to illustrate this book: EMAP Consumer Magazines for *Elle*, *New Woman*, *Minx*, *Red* and *Frank*; IPC Media for *Honey*, *Options*, and *Marie Claire*, *Cosmopolitan*/copyright © The National Magazine Company for *Cosmopolitan*; copyright © Sian Frances/Times Newspapers Limited, London for the illustration of 'The New Woman'; and Wintour Publications for *Working Woman*. Every effort has been made to obtain permission to reproduce the images in this book. If any proper acknowledgement has not been made, we invite copyright holders to inform us of this oversight.

Figure 1 'The New Woman', *The Times*, 23 May 1988 (copyright © Sian Frances/Times Newspapers Limited, London).

INTRODUCTION

In May 1988, a picture of a women's magazine called *The New Woman* appeared in *The Times*. Like many other women's magazines of the period, a well-groomed, female model beamed cheerily out from its cover. Yet the rest of the magazine did not bear the hallmarks of a typical women's title. To begin with, the woman on the cover was wearing a business suit, and in her hand she held her credit card. Over her shoulder was slung – somewhat incongruously – a bulging sports bag. In the woman's arms was an over-sized, slightly grumpy, wriggling toddler. The cover lines were also unusual. 'Does she want to gain ££££££s?', they asked, and 'Is she seriously glamorous or glamorously serious?' 'Does she think a nanny less expensive than a nervous breakdown?', they wondered, or 'Can she housetrain her high-flying husband?' 'When she gives a dinner party does she cook?' 'Is she fit (or fit to drop)?' (Slaughter, 1988: 21).

The New Woman, of course, never actually appeared on newsagents' shelves. It was a spoof, existing only as an amusing illustration to accompany an article on the changing business of women's magazines. Nevertheless, although the magazine itself was a fiction, the image and sell-lines on the cover can be seen as bringing together many elements of the story of women's magazines in the late twentieth century that this book sets out to tell. As the accompanying article by ex-magazine editor Audrey Slaughter (1988: 21) observed, the women's magazine industry was trying to construct new readerships of women, but there was little agreement about how a 'New Woman' would want to be addressed. According to Slaughter, one new magazine imagined the 'New Woman' as '[s]harp, avid and with a short attention span', wanting a magazine that could provide her with 'information doled out like hormone implants', whilst 'keeping her fit and young while she copes efficiently with her career and her marriage' (Slaughter, 1988: 21). Another believed her to be 'a worrier', 'agonizing over whether she is being selfish if *her* preference, *her* television programmes, *her* wishes have priority, requiring reassurance that her needs are valid and important' (Slaughter, 1988: 21). A third magazine fancied the 'New Woman' as 'stylish, curious and anxious to understand what is going on beyond her immediate ken'

1

(Slaughter, 1988: 21). There was evidently much argument about the 'New Woman', and about what – if anything – she would want from a women's magazine. Indeed, perhaps the only agreement about her was that she was a component of a target market of 'nine million' middle-class women with 'up-market aspirations' (Slaughter, 1988: 21).

I argue in Chapters 4 and 5 that new forms of market research were central to the appearance of a 'New Woman' as a target market for women's magazines in the 1980s and 1990s. In the immediate post-war years, the women's magazine industry had used demographics to help them imagine and classify their readerships and to predict their consumption patterns. Demographics ranked women by social class based on the occupation of the (usually male) head of the household, and combined this data with other factors such as age and marital status. Thus, a classic demographic segmentation used by the magazine industry had been 'ABC1 housewives with children', and a classic magazine for this consumer market had been the domestic weekly title, *Woman*. From the late 1950s onwards, however, there had been some attempt by the women's magazine industry to shift away from demographics towards segmentation by 'attitude' (Winship, 1987: 46).

According to Janice Winship (1987: 46–7), the move of the women's magazine industry away from demographics was largely spurred on by their engagement with forms of 'motivational' market research. Through qualitative data produced by research into the behavioural psychology of consumers, a picture of a very diverse 'women's market' was constructed. This data also spurred on a number of attempts to produce magazines for a 'New Woman', who was believed to be distinguishable from the traditional mass-market 'housewife' through her broader range of life experiences and 'motivational distinctions' (see Nixon, 1996: 93). IPC's ill-fated *Nova* (1965–75) ('the new magazine for the new kind of woman') and *Candida* (1972), for example, along with National Magazines' more popular venture *Cosmopolitan* (1972–present), were all products of the magazine industry's attempts to identify the 'needs' and motivations of women consumers of the 1960s and early 1970s. By the late 1970s, however, 'motivational' research per se began to lose ground with some market researchers. It was replaced by 'lifestyle' segmentations produced through qualitative research techniques. Lifestyle research represented consumers as more diverse and changeable than ever before, and produced more individualistic images of them. Moreover, lifestyle research emphasized the differences between consumer groups in cultural, as well as economic and motivational terms (Nixon, 1996: 92–6). The take-up of these techniques by the women's magazine industry, I argue, helped to shape its representations of a 'New Woman' in glossy women's magazines from the mid-1980s onwards.

As I discuss in Chapter 1, the account developed in this book has been shaped in relation to a range of discourses about, and interpretations of, these new 'lifestyle' images of young, middle-class femininity. A plethora of

commentary and analysis about a 'New Woman' appeared within the magazine and advertising trade press of the 1980s and 1990s, and sometimes (as we
have already seen) extended into the broadsheet newspapers. There was also
a small amount of academic analysis of the significance of this 'New Woman'.
In an account of women's magazines in the 1980s, Janice Winship (1987: 150)
offered a reading of the 'New Woman' that saw her as a commercial 'appropriation of the cultural space of feminism opened up minus most of the
politics'. Arguing that the 'New Woman' was, in effect, an unrealizable
'Superwoman', Winship maintained that the basis for these new magazines lay
in the growing financial independence of middle-class women in their
twenties and thirties. 'Not only is this group growing numerically', Winship
(1987: 156) observed:

> but the steady post-war rise of married women's employment and the
> effects of sixteen years of the women's movement have meant that
> these women tend to have personal spending money beyond the
> purely domestic sphere. If the High Streets in Britain have witnessed
> a crop of Next, Principles and Country Casuals shops springing up to
> provide for these 'mature' women's fashion needs, so too the
> magazine world has begun to look to her custom.

My account here partly pursues Winship's ideas. Indeed, in Chapters 2 and 7
it seeks to understand the significance of images of a 'New Woman' in relation
to formations of middle-class femininities in the late twentieth century.
Unlike Winship, however, I do not concern myself with exploring the
contradictions between feminism and femininity in the pages of the
magazines, or the possible 'effects' of the magazines on their readers. As I
show in Chapter 1, such questions are important for the analysis of women's
magazines, and have already received considerable attention – and produced
much debate – within feminist magazine scholarship (see, for example,
Ballaster et al., 1991; Hermes, 1995; Winship, 1987). This book leans instead
towards an exploration of discourses about a 'New Woman' in the spheres of
production and circulation. It therefore explores how images of new markets
of potential readers were discursively constructed by media professionals,
including publishers, journalists and advertisers. Fundamental to this
analysis, therefore, is a need to understand how a complex nexus of power
relationships produced particular discourses about a 'New Woman', helping
to define how femininity was thought about – and imagined – within women's
magazine production. My methodological approach, and the reasoning
behind it, are discussed in some detail in Chapter 1. But, readers should note
here, that this book reflects less upon the 'language' of women's magazines
themselves, and more upon the rise of a 'New Woman' as a subject for debate
in the advertising, marketing and magazine industries, and particularly in
their trade press. It is therefore in relation to the 'New Woman' as she was

represented within the discourse of media industries that I advance an argument about her cultural – and economic – significance. In Chapter 4 I detail the importance, in particular, of the advertising trade press of the mid- to late 1980s in promoting the figure of a 'New Woman'. The remainder of the book charts the discursive formation of a 'New Woman' in the women's magazine industry. Chapters 5 and 6 focus on the elaboration and solidifica- tion of a 'New Woman' figure in the discourses of advertisers and magazine professionals from the mid-1980s and early 1990s. Chapter 7 explores the 'New Woman' as a space of projection for media professionals, and speculates on its function as a distinctive social space for some magazine readers. Chapter 8 considers more recent attempts to break away from a 'New Woman' as she was figured in the latter years of the twentieth century.

The historical specificity of the 'New Woman' as she was deployed by media professionals is, therefore, a central concern of this book. The story I tell here is best read as a cultural history of shifting discourses about a 'New Woman' as she was deployed by magazine and advertising professionals in the 1980s and 1990s. As I demonstrate in Chapter 3, these decades were particularly active for the magazine industry in the United Kingdom. In the late 1970s the magazine sector had faced many disheartening predictions of future demise in the face of increased commercial competition from new media. Yet, as Tony Weymouth and Bernard Lamizet (1996: 52) have observed, this view of the sector was mistaken. Indeed, the British magazine industry – in line with a European trend – experienced a period of significant expansion in these decades. Most notable here was a revitalization of the women's magazine market. Whilst traditional domestic titles such as *Woman's Own* had experi- enced a great decline in their sales figures, other magazines had appeared to take their place. Most conspicuous here were a range of monthly 'glossy' women's titles – including *Elle* and *Marie Claire* – that had achieved high circulations amongst groups of young professional women (Weymouth and Lamizet, 1996: 52).

As I suggest in Chapter 8, women's magazines of the twenty-first century continue to design new editorial mixes for women. Some magazines have attempted to break from the 'New Woman', as she was conceived and elaborated upon throughout the mid-1980s to the late 1990s. Indeed, they have tried to produce new images of femininity that are distinguished from those discussed in Chapters 5, 6 and 7. The women's magazine industry has not, however, tried to move away from targeting readerships of young, professional middle-class women. Yet, as Anne M. Cronin (2000: 51–3) has noted, 'young' is viewed by media industries as an increasingly 'elastic' category and many women's magazines (for example, *Red* and *Eve*) now seek core readerships of women in their mid-thirties. Indeed, this suggests that some media professionals are seeking to devise new titles and editorial mixes to target many of the same women readers they sought in the late 1980s and early 1990s.

This book is very concerned with the cultural shifts that had an impact on the formation of discourses about a 'New Woman' in the late twentieth century. Yet it also contends that there were economic and politically driven factors that helped produce these images of contemporary femininity. In the first part of Chapter 2, I explore debates about the 1980s in the UK: the 'enterprise culture' and its characteristic economic, political (and to a degree social and cultural) dynamics. I engage here, particularly, with a body of work that attempts to frame these shifts within a Fordist/post-Fordist paradigm. This examines the crisis of mass production and traces shifts towards a new economic era characterized by more flexible forms of manufacturing and new strategies of economic regulation. Chapter 3 also draws on the Fordist/post-Fordist model as a means for understanding transitions in the women's magazine industry of the 1980s and 1990s, and its emphasis on developing more flexible organizational forms and practices. The Fordist/post-Fordist paradigm remains central to the discussions of institutional practices throughout this book. I argue that the changes in the organization and practices of women's magazine and advertising production during the late twentieth century are related to this wider process of economic restructuring. Indeed, the development of cultures of flexibility within advertising – and subsequently the magazine industry – ultimately *facilitated* the introduction of more flexible techniques of production and organization, and the development of titles for a 'New Woman' within the women's magazine sector.

Whilst this analysis is sensitive to institutional practices and processes, it does not attempt to represent these in a 'deterministic' sense familiar in many studies of the 'political economy' of the media. In contrast, I adopt an analytical framework known in cultural studies as 'cultural economy', and view 'economic' activities as profoundly 'cultural' phenomena (see du Gay, 1997a; du Gay and Pryke, 2002). One consequence of this approach is that I view the processes of production and systems of organization of the magazine and advertising industries as discursive. These industries carry meanings about how such sites should be thought about and responded to by others. Similarly, I do not view the organizational structures of these industries as forms that are simply 'inhabited' by those within. As is particularly evident in my discussion of magazine editors as cultural intermediaries in Chapter 7, working practices are profoundly 'cultural' practices – carrying particular meanings and constructing certain forms of action amongst people subjected to them. Chapter 1 of this book discusses in more detail the conceptual frameworks and research model I have adopted in this study – and their inevitable limitations. It also explains, however, ways in which this study can open up a new and challenging way for 'understanding' women's magazines and other cultural industries, and for considering the processes of cultural production, circulation and consumption in the modern world.

1

UNDERSTANDING
WOMEN'S MAGAZINES

How can we 'understand' women's magazines? Previous scholars in this field have offered contrasting accounts of how women's magazines might be 'understood', and how they should be studied. Many have focused on women's magazines at a textual level, and analysed them for their ideological content. Others have argued that women's magazines can be understood by exploring the ways in which their readers consume them. A few studies have maintained that women's magazines are best approached through an analysis of their conditions of production. In this chapter I explore and unpack these various approaches, clarifying exactly what is at stake when we talk about 'understanding' women's magazines.

A survey of existing research both alerts us to some of the complexities involved in the study of women's magazines and highlights the variety of ways in which the field has been accorded significance within the social sciences. A review of earlier scholarly work also allows the context and concerns of the present study to be mapped out. In outlining the nature and implications of earlier studies, this chapter explores the ways in which women's magazine research could benefit from a re-evaluation of its methods of cultural analysis. In particular, I argue for an account of women's magazines that gives close attention to the ways their meanings are produced and circulated at 'economic' sites. I am especially concerned with how practitioners in the women's magazine industry (together with those working in the closely allied fields of advertising and marketing) understand, represent and relate to their product. I explore the ways in which these conditions of existence impact upon the management and organization of the magazine industry, the way they influence the relationships between women's magazines, advertisers and marketers, and the way they ultimately shape the character of the magazines that appear on the newsagents' shelves. Rather than being the exclusive province of economic imperatives, therefore, I argue that the business of women's magazine production should also be seen as a *cultural* realm. Yes, it is a commercially led, market-oriented industry. But one that depends heavily on *social* and *cultural* processes for its effective operation.

As will become evident, while I emphasize issues of methodology in this chapter, I acknowledge that the research model I ultimately adopted for this study has inevitable limitations. The strength of the analysis lies, however, in the attention it gives to the economic and social facets of the business of magazine production – areas almost entirely ignored in previous studies of women's magazines, where textual analysis has tended to be prioritized over issues of production and industry organization. In doing so, existing scholarship has, I argue, disregarded aspects in the 'life' of women's magazines that are crucially important in the generation and circulation of their meanings. This chapter, therefore, outlines existing work in the field of women's magazines and explains how my own study of a particularly important moment in their development – the 1980s and 1990s – opens up new and challenging ways for 'understanding' these texts' production, circulation and consumption.

Women's magazines, feminism and ideology

Studies of women's magazines have been conducted largely by feminist media scholars. As Joke Hermes (1997: 223) has pointed out, such studies have invariably configured these texts as a 'problem' for women. Whilst the work of feminist media critics has diverse disciplinary origins, the majority have argued that the media contribute to the reinforcement of gender differences and inequalities in contemporary societies. From this perspective, media representations are seen as a key site through which oppressive feminine identities are constructed and disseminated. In these terms those working in media production are seen as conspiring in the promotion of both capitalism and patriarchy. Classically, then, feminist critiques of the media industries portray them as ideologically manipulative – and the role of the critic is seen as highlighting and challenging their system of domination.

Such assumptions about the manipulative role of media producers are evident in most studies of women's magazines. The women's magazine industry is understood as a monolithic meaning-producer, circulating magazines that contain 'messages' and 'signs' about the nature of femininity that serve to promote and legitimate dominant interests. This book argues that such accounts of women's magazines offer, at best, only a partial account of the industry. In particular, I contend that 'classic' feminist perspectives tend to neglect the ways in which cultural production involves, as Richard Johnson puts it, 'raw materials, tools or means of production, and socially-organized forms of human labour' (1986/7: 99). Many feminist accounts of women's magazines, I argue, overlook these vital issues. Existing perspectives effectively marginalize the specificities of social, political and economic formations and their impact upon not only women's magazine production, but also the lived cultures of the magazine producers themselves. Taking the text itself as the key point of analysis, existing scholarship has hitherto ignored the roles of *producers* in using (and transforming) discursive and ideological elements within the development of women's magazines.

7

Early feminist accounts of women's magazines (and their interpretation of the relationship between the texts and their readers' self-perception) were concerned with the ways that magazines offered 'unreal', 'untruthful' or 'distorted' images of women. These studies, therefore, called for more 'positive' images of women, ones that were more in line with the ethos and ideals of the feminist movement. Betty Friedan (1963) and Tuchman *et al.* (1978), for example, both offered seminal accounts of women's magazines that viewed the texts as highly problematic for feminism. From this perspective, women's magazines were seen as a powerful force for the construction and legitimation of gender inequalities. In these terms, women's magazines did not simply offer their readers innocent pleasure – they were a key site for the development of a self-identity that undermined women's essential, 'real' feminine identities. Both Friedan and Tuchman presented women's magazines as pernicious and alienating, as texts that worked to estrange and separate women from both one another and from their 'true' selves. The media (and implicitly those involved in their production), therefore, were presented as a 'problem' for the women's movement – a 'problem' to which Friedan and Tuchman offered similar solutions. Both authors concluded their studies by advocating the 'liberation' of women's magazine readerships through the 'enlightening' force of feminism. And this, they hoped, would ultimately sweep away the women's magazine in its contemporary (and lamentably patriarchal) form.

The late 1970s saw a shift away from conceiving women's magazines simply in terms of their 'negative' or 'positive' images of women. Instead, moving beyond the liberal feminist perspectives advanced by Friedan and Tuchman, many critics found a more sophisticated theoretical model in the work of the neo-Marxist philosopher, Louis Althusser (1970). Influenced by Althusser's challenging reworking of the Marxist notion of ideology, many feminist authors began to suggest that the representations of women prevalently offered in women's magazines were not simply 'ideological' chimera, but had repercussions in women's lives that were both concrete and material.

The significance of Althusser's work lies in his insistence that ideology is not just a set of illusory ideas, or a form of mental state or consciousness. Instead, he understands ideology as having material form, existing as something that is carried out by groups and institutions in society. In order for ideology to be effective, Althusser argues, the people living this imaginary relation to the real conditions of existence must engage in rituals and practices. These, he contends, are ideologically inscribed into the 'Ideological State Apparatuses' (ISAs) of society. These institutions work to form people as subjects of ideology. They also ensure that people place (and understand) themselves in terms of ideological frameworks. Feminist media critics who employed Althusser's model in their analyses of women's magazines believed that women would recognize themselves in terms of the ideological frameworks generated within the texts (see Glazer, 1980; Leman, 1980; Winship,

1978). The representations of femininity in women's magazines, therefore, were seen as 'naturalizing' an ideologically charged image of women and their place in society. Consequently, these texts were seen as instruments of domination that contributed to the overall subordination of women's 'real' identities (Hermes, 1997: 223). As with the earlier (liberal feminist) studies, the practices of magazine producers went largely undiscussed within the neo-Althusserian model – the implicit assumption being that the producers were either cunning publishing entrepreneurs or exploited media workers dragooned into the dissemination of dominant ideas and values.

Nevertheless, the strength of this 'Althusserian' model of analysis lay in its capacity to move away from the earlier obsession with 'positive' and 'negative' images of femininity. Instead, greater recognition was given to the place of women's magazines in the wider universe of cultural politics, and better attention was given to their role in fixing and containing feminine identities. At the same time, however, these approaches were not without their flaws. As subsequent studies observed, the implications of accounts informed by Althusser's ideas were that women's magazines were essentially 'closed' texts that imprisoned their women readers within a dominant set of ideologies. For some, such an approach offered an overly pessimistic account of readers' relationships with their magazines, reducing the text to little more than an agent in the service of patriarchal capitalism.

Women's magazine scholarship and 'the turn to Gramsci'

By the 1980s a number of feminist authors had begun to develop textually based approaches to women's magazines that addressed some of the short-comings of the earlier scholarship. Influential in this respect was the work of the Italian Marxist intellectual Antonio Gramsci (1971). Gramsci's notions of 'civil society' and the production of hegemony were of particular interest. For many theorists they allowed women's magazines to be conceived of as an arena of political contest rather than simply a site of ideological manipulation.

Generally, Gramsci conceives of hegemony as a situation in which a class or class faction is able to secure a moral, cultural, intellectual (and thereby political) leadership in society through an ongoing process of ideological struggle and compromise. Hegemony, therefore, is not a 'given'. Rather, it is a *process* requiring strategies of accommodation in which a degree of 'space' is accorded to oppositional ideas and interests. Hence hegemony is understood as a 'compromise equilibrium' – though it is an equilibrium that ultimately works to articulate the interests of subordinate groups to those of the dominant (Gramsci, 1971: 161). According to Gramsci, this is achieved in the realm of what he calls 'civil society'. This is an aggregation of social institutions that includes trade unions, religious organizations, the media and all the other organizations that are formed outside the parameters of the more coercive state-funded organizations and bureaucracies. In employing a

Gramscian framework, therefore, women's magazines could be conceived as constituent in the play of dominant and subordinate interests that took place within the realm of 'civil society'. As such, magazines were seen as a site where women's oppression was debated and negotiated, rather than merely reinforced.

Sandra Hebron's study of *Jackie* and *Woman's Own* (1983) was one of the first to adopt this approach. Hebron argued that whilst ideology played a crucial role in maintaining women's subordinate position in society, women's magazines constituted a site where marked elements of ideological negotiation were discernible. Janice Winship took a similar line. Winship's influential work on the changing contours of the British women's magazine market from the 1950s to the 1980s attempted to pursue the full implications of Gramscian theory. In her key study, *Inside Women's Magazines* (1987), Winship examined the shifting content of women's magazines in relation to wider changes in the social position of women in modern Britain.[1] From the late 1960s, Winship argued, the rise of the women's movement brought with it a growth in magazine coverage of political issues, including those previously dismissed as unacceptably 'feminist' (Winship, 1987: 92). She asserted, however, that women's magazines still adopted a characteristically 'pragmatic' approach to such issues. So, while the magazines *appeared* to offer solutions to women's socio-economic oppression, this was essentially a superficial resolution, which effectively worked to block perspectives deemed radical or 'too controversial'. This ideological work, Winship contended, was accomplished through women's magazines' characterization of gender inequality as an issue to be resolved by the *individual* acting in their everyday lives rather than as a deep-rooted problem that demanded wide-ranging social transformation. Thus, whilst *appearing* to engage with questions of political liberation, women's magazines actually inhibited its realization by emphasizing a 'post-feminist' individual whose life could be 'whatever you, the individual, make of it' (Winship, 1987: 149–50).

Winship, however, went farther than Hebron in conceding the potential pleasures offered by women's magazines. Indeed, Winship acknowledged that she was, herself, an avid reader. Women's magazines, she observed, were a 'chocolate box' of treats that were read in a variety of contexts:

> we escape with them in nervous moments at the doctor's or during tedious commuting hours. We read them as relaxation at the end of a long day when children have at last been put to bed, or to brighten up the odd coffee break and lunch hour when life is getting a bit tough, or simply dreary.
>
> (1987: 52)

Winship warned, however, that pleasure was not an experience that existed 'beyond' ideology. Pleasure, she explained, might feel 'like an individual and

10

spontaneous expression', but it was highly coded and structured, offering women little opportunity of escape from the limited social spaces they inhabited (Winship, 1987: 52). In these terms, readers' 'resistance' to the ideological messages of women's magazines was (at best) partial and temporary.

Similar approaches were adopted in subsequent studies.[2] Ros Ballaster *et al.* (1991), Ellen McCracken (1993) and Gigi Durham (1996), for example, all arrived at comparable conclusions in their various analyses of ideology and femininity in women's magazines. They all called the power of the ideological text into question, revealing the possibilities of negotiated and oppositional meanings that readers could develop. Nevertheless, while these authors recognized the potential spaces for counter-hegemonic, 'resistant' readings, they regarded these as lacking the substance needed to effect meaningful change in either wider society or the magazine genre itself.

Other accounts, however, were more optimistic about the power of the contemporary reader to resist the ideological interpellations in women's magazines. Eva Illouz (1991), Linda Steiner (1991), Jacqueline Blix (1992) and Myra Macdonald (1995), for example, all argued that the texts offered small – but still very significant – spaces for resistance and alternative readings of women's lives. Steiner's optimism was especially pronounced in her account of the American pro-women's movement magazine, *Ms.* For Steiner, the magazine offered possibilities of genuine political impact through its attempt to challenge and 'de-naturalize' the feminine styles and identities articulated in other media texts. The questions raised in *Ms.*, she argued, might even precipitate a change in the codes and conventions operating in other women's magazines – and even held potential for the development of a new, more progressive, hegemonic account of gender (Steiner, 1991: 343).

Feminism, postmodernism and ethnographic approaches to women's magazines

During the mid-1980s postmodern and poststructuralist theory began to register significant impact on feminist approaches to popular culture. This shift had important implications for the study of women's magazines, with the development of a strong critique of earlier, textually based, analyses. Feminist researchers informed by postmodern and poststructuralist theorists (especially the French intellectual Michel Foucault (1997a; 1997b)) argued that the meanings of women's magazines – or indeed any other form of culture – were not pre-existent messages waiting to be 'discovered' by the researcher. Instead, they employed the concept of discourse, and began to consider the meanings of women's magazines as 'dialogical', and in potential struggle with other historically and culturally specific uses of language, other forms of culture, and practices. This helped feminist researchers to develop a critique of the epistemologies prominent in philosophical thought since the

Enlightenment, and to seek new ways of interpreting the 'truth' and 'meaning' of women's lives and experiences, and new ways of analysing the cultural artefacts consumed by women (see, for example, Hekman, 1990; Ramazanoglu, 1993; Scott, 1990).

Influenced by these perspectives, some authors began to embrace interpretative and ethnographic methodologies in their study of women's magazines. If the meaning of magazines was produced through discursive formations, it was argued, interpretative ethnography offered potential for discerning how *particular* readers make women's magazines meaningful in *specific* social and historical contexts. Furthermore, this method openly acknowledged the role of the researcher, refusing to elevate the scholar to a position of informed 'enlightenment' that eluded 'ordinary' readers. According to Joke Hermes the rise of this approach marked an identifiable 'ethnographic turn' in audience research within media and cultural studies (1997: 217–18).

One of the earliest ethnographic approaches to women's readings of women's magazines featured in the final chapter of Ros Ballaster *et al.*'s study, *Women's Worlds* (1991).[3] A 'postmodern' scepticism to notions of ultimate 'truth' was clearly apparent in these authors' assertion that 'any critical reading or data collection or textual analysis which presents itself as value- or theory-free is *mis*representing itself' (Ballaster *et al.*, 1991: 127). From their interviews with groups of women, they concluded that readers were actually very conscious of women's magazines as 'bearers of particular discourses of femininity', with many in the groups even making what the authors termed a 'critical assessment' of the magazine content (Ballaster *et al.*, 1991: 126–37).

Nevertheless, the account offered by Ballaster and her associates remained anchored around an analysis of the text itself, whose 'meanings' they tended to privilege over the reading practices of the audience. As they explained themselves:

> it is not our view that the constructions of femininity we find in magazines are harmless and innocuous . . . [w]hile we reject any straightforward causal relation between representation and behaviour, or the idea that these texts simply 'brainwash' their readers, we would argue that certain readings are privileged and that frequently the terms of our criticism can only remain within the terms of the magazine discourse itself. ... [The] disagreement [of readers] is a response to, a reaction to, these versions [of femininity], rather than a reshaping or a destruction of them.
>
> (1991: 131)

This assertion that women's magazines can in some way 'harm' readers was challenged by Joke Hermes (1995: 3). In her study of women's magazines and everyday media use, Hermes contended that a thorough-going critique of women's magazines needed to combine self-reflexivity on the part of the researcher with a methodology 'that let readers speak for themselves' (1995: 5). Hermes sought to negotiate a pathway between those studies of media that privileged the analysis of genre and text, and those that dealt with the 'situatedness' and 'everydayness' of media use. In this way Hermes aimed to address the manner in which women's magazines 'become meaningful exclusively through the perception of their readers' (1995: 6). At the same time, however, Hermes maintained a commitment to 'postmodern' self-reflection, acknowledging that this research was her own 'interpretation of how readers interpret women's magazines' (Hermes, 1995: 6).

Drawing on seventy-five interviews with readers of women's magazines, Hermes was initially disappointed with her research material. As she explained, '[t]he emancipated audience didn't strike me as all that active and celebrating. Nor did the interviews, at first sight, make any clearer how women's magazines or other media are made meaningful' (Hermes, 1993: 495). It was the interview process itself, however, which prompted her to realize the impossibility of distinguishing between the magazine text and the context of reading.

Hermes asserted that her interviewees did not differentiate between their explanations of reading women's magazines and their explanations of their everyday lives. Her interviewees often seemed to have very little to say *at all* about the magazines themselves, talking much more about how the magazines they read fitted into their daily routines. In fact, readers gave meanings to women's magazines which Hermes found to be quite independent of the text, employing them at particular moments as tools in the formation of fantasy and imagined 'new selves' (1995: 146). The implication of this, Hermes argued, was that women's magazines were not meaningful when analysed outside the context of the readers' everyday lives. Indeed, for Hermes, the texts themselves were not really all that significant, as there was 'no essential meaning that can be actualized nor is there an essential viewing mode or practice of media use' (Hermes, 1993: 504).[4]

Production-based studies of women's magazines

Despite the substantial amount of research on women's magazines outlined above, there remain important areas of knowledge that need to be developed more fully. As I have already outlined, early scholarship in the field was dominated by textually based studies focused on issues of representation. More recent accounts, influenced by the 'postmodern' feminist re-evaluation of ethnographic method, have delved into issues of consumption. In different ways both the earlier and more recent studies have attempted to examine the relationships between feminism, femininity and women's magazines, exploring the extent to which these texts foster dominant forms of femininity among their readers. Conclusions have, as we have seen, been various and there exists little consensus regarding the role of women's magazines in producing feminine subjects. Overall, it is the sheer unpredictability of the relationship between reader and text that emerges from the recent studies of women's magazines and their audience.

While the reading practices and meanings of magazine readerships (and the extent to which these are determined by the industry) have been subject to considerable analysis by feminist media critics, the practices and meanings of magazine *producers* have gone relatively unexplored.[5] One exception to this is Marjorie Ferguson's (1983) study of production, consumption and the women's press which, to date, has offered the only in-depth consideration of women's magazine production. This, therefore, is a study of particular relevance to my own work. Ferguson, herself a former employee of a women's weekly, adopted an innovative approach in her magazine research. Rather than focusing on the *readership* of women's magazines, she sought to combine a content analysis of specific titles with her inside knowledge of industry concepts and practices.

Ferguson's study was also notable for the way it was informed by Émile Durkheim's writings on the sociology of religion. She argued that the relationship between women's magazines and their audiences was akin to that which Durkheim outlined between religious cults and their adherents. Paraphrasing Durkheim, Ferguson argued that in a religious cult, a woman can 'worship her own society through its religious observances, and acquire that society's essentially social concepts through them' (Ferguson, 1983: 11). In a similar fashion, Ferguson argued, femininity can also be regarded as a 'cult' – a denomination, moreover, in which magazines represented the holy testament. As Ferguson explained, there were a number of direct parallels between the 'cult' of religion and that of 'femininity':

> the oracles that carry the messages sacred to the cult of femininity are women's magazines, the high priestesses who select and shape the cult's interdictions and benedictions are women's magazine editors; the rites, rituals, sacrifices and oblations that they exhort are to be performed periodically by the cult's adherents. All pay homage to the cult's totem – the totem of Woman herself.
>
> (Ferguson, 1983: 5)

For Ferguson, then, magazine editors were extremely important as 'custodians' of the feminine 'cult'. By setting the 'feminine agenda' within the 'scripture' of women's magazines, the editors were in a powerful position – occupying a pulpit from which they could decree the character of femininity. In these terms, magazine readers were willing disciples, often showing an unshakeable faith in particular titles that they adopted as a gospel for everyday life. Moreover, while the women's movement might seem to offer a perspective that challenged the magazines' credo, for Ferguson feminism was actually an extension of the same 'cult'. As she explained, while the women's magazine:

> determinedly defines the female condition positively and, ultimately around 'finding a male' . . . [t]he movement, equally determinedly defines women negatively in term of their common oppression by men. . . . In one sense the women's movement offers a counter culture, but in another sense it is an extension of the cult.
>
> (1983: 187)

While elements of Ferguson's study touched on the producers of women's magazines, her approach was still primarily focused on the text. As such, she gave only limited attention to either readers' understandings of magazines or the everyday practices of the texts' producers. In the case of the latter, patterns of economic ownership within the magazine industry were presumed to determine fairly directly the activities of those working within it. Such activities were generally assumed to be explicable in terms of the way they administered production processes in the interests of capital. Any creative activity was perceived as being largely framed by dominant ideology, and the production of magazines was presented as a standardized, rational and (for the most part) thoroughly predictable process.

It is unlikely that Ferguson would, following the impact of postmodern feminism, carry out her research in exactly the same way today. Nor is it likely that she would arrive at precisely the same conclusions. Nevertheless, her study remains the most detailed analysis of the women's magazine industry to date. Two other studies, however, also deserve mention. Sammye Johnson (1993) and Barbara Straus Reed (1996) have both conducted empirically based research on working practices within the magazine industry. Both authors observed the lack of empirical research on industry routines and were interested in exploring the position of women within American magazine publishing. Whilst Johnson's study examined statistical data on women's changing employment and status within the magazine industry (1993: 135), Reed (1996) chose to focus on one publisher, Hearst Magazines. Drawing on a combination of personal interviews and statistical data, Reed argued that the position of women within magazine publishing had improved greatly over the preceding two decades. This, she claimed, had mainly been a consequence of women's 'hard work, dedication, and willingness to make sacrifices' (Reed, 1996: 271). Reed's most interesting observation, however, was that female employees had become especially prominent within women's magazine publishing. In the words of the director of Hearst Magazines International, they 'understand better what other women want' and 'work harder, are tougher, and aggressively want to succeed' (George Green, cited in Reed, 1996: 261). Women were also seen as more empathetic, bringing new working cultures and practices to the industry itself, as well as 'listening to readers' views' more attentively than their male counterparts (Reed, 1996: 271).

Although it did not aspire to be a comprehensive study of production practice, Reed's project at Hearst Magazines raised some interesting questions about the role of the magazine producer. She emphasized the important shifts that had taken place in the magazine industry's working practices, suggesting that these had (in turn) also brought about a profound set of cultural changes within the industry. Industry concepts of their readers were also significantly modified, this ultimately having an impact on the codes of representation within the magazine texts themselves. Reed, in fact, urged readers who were unhappy with magazine content to write to the publishers and producers, as she claimed that 'they will be heard, now perhaps as never before' (1996: 271).

'Bridging the gap': production, consumption and women's magazines

The inter-relationships between the moments of production and consumption in magazine publishing were pursued further in work by Angela McRobbie (1996a). In a study of the 'new' women's magazines of the 1990s, McRobbie reconceptualized what she called the 'interdiscursive space' of production, arguing that the project of magazine analysis should be 'to generate a more rigorous account of the complex and multilayered relation between the production of meaning in the magazine and the diverse ways in which these meanings are consumed by readers' (1996a: 178). With this in mind, McRobbie (1996a: 193) proposed a 'more sociological approach' in magazine scholarship. This, she suggested, should employ a synthesis of ethnographic method, the use of hard empirical data and textual analysis – a triangulation of methodological approaches that should also be informed by a postmodern feminist understanding of gender and subjectivity.[6] Through this combination of methodologies McRobbie argued that it was possible to understand the complex ways in which 'the reader' operated as a discursive category within the magazine industry.

'The reader', McRobbie argued, could also be seen as a space of 'projection' for the magazine editor, entrepreneur and journalist. Within magazine production, 'the reader' was understood in an emotional and intimate way, practitioners even describing 'the reader' as one of their 'own circle of friends and acquaintances' (McRobbie, 1996a: 180). Market researchers also participated in this process, acting as industry intermediaries in the way they shaped the 'reader' into a concrete consumer profile. This profile could be offered to existing and prospective advertisers, demonstrating that the magazine was keeping its finger on the pulse of young women's cultures. Recruitment policies at the magazines also figured in this process by ensuring that (as much as possible) the workforce *embodied* the qualities of this 'ideal' reader –

women employees understanding themselves, when appropriate, as *Just Seventeen* or *Cosmo* 'girls'.

McRobbie went on to argue that the discursive category of 'the reader' was one that changed over time. To demonstrate this, she returned to textual analysis. Investigating commercial constructions of feminine identities through an analysis of the pages of various young women's magazines, McRobbie argued that the currency of feminist discourses within contemporary society had meant that sexuality had displaced romance as the magazines' ideological focus – with a much more pronounced emphasis on 'strong, frank, and explicitly sexual representations' (McRobbie, 1996a: 192). In addition, the employees of the magazines were well versed in these languages of sexual politics. Keen magazine readers themselves, they were frequently graduates of university degree courses that had encouraged a critical understanding of media texts. Indeed, some of them retained an interest in media and cultural studies research, even identifying themselves as 'feminists' and concurring with feminist criticisms of women's magazines. Moreover, these employees asserted that their readers shared a similar worldview. New magazines such as *More!* and *Marie Claire* thus spoke to readers about sexuality in an idiom that was 'mocking and ironic' (1996a: 183), this providing a counter-hegemonic space for 'critical reflection' that effectively turned the tables on the men and boys who had traditionally scrutinized women as sexual objects within the universe of glossy magazines.

Using interviews and observation, Caroline Oates's (1999) study also investigated the position of readers of 'new' women's weekly magazines in the minds and practices of both readers and journalists. Oates's work generally supported McRobbie's assertions about the parity between magazine employees and readers, but also identified dimensions of tension between editorial staff, advertisers and readers that were 'constant and ... played out against a highly competitive environment of rival magazines and fluctuating sales' (1999: 16). As a consequence, Oates argued, McRobbie's stress on the *shared* knowledges and aspirations of readers and magazine employees was somewhat idealistic, because ultimately:

> the agenda of women's weekly magazines . . . and the way they represent women, remain largely outside the realm of the reader, yet the illusion of readers being allowed to participate in and even write their own magazine is an image offered by editors.
>
> (Oates, 1999: 18)

Oates argued, therefore, that what differentiated the 'new' weekly magazines such as *Best* and *Bella* from 'old' weeklies such as *Woman* was the 'illusion of participation' they offered their readers (1999: 17). Rather than marking a profound reconfiguration of the divisions between producer and consumer, Oates understood the new sense of 'participation' as largely a marketing gimmick that left the industry's traditional attitudes to their product (and its traditional perception of readers) essentially unchanged.

Cultural production and the 'sovereign consumer'

Recent years have seen the appearance of a number of valuable studies of working practices in other cultural industries. These have made key interventions into the understanding of relationships between cultural production and consumption. In particular, Paul du Gay's study of working practices in the retail industries, *Consumption and Identity at Work* (1996), reconceptualizes the model typically deployed in the social sciences for understanding the relationship between producers and consumers. Building on Michel Foucault's studies of discourse as a system of representation (Foucault, 1980), du Gay highlights the discursive figure of 'the customer' that operates within new retail outlets in Britain. Du Gay's approach is influenced by Foucault's later work and its focus on the discursive practices of specific institutional settings. Du Gay draws, in particular, on Foucault's ideas regarding the ways discourse regulates the conduct of its subjects and those who are subjectified by it – du Gay applying these concepts to the institutional context of modern retailing. Here, du Gay argues, the customer has been increasingly envisaged as a 'sovereign consumer' whose consumption practices are characterized by unpredictability. In an attempt to deal with the inconsistencies of their 'sovereign consumer', therefore, du Gay argues that retailers have initiated new methods of staff training that encourage employees to become more flexible and enterprising in their work lives.

Within retailing organizations, du Gay argues (1996: 145), retail staff are required not only to *be* at work, but to become 'individuals who calculate about themselves and work upon themselves in order to better themselves'. In other words, retail staff are encouraged to shape themselves into people who live their lives as 'an enterprise of the self' (1996: 145). Nor are retail staff the only ones who have been required to rethink 'the customer'. Du Gay argues that marketers, designers and advertisers have also had to become more customer-focused, designers and visual communicators using their symbolic expertise to create an 'image' or 'look' for retailers that articulates the attitudes and aspirations of consumers and (hopefully) translates these desires into sales (du Gay, 1996: 111).

The discursive production of identities within the work context also features in Angela McRobbie's study of the British fashion design industry (1998). Focusing on the careers of young fashion designers and the formation of their occupational identities, McRobbie explores the role of discourses of 'creativity' and the 'creative individual'. These, she argues, protect young fashion designers against failure when times are hard. They also provide an 'incentive to work even harder, in an unambiguously commercial capacity, on the basis that what they are doing now counts as creative work' (McRobbie,

1998: 179). Whilst this romantic image of 'the artist' has strong currency among cultural professionals, McRobbie maintains that the reality of the contemporary fashion economy works against such individualism, forcing fashion designers into unstructured relations of dependency and reciprocity with other designers and cultural professionals. So, whilst the discursive figure of 'the creative individual' is articulated through a number of institutional sites (including art education and fashion journalism), economic contingencies dictate that the fashion industry operates with practices that are ruthlessly consumer-led and commercial, and which ultimately work against 'creative individuality'.

Sean Nixon (1996) and Frank Mort (1996) also consider the discursive construction of consumer identities in their surveys of masculine narratives of production and consumption in modern Britain. Mort's study of commercial masculinities during the 1980s examines the role of advertising, marketing and retailing in the development of new projections of masculinity. Focusing on the practices of a collection of fashion journalists, designers, photographers, models and 'urban *flâneurs*', Mort argues that this group identified themselves as metropolitan 'taste leaders' whose 'intuitive' knowledges were drawn upon, and professionalized, by those involved in mainstream commerce (1996: 8–9, 11). Mort eloquently situates these commercial masculinities against the economic backdrop of 1980s entrepreneurialism, but also relates them to the shifting 'social geography of masculinity' during the period. Focusing on London's Soho and West End, he argues that a significant part of the discursive struggle over emerging masculine identities took place amongst those who *themselves* consumed and experienced these representations, Mort charting the emergence of a fashionable coterie whose cultural practices and forms of self-representation drew on the symbolic narratives of 'stylish' city life.

Focusing on the same historical period, Nixon's (1996) study examines the practices of retailers, advertisers and magazine producers and their role in the discursive formation of the 'new man' archetype – an emergent masculine identity predicated on the narcissistic pleasures of visual display and commodity consumption. Like du Gay (1996), McRobbie (1998) and Mort (1996), Nixon points to the significance of new technologies and modes of flexible production in this process. He also examines the ways in which the 'new man' was constructed and mediated by cultural intermediaries who articulated this consumption-oriented version of masculinity via new codes and practices of representation. These, Nixon argues, encouraged not only new modes of spectatorship and desire among male consumers, but also new, more style-conscious and hedonistic forms of consumer practice.

Such accounts of contemporary cultural industries indicate a significant theoretical shift in the way the relationships between practices of cultural production and consumption are perceived. This is particularly relevant for the study of women's magazines, given that existing studies in the area have tended to characterize these texts as a force working to undermine women's autonomy, creativity and cultural freedom. In contrast, what the studies of du Gay (1996), McRobbie (1998), Mort (1996) and Nixon (1996) all demonstrate is that cultural industries cannot be represented as homogeneous and stable entities. Instead, they are fluid and variable, relying on specific systems of micro relations to function. Particularly important for these industries is the complexity of micro-relations that exist around notions of identity. The perception and articulation of identities is especially crucial to cultural producers because, as they struggle to compete in the competitive commercial sphere, they have to present a construction of both themselves and their intended consumers.

This study explores the nature of such strategies of 'identity construction' in the production of women's magazines during the 1980s and 1990s. The choice of period is not random. These decades occupy a position of special significance in the development of the women's magazine industry. The period, I argue, witnessed a marked increase in the 'culturalizing' role of those involved in women's magazine production, with the rise of more pronounced and self-conscious strategies geared to construct not only the identity of the magazines' readerships, but also the 'personality' of the texts themselves. As I outline in Chapter 2, these processes were linked to wider economic shifts that were associated with the transition from an era of mass-produced and mass-marketed consumer goods to an era of 'flexible specialization' and market differentiation. This was a transition, I argue, that did not simply impact upon manufacturing systems and production processes. Rather, the changing dynamics of consumer culture and the émerging organizational forms of flexible specialization also transformed culture industries, as the possession of 'cultural' expertise became increasingly prized as an indispensable commercial commodity. While identifiable in such fields as advertising and marketing, I argue that it was in the realm of women's magazine production that these developments were especially pronounced – their impact registering on the texts' production and producers, and doubtless on the cultural values, tastes and commitments of the women who read them.

This book's key area of analysis is a group of women's magazines that were at the heart of this transformation – a collection of monthly titles known collectively as 'the glossies'. Any account of developments in the women's magazine industry during the 1980s and 1990s would point to the way this publishing sector managed to rejuvenate itself in an inhospitable business climate. As Weymouth and Lamizet observed, however, it was a group of 'glossy' newcomers who emerged as especially dynamic in this 'aggressively contested area of the [UK] market' (Weymouth and Lamizet, 1996: 53). Particularly successful were titles that seemed to offer a new image of femininity, an image that won particular appeal among 'young, professional women' (Weymouth and Lamizet, 1996: 53). It is the rise of these titles, their specific construction of femininity and their overall significance within the history of women's magazine publishing that are the specific focus of this book.

The overarching argument of this study is that the changes characteristic of the organization and production processes of the women's magazine industry during the 1980s and 1990s cannot be understood in economic terms alone. Informed by recent studies of cultures of production, I contend that industrial organization and practice is not driven solely by the 'motor' of economic contingency. Rather, this analysis of a particular moment in the history of women's magazines shows how *cultural* discourses around particular forms of feminine identity were also a crucial factor – one that not only featured in the lives of magazine producers, but also impacted upon the form of their products and the structure of the industry in which they worked.

Questions of method

Developing a framework for research was a challenging task. For this reason it is important to outline my rationale for the way I present my account of the business of women's magazines in the 1980s and 1990s. Originally, I intended qualitative research methodologies to be at the heart of my enquiry. Qualitative investigation has long been recognized as a valuable method for exploring and analysing the nature of media organizations and institutional practice (Cottle, 1995; Helland, 1996b). Indeed, qualitative research has produced many significant insights into the routines, ethos and professional ideologies of the media and its workers, qualitatively oriented studies offering important new methodological and theoretical models through which the media can be understood.[7]

In this methodological tradition, the contribution of ethnography has been especially distinctive (Helland, 1996a: 50). The ethnographic study of media organizations and practice has taken a variety of forms. Some authors have embarked on extended periods of participant observation within media industries,[8] while others have combined elements of ethnographic work with structured and unstructured interviews, focus group research and surveys. Studies based on such methodologies have been especially valuable in high-lighting the dynamic and unpredictable nature of processes of media production (particularly in the realm of the news media). Moreover, as Pertti Alasuutari (1995: 86–90) has observed, since it raises ethical questions that foreground the complex power relationships implicit within research situations, ethnographic research is congruent with many political concerns at the heart of feminist research. Furthermore, ethnographic method is especially adept at highlighting the subtle complexities of media industries. Rather than depicting the processes of media production as 'billiard ball smooth', ethnographic research has painted a picture that is 'less clean, less tidy, more happenstance, more leaky' (and therefore more accurate) than the sterile and mechanical image that emerges from accounts based around theoretical abstraction (Cottle, 1995: 46).

With this in mind, I originally perceived ethnographic method as a strategy particularly suited to the exploration of the world of women's magazine production. Initially, therefore, I had hoped to carry out 'behind the scenes' research in the contemporary women's magazine industry, with the intention of exploring the complex constraints, pressures and ethos that surround its operation. During the 1990s women's magazine production seemed ripe for such an approach. Since Marjorie Ferguson's study of the industry in 1983 dramatic shifts had taken place in the media landscape, hence a new assessment of the practices involved in the production of women's magazines promised to be a timely intervention. However, many of the difficulties commonly encountered in ethnographic media research quickly made themselves felt.

Almost from the outset I found that my original methodological intentions were over-ambitious. Issues of access always loom large in ethnographic studies of media production – the degree and nature of access inevitably determining the character of the data the researcher collects. Ferguson's experience as a journalist working for women's magazines had afforded her 'special' access to many areas of the industry, securing her an intimate vantage point on many aspects of magazine production. As an academic, I was in a less fortunate position and encountered a range of difficulties typically faced by researchers hoping to gain access to fields of media production.[9]

My initial plan to gain formal access and carry out fieldwork in the women's magazine industry soon floundered. Rather than making written requests for access, I outlined my fieldwork plans over the telephone – hoping that this strategy would elicit a more positive response. Results, however, were disappointing. As other researchers have found, junior editorial staff acted as effective 'gatekeepers' (see Hammersley and Atkinson, 1995: 63–7). Some referred me to an endless chain of other staff, while others simply blocked off my lines of enquiry by insisting (perhaps understandably) that fieldwork was not permitted because it would disrupt the workplace. Attempts at achieving access through letter proved little more successful. While some within the industry agreed to see me, meetings were frequently cancelled by telephone with less than an hour's notice – and sometimes when I was already waiting in the office foyer. To be fair, this is understandable. Like all professionals, women's magazine practitioners are necessarily concerned with the job in hand. And, in fact, I eventually succeeded in speaking to all those who had initially agreed to a meeting. The interviews that took place were semi-structured and enabled me to build up a general understanding of the industry's personnel structure and the functions of various staff. But the meetings did not, as I had hoped, lead to permission for further informal contact. Interviews were invariably short, while their formality made it difficult to raise the possibility of fieldwork access.

Issues of access were not the only problem with this methodology. It quickly became apparent that interviews and ethnography, in themselves, would not provide the kind of material needed for a thorough-going, critical account of the operation of the women's magazine industry. Perhaps predictably, such approaches did not allow practitioners to talk openly about their work and the operation of their company. Media professionals are understandably concerned about how they will be depicted in research and, in my own case, the practitioners I approached seemed especially worried that I would criticize them for the ways their magazines depicted contemporary femininities. As Oliver Boyd-Barrett has observed, such tensions are not uncommon. Boyd-Barrett suggests that the prominence of issues of political economy, ideology and cultural hegemony in academic analyses of media occupations and media output has not helped to 'open doors for further research' (Boyd-Barrett, 1995: 271). Studies of media practice have often been critical in tone and historically have had little use value for media professionals. As a consequence, Boyd-Barrett argues, media industries have shown limited interest in facilitating academic research. Indeed, this is borne out by my own experience. Within the women's magazine industry I encountered attitudes of both mistrust and disdain towards academic media research – a negativity that was frequently reinforced by calculations about my political investments, based upon a knowledge of previous academic studies in the area. As a woman and an academic, it was assumed that my intellectual stake in studying the women's magazine industry must have its roots in what was perceived to be a 'retrograde' form of feminist politics. Given that many previous feminist academic studies had been highly critical of women's magazines and their producers, it is perhaps unsurprising that the prospect of assisting yet another hatchet job did not seem especially attractive.

With my original research plans facing such insurmountable obstacles, I looked towards alternative methodological strategies. In particular, I began to seek other published accounts of women's magazine production and their professional processes. Whilst there are few academic articles on this subject, accounts of contemporary magazine production in Britain were available in the Periodical Publishers Association (PPA) magazine, *Magazine News*. Launched in 1989 as part of a PPA public relations exercise, *Magazine News* had been designed to promote interest in, and awareness of, the contemporary magazine sector among advertisers, marketers, potential sponsors and retailers. A British trade publication produced as a response to dwindling magazine circulations and advertising revenues in the 1980s, *Magazine News* was especially anxious to argue for the commercial benefits of advertising and investing in magazines over other media, and generally to reorient the opinions of colleagues, competitors and clients more favourably towards the magazine industry. Though this source was obviously partisan, I found it was actually possible to learn a great deal about the practices of the women's magazine industry from the self-promoting accounts offered by practitioners in its pages.

The narratives of magazine publishing in *Magazine News* also turned my attention towards other (often conflicting) accounts of women's magazine production practices that appeared in the advertising and marketing trade press. An examination of titles such as *Campaign*, *Media Week* and *Marketing Week* reveals that until the mid-1980s they had relatively little to say on the subject of women's magazines or about marketing to women. The mid-1980s, however, saw a flurry of interest in the marketing potential of the glossy women's titles that were beginning to appear. In particular, the magazines *Working Woman*, *Elle*, *Marie Claire* and *New Woman* prompted a great deal of interest among advertisers keen to find appropriate media vehicles for the targeting of professional women.

Though partial and value-laden, such sources represent a valuable avenue for the analysis of the professional practices and cultures of production within the women's magazine industry. Obviously, such accounts are not a neutral reflection of 'what went on' in women's magazine publishing during the 1980s and 1990s. Instead, the value of the trade press accounts lies in the way practitioners sought to represent their production processes and practices to one another. They are attempts by practitioners to organize *their own* understanding of what they do, and to represent it to other culture industry professionals. In other words, there is a politics of representation at issue that aims at modifying, reshaping and redirecting the relations not simply between the magazines and their readers, but also between various colleagues, professionals and clients from the wider world of commercial industry.

Readers will notice that I have steered away from any attempt to anchor the meaning of women's magazines through close textual analysis. Instead, I have drawn upon trade press descriptions and assessments of magazine texts to demonstrate the ways in which industry practitioners and commentators developed a particular set of discourses around their products. Rather than being based on a semiotic analysis of women's magazines, therefore, this study deals primarily with the *discussion* of texts that took place in the trade press and newspaper commentaries. The strengths of such an approach lie in its capacity to situate magazines within their specific institutional contexts. Unlike the textual analyses of women's magazines, this method draws attention to the ways in which the 'meaning' of women's magazines is not generated simply at the moment they are read by their audience. Instead, it highlights the existence of a *range* of discursive sites where meanings are read, re-read and reconceptualized – discursive sites that not only exist at the point of consumption, but also at the point of *production*. Women's magazines, this study contends, are objects of discourse and sites of contestation not only for their readers, but for their producers as well.

This study does not pretend to be neutral and dispassionate. It would be neither possible nor desirable to try to produce a 'true' account of the production of commercial femininities within the magazine industry of the 1980s and 1990s. Instead, like any other account of media culture, this research needs to be situated within a continuum of debates about positivism, realism and inter-pretation within social science practice and epistemology. The organization of my research material uses a series of case studies to develop a theoretically informed account of the social, economic and political discourses that underpinned the development of women's magazines during the 1980s and 1990s. At the same time, however, it examines wider relationships between the producers and consumers of commercial media aimed at women and, as such, explores more general questions about the relationship between com-mercial cultures and identity. In this capacity the analysis that follows hopes not only to advance our understanding of women's magazines, but also to offer insights useful for future feminist research dealing with media culture.

2

POST-FORDISM, POST-FEMINISM AND THE 'NEW WOMAN' IN LATE TWENTIETH-CENTURY BRITAIN

To 'understand' the texts that are the focus of this book – women's magazines of the 1980s and 1990s – it is necessary to situate them within their broader cultural, political and socio-economic context. In particular, we need to think about the way in which shifts in women's employment and cultural experience impacted upon the themes, imagery and modes of address that characterized the changing face of women's magazines during the late twentieth century. As we shall see, within the magazine industry there developed a specific set of perceptions regarding the nature and trajectory of change in women's lives during this period – perceptions which were a fundamental influence on the symbolic meanings and associations inscribed within the monthly 'glossies' which came to dominate the women's magazine market.

A thorough-going analysis of women's magazines as a 'culture industry' demands an approach which understands them as both 'economic' and 'cultural' phenomena, and which teases out the precise nature of the relationship between the planes of culture and economy. The first part of this chapter, therefore, explores competing accounts of the nature and scale of economic and cultural change in advanced industrial societies and, in particular, assesses what light notions of 'post-Fordism' might shed on developments in the British economy during the 1980s and 1990s. Though such perspectives certainly influence and inform this study, existing accounts of post-Fordism tell us relatively little about the specific ways in which these patterns of economic and cultural change impacted upon *women's* lives.[1] The second part of the chapter, therefore, explores the range of feminist, sociological and cultural studies that have dealt with shifts in women's cultural and economic experience during the 1980s and 1990s. These patterns of change (and the ways they were interpreted) are vital to an appreciation of the transformation that took place in the women's magazine industry – the lifestyles, interests and values of *particular* groups of women emerging as the principal constituency in British magazine publishing and related commercial fields.

Fordism and its discontents

A plethora of academic work has analysed and accounted for the significant changes that have occurred in international economic structures since the Second World War. For many theorists, this period has been characterized by a shift from a 'Fordist' era of mass production for mass consumer markets, to something different – something variously termed 'post-Fordism' (Murray, 1989), 'neo-Fordism' (Aglietta, 1979; Lipietz, 1987), 'disorganised capitalism' (Lash and Urry, 1987) and 'flexible specialization' (Hirst and Zeitlin, 1997; Piore and Sabel, 1986). These accounts disagree about the precise nature of the routes Western economies have taken out of Fordism,[2] but they share a common belief that patterns of economic change during the 1970s and 1980s brought about significant social transformation. Generally, the Fordist era of mass production and mass consumption (and their associated economic, political and social structures) is seen as giving way to a new epoch characterized by more flexible approaches to manufacturing and the rise of plural consumer markets. These transformations, moreover, are not explained solely in economic terms. Rather, they are generally seen as (at least partially) both responding to and reproducing *cultural* discourses about the nature of capitalism in the late twentieth century.

But, before I explore the various 'post-Fordist' pathways in greater depth, it is useful to begin by establishing a better sense of 'Fordism' as a distinct industrial era. In his influential essay on the transition from Fordism to post-Fordism, Robin Murray (1989: 38–42) identifies a set of characteristics and structures that distinguished 'Fordism' as the dominant mode of production in twentieth-century Western economies. Fordist industries, he observes, were marked by large-scale production of standardized products – exemplified by the mass-production systems pioneered by Henry Ford at his car works at Dearborn, Michigan, at the end of the First World War. Such modes of mass production, Murray argues, were supported by a system of protected national markets that enabled industry 'to recoup its fixed costs at home and to compete on the basis of marginal costs on the world market' (Murray, 1989: 39). These structures of production were accompanied by new sets of centrally managed working practices and systems of work relations that were inflexible, hierarchical, and de-skilling in character. Whilst this enabled rigid control of production by the manufacturers, it also produced bureaucracies that were vulnerable to sudden falls in demand – particularly falls caused by economic recession. In order to maintain its stability, therefore, Fordism necessitated state intervention in the national economy through Keynesian demand and monetary management. 'Mass consumers' were also essential as the all-important market for the standardized products, while the rise of mass advertising 'played a central part in establishing a mass consumption norm' (Murray, 1989: 39). Combined together, these strategies allowed the Fordist system of production to proliferate in the manufacture of everything from cars and ships to clothes, food and even popular entertainment.

From the late 1960s onwards, however, the Fordist regime in America and Europe was beginning to experience problems that would gradually come to a head. Exactly *why* Fordism reached this point has been a subject of much debate. Two factors, however, loom large in accounts of its decline (Allen, 1992: 187–8; Aglietta 1979). First, a system geared towards mass production and consumption faced the dual difficulties of dealing with fluctuating demand for products and shifting patterns of taste amongst consumers. This instability was exacerbated by an excessive bureaucracy and a de-skilling of labour that produced unfulfilling working environments and a consequent high turnover of workforce and the constant threat of strike action. Second, Fordist structures were not able to respond to global shifts in post-war patterns of demand. Whilst Fordism was founded upon the hegemony of America within the world economic order, by the late 1960s the US was facing new competition from countries such as Japan and Germany. The emergence of these new players broke down oligopolistic methods of pricing within national markets, the new dimension of competition producing global economic instability and an increase in the prospect of international recession. The structures of Fordism, therefore, were unable to cope with the unpredictability of these shifting dynamics within the spheres of production and consumption. Moreover, trends in government policy towards deregulation and free-market ideology robbed Fordism of its 'safety net'. In this context of instability, change and vulnerability, therefore, Fordist modes of production were increasingly transfigured.

After Fordism?

Studies of the resolution of this Fordist 'crisis' have tended to take either a broadly 'neo-Fordist' or a 'post-Fordist' stance (Allen, 1992: 188).[3] For the neo-Fordist school, the 'crisis' of Fordism has partially resolved itself through the development of greater economic flexibility. This has been achieved through employing new technological innovations; maximizing the use of a small and skilled (rather than large and unskilled) workforce; and through introducing greater flexibility in the scale of production (Aglietta, 1979). The new technologies of production have also enabled decentralization, with many firms moving aspects of their production to previously peripheral locations – including countries such as Hong Kong, Taiwan, Singapore, South Korea and Brazil. According to neo-Fordists, these trends do not actually represent a *break* with Fordism. Instead, Fordism has continued in a new form, seeking new markets, maintaining high levels of productivity and bureaucracy and employing new groups of workers to perform unskilled and poorly paid labour (Lipietz, 1987).

Theorists of post-Fordism, on the other hand, argue that there has been a move *beyond* Fordism, involving profound shifts in economic organization and the nexus of regulation. Like neo-Fordists, advocates of post-Fordism point to the new, more flexible, manufacturing systems and to the new forms of working practice with which they are associated. Post-Fordist theorists, however, are more optimistic than neo-Fordists about these developments. For post-Fordists, there may be a more positive side to the rise of new production technologies because, in return for flexibility, post-Fordist industries offer employment and institutional security – post-Fordism generating both a more multiskilled labour force and a less hierarchical work environment (Murray, 1989).

Additionally, theorists of post-Fordism highlight a series of production changes generally ignored in the neo-Fordist model. Robin Murray, for example, points to the ways in which manufacturing organizations (driven by the demands of newly computerized retailers) use new technologies to 'overcome the limits of the mass product' (1989: 43). Murray details the ways that technology facilitates change in manufacturing processes, helping producers to develop and sell products in response to the vagaries of demand. In addition, manufacturers and retailers have come to rely on 'ranges of products geared to segments of the market' (Murray, 1989: 43) – with the rise of new, more specialized forms of design and marketing strategy geared to more specific market 'niches'. Indeed, in contrast to the neo-Fordist accounts, consumption has a starring role in post-Fordist narratives of economic change. Frank Mort (1989: 167–8), for example, notes that manufacturers, marketers and retailers have increasingly resorted to '[g]reater market segmentation [which] demands different methods of communication ... [with an] upbeat stress on design and visual awareness'. In turn, he observes, consumers expect something more from consumption, requiring it to fulfil rational and informational, as well as 'emotional', needs. Advertisers and marketers, therefore, 'appeal to the unique *you*', offering 'a proliferation of individualities, of the number of "yous" on offer' (Mort, 1989: 168). Moreover, this shift towards pluralization within production, Stuart Hall argues, is part of a more general trend towards pluralism in social life across the industrialized world, this trend demonstrating the acceptance of new 'positionalities and identities available to ordinary people ... in their everyday working, social, familial and sexual lives' (Hall, 1989: 129).

Fordism, post-Fordism and the modern British economy

Despite their differences, post-Fordist and neo-Fordist theorists share the view that the late twentieth century saw the global economy increasingly characterized by changes that were both profound and complex. This complexity, moreover, is compounded by the fact that there is no single economic dynamic. Rather, different national economies have taken their own trajectories out of Fordism – with distinct and diverse economic strategies being developed in Europe, the US, Japan and so on. Indeed, Sean Nixon (1996: 23) has observed that British moves towards flexible specialization (or post-Fordism) may be very different to those typical of elsewhere in the West. The UK national economy, Nixon argues, was *never* underpinned by a classically Fordist system of mass production. While the British model of capitalism was based on the same ideological theories as that in the US, its institutional and political structures were very different and markedly less efficient. Compared to other nations, therefore, Britain's move into an era of flexible specialization was noticeably distinct – and relatively less successful.

Attempts to account for the underlying weaknesses of the British capitalist model are highly controversial. Will Hutton (1996: 293), for example, has traced the problems back to the character of Britain's early industrialization and the 'largely spontaneous and market driven' economic ethos which emerged during the eighteenth century. The subsequent reluctance to countenance state intervention in the economy, Hutton argues, was a key factor in Britain's steady decline as the leading industrial power. Bob Rowthorn (1983: 67), on the other hand, has argued that it was the international organization of British capital that ultimately led to economic decline – a historical dependence on Empire and production centres outside the UK leading to a weakened manufacturing base after 1945, as the structures of Empire were dismantled.

While accounts of the roots of British economic decline vary, there is general agreement that the slide accelerated during the mid-1960s. British industrial growth remained relatively strong until 1966, but then began to falter. This is the point, it has been argued, when the first signs of British 'de-industrialization' begin to appear, with a significant fall in levels of manufacturing employment (see Rowthorn, 1983: 70; Hirst and Zeitlin, 1997). The downturn then became unmistakable, the world oil crisis in 1973 leading to an international slump that exacerbated Britain's economic stagnation and pushed the national economy into further decline. In addition, a growing imbalance of international trade led to a greater state of economic instability. More buoyant economies such as West Germany and Japan were in surplus by the mid-1960s and continued to grow through a reliance on export markets. In Britain, however, the economic policies of both Labour and Conservative governments were geared towards stimulating domestic demand, a strategy that encouraged more imports and increased balance of payments problems (Currie, 1983: 87). As Sked and Cook (1990: 327) have observed, by the time of the Conservative Party's 1979 general election victory, the popular view of the electorate was that Britain was 'the sick man of Europe' and – whatever the origins of its inefficiency – it was clear that the British capitalist model could not continue along the same path.[4]

The free-market outlook of the Conservative governments of Margaret Thatcher and John Major was an important factor in British manufacturing's uneven transition into flexible specialization and post-Fordism after 1979. Where the 'consensus' politics of earlier Conservative and Labour governments had advocated Keynesian economic intervention geared towards maintaining levels of demand, 'Thatcherite' doctrine argued for an economy based on free-market competition and monetarist principles. Across the economic spectrum, therefore, post-1979 Conservative governments championed competition, entrepreneurialism and profit, with an ethos that venerated private property and individualism (Hayes, 1994: 62). And, in line with monetarist dogma, a tight control of the money supply was exercised through the Bank of England, thus maintaining high rates of interest and forcing individuals and firms to reduce borrowing. Monetarist policies dictated that economic success could only be achieved through a relentless pursuit of competition. To keep costs down, therefore, industries would have to lay off workers and adopt more streamlined modes of operation. Only the firm that could be ruthlessly competitive, both at home and overseas, would survive (Lowe, 1984: 484–5).

The Conservative government's commitment to free-market enterprise also sought greater scope for foreign investors in British business. By the late 1980s, twenty of Britain's top thirty employers were multinational companies – a trend applauded by the government for its creation of jobs and promotion of technological innovation. In addition, overseas companies (particularly from Japan) were encouraged to use Britain as a resource for cheap labour and develop centres of production in the poorer areas of central Scotland, the north-east of England and south Wales. Simultaneously, industrial relations were transformed, with a significant reduction in union power (though workers in some, newer, industries enjoyed an increased participation in decision-making) (Marwick, 1990: 313–14).

Conservative governments were shrewd in the way they secured consent for their policies of free-market individualism. As Frank Mort has demonstrated (1989: 163–4), whilst the abstract concepts of Keynesian theories sometimes made them difficult to explain, monetarism was easily translated into a 'popular', 'common-sense' rhetoric. Thatcher, for example, frequently referred to the British economy as if it were the contents of her own purse and made periodic references to 'balancing the books' and the 'housewife's budget'. The popular adage 'you cannot spend more than you earn' was also employed to illustrate and popularize management of the national economy (see also Hayes, 1994: 77). Breaking from traditions of welfarism, Conservative governments also promoted what Deborah Cameron has called 'enterprise values' – values that not only govern '"individuals" conduct in the public sphere of industry, commerce and politics, but also . . . their private lives as community and family members' (2000: 9). And, as Leadbeater notes, some social groups were understood to be more 'enterprising' in their values and actions than others. These 'rising classes' – the socially mobile and affluent working class, the entrepreneurial classes, the private-sector middle class, the young urban professionals – all asserted their support for extensive privatization (Leadbeater, 1989: 143). Conservative governments actively sought to secure the consent of these 'enterprising' groups, offering them rewards and incentives that included cuts in income tax and corporation tax, a rise in the threshold on capital gains tax and a reduction in the upper tax band on investment income. The figure of the 'enterprising individual' was, therefore, used by Conservative governments to secure consent not only for a free-enterprise consumer society, but also for a more general philosophy of 'how society should be organized ... [that had] individual morality at its centre' (Leadbeater, 1989: 141).

These discourses of enterprise and individualism were crucial to the restructuring of areas of British manufacturing along the lines of flexible specialization (or post-Fordism) during the 1980s and 1990s. The fundamental ethos of the period's 'enterprise culture' promoted ideals of creativity, competition and self-interest, together with the rational maximization of potential. These values, moreover, were not confined to individual morality, but found their economic correlative in the structures of flexible, 'post-Fordist' manufacturing and service. As Anna Pollert suggests, the drive towards post-Fordist industrial flexibility can be seen as symptomatic of not only economic change, but also significant political and ideological shifts (1988: 62–3). For Pollert, the rhetoric of 'flexibility' and 'post-industrialism' is based on a 'false premise of initial homogeneity' which ignores the 'long-standing segmentation' of capitalist firms since the earliest days of the factory system' (1988: 62–3). Though distorted and a-historical, Pollert contends that the discourses of 'post-industrial flexibility' had significant ideological impact, helping to promote the credo of 'competitive individualism' within the small business sector at a time of recession and working to obscure the extent of exploitation in this sector by promoting 'the illusion that the self-employed are all independent, profit-making entrepreneurs' (Pollert, 1988: 63–4).

Post-Fordism, post-feminism and gendered inequality

Feminist commentators have also found fault in the rhetoric of 'flexibility' and 'post-industrialism'. Linda McDowell (1992: 182–3) and Sylvia Walby (1997: 75), for example, have both been critical of those accounts (such as that offered by Piore and Sabel, 1986), which present practices of flexible specialization as having emancipatory potential for 'marginal groups' such as immigrants, minority ethnic populations and women. Adherents of the 'emancipatory' thesis find support for their position in the growing number of women in the labour force after 1945, especially in many 'high-skill' and 'high-wage' industries.[5] As McDowell points out, however, this thesis ignores a growing divide in the 'post-Fordist' labour market between a 'skilled and permanent core', in which women are underrepresented and generally subordinate, and 'a temporary, exploited periphery' where women make up the bulk of the workforce (McDowell, 1992: 183).[6]

One of the major criticisms of Fordism from a feminist perspective was that its labour-market regulations, combined with traditional ideologies about gender roles, clustered women at the bottom of the occupational hierarchy (see, for example, Beechey, 1982; Wood, 1982). In Britain in 1975, for example, the upper socio-economic groups of professionals, employers and managers included only 5 per cent of economically active women – a figure which compared to 20 per cent of economically active men. In contrast, the lower socio-economic groups of semi-skilled manual, service personnel and unskilled manual workers included 40 per cent of economically active women, compared to just 22 per cent of economically active men (OPCS, cited in Walby, 1997: 35). Women workers in 'Fordist' Britain were also accorded lower pay, less occupational security, fewer promotion prospects and fewer employment rights than their male counterparts. The emphasis on women's domestic labour in the home, meanwhile, further ensured a disproportionately heavy workload for the majority of women (see Gershuny *et al.*, 1994).

As feminist critics note, however, the shift into post-Fordist forms of flexible production has done little to 'emancipate' women. McDowell (1992) and Walby (1997) acknowledge that the proportion of women within the workforce has increased – from 55 per cent of British women of working age in 1971, to 71 per cent in 1991 – but they insist that gender inequalities persist in patterns of employment (McDowell, 1992: 183; Walby, 1997: 64). More women than men, they argue, take up short-term contracts and temporary work, while women are more likely to experience intermittent periods of unemployment and to be less eligible than men for so-called 'fringe' benefits such as sick pay and pension schemes. In this way women can be seen as the 'new model workers' in the age of post-Fordist flexibility (McDowell, 1992: 181–2; Walby, 1997: 78–9). McDowell and Walby both argue, moreover, that post-Fordism has intensified class divisions between women. It is, they contend, a minority of mainly white, middle- and upper-class women who can reap the rewards of developing opportunities in labour markets traditionally reserved for men. The economic position of working-class women, however, has declined, so that the possibility of economic independence without an income from a male partner looks increasingly bleak (McDowell, 1992: 188–9). Indeed, as Walby explains:

> [t]he higher the socio-economic group of the woman, the more likely she is to be in employment and the more likely that employment is to be full- rather than part-time. The notion of the 'bourgeois family' model where women stay at home is empirically incorrect. The class that could most afford for women to stay at home is the one in which women do so least. Amongst professional and managerial women, 85 per cent are economically active, 65 per cent full-time, while only 68 per cent of unskilled manual workers are economically active, 7 per cent full-time.
>
> (1997: 59–61)

Furthermore, Walby asserts that class-based inequalities between women are amplified when children are brought into the equation. Mothers in professional and managerial occupations, she observes, are far more likely to work full-time than those in unskilled, manual work. This is because the costs of childcare are much more bearable for women in professional work, and so maintaining a career is a feasible option. For women in unskilled occupations, on the other hand, the cost of childcare means that continuing in full-time work is less viable. In 1992–4, for example, only 3 per cent of women with dependent children in the unskilled manual socio-economic group remained in full-time work, but this figure leapt to 47 per cent among professional or employer manager women (OPCS cited in Walby, 1997: 60).

Empirical evidence, then, suggests that gender-based economic divisions and inequalities remained pronounced in late twentieth-century Britain. Paradoxically, however, this period saw a welter of popular media discourses celebrating 'improvements' in women's lives. According to this account, women's equality with men had finally been 'achieved' and so feminism had become an irrelevant anachronism. Myra Macdonald (1995: 91–2), amongst others, has argued that such 'post-feminist' discourses were particularly visible in the context of consumer culture, where an image of the post-feminist 'New Woman' was strongly promoted. This archetype incorporated a 'feminist' language of 'freedom', 'independence' and 'pleasure', but reduced these to matters of lifestyle and consumption.[7] In particular, Macdonald points to advertisements of the 1980s and early 1990s that suggested that women could now 'do their own thing' and 'be comfortable with who you are' through the purchase of 'an independently-minded new hairstyle, new look and new bra' (Macdonald, 1995: 93). Self-fulfilment, therefore, could be achieved not through collective feminist action, but through the individual woman's consumption of consumer products.

Certainly, as Walby acknowledges (1997: 63), the 1980s and 1990s saw some moves towards greater gender equality in the realms of education, employment and political life. Nevertheless, she argues, these shifts did not amount to the dawn of a new era of gender equality in which feminist politics had become redundant. Excluded from 'post-feminist' freedoms, for example, were large numbers of older women, women from minority ethnic groups, women with children and women with fewer educational qualifications. These were women who had, at best, an ambiguous relationship with the sphere of life central to notions of 'post-feminist' identity and individuality – consumption.

According to Anne M. Cronin (2000), women's unequal access to the realm of consumption does not simply have consequences for what they are able (or unable) to purchase. Additionally, she asserts, women's access to consumption also has serious consequences for their status as citizens. As evidence, Cronin points to the Conservative government's 1991 White Paper, *The Citizen's Charter: Raising the Standard*, which configured a notion of the

British citizen as an individual who qualified for citizenship through being a 'consumer of goods and public services and . . . [a] taxpayer' (Cronin, 2000: 32). Those not embraced by this discursive framework, therefore, were implicitly configured as subordinate to other, more 'active', citizens. Women, in particular, were peripheral to this notion of citizenship. By implication, poor women, unemployed women and women in receipt of state welfare all lacked recognition as citizens of their national community through their inability to participate fully in the consumer society.[8]

In this light, media proclamations of gender equality during the 1980s and 1990s seem unduly premature. Certainly, many middle-class women *did* reap rewards from, for example, equal opportunities campaigns, shifts in trade union policies and changes in family practices. But such transformations did not, by any stretch of the imagination, involve *all* British women. Indeed, as Walby (1997) and Cronin (2000) suggest, the differences between groups of British women along the lines of class and 'race' were actually accentuated during this period, indicating that the aims of second-wave feminism had only been 'won' for the few. In these terms, the media celebration of 'post-feminist' freedom and pleasure can be seen as addressing the experience of a comparatively select group of women – those white, young and middle-class women who were able to exercise their 'empowerment' through consumption.

Backlash? Gender, politics and a taxonomy of 'post-feminism'

In her book *Postfeminisms*, Ann Brooks (1997: 4) has usefully distinguished between media configurations of 'post-feminism' and academic concepts of 'postfeminism'. The former, she argues, is essentially depoliticized and incorporated – configuring gender-based inequality as a (steadily waning) problem, to be faced and resolved at the level of individual experience. Focused around issues of '"women's rights" and equal opportunities', it amounts to a 'white, Western, middle-class, mainly northern hemispherical conception of feminism' (Brooks, 1997: 4). In contrast, Brooks argues, feminists in academia have never argued that the need for feminist politics has passed, though since the 1980s many have proposed 'a political shift in feminism's conceptual and theoretical agenda' focused around concepts of 'difference' (Brooks, 1997: 4). In this respect, academic postfeminism draws inspiration not only from the intellectual heritage of the women's movement, but also from an engagement with concepts of postmodernism, post-structuralism and post-colonialism, together with attention to the interests of 'marginalised, diasporic and colonised cultures' (Brooks, 1997: 4). In this way, academic postfeminism can be seen as posing a major challenge to a key tenet of second-wave feminism – the idea of bringing about change through a feminist alliance based upon common experience and the unifying concept of 'women' (Brooks, 1997: 23).

Other theorists, however, see the distinction between media and academic forms of 'post' feminism as less clear-cut. In a fierce critique, Georgina Murray (1997: 46) argues that academic postfeminism (like media post-feminism) *also* excludes most women. In particular, Murray points to the complex theoretical language employed in academic postfeminist writing. Such rhetoric, she argues, is meaningless to, and works to exclude, the 'ordinary woman'. Worse still is the abstract and theoretical emphasis of postfeminist work. This, Murray argues, obscures the realities of the social, economic and political problems that women meet and masks points of convergence other than 'womanhood' on which collective battles can be fought.

Such criticisms are harsh, and perhaps underplay academic postfeminism's meaningful contribution to feminist political practice (see Brooks, 1997). Nevertheless, Murray's arguments do alert us to the problems academic postfeminists have faced in developing interventions outside the academy. Arguably, writers working within more 'traditional' feminist perspectives achieved greater success during the 1980s and 1990s. Naomi Wolf, for example, won popular acclaim with *The Beauty Myth* (1991), a book whose attack on the trappings of consumer femininity echoed many of the concerns of 'second-wave' feminism. Denouncing women's magazines and advertising for heightening women's insecurities and for maintaining their patriarchal subordination, Wolf argued that commercial representations of femininity were responsible for the growth of the perniciously manipulative diet, beauty and plastic surgery industries. In this way Wolf hoped to alert women to their participation in a 'hopeless' quest to achieve an impossible standard of beauty – and ultimately to their place in the operation of patriarchy.[9]

Journalist Susan Faludi (1992) also achieved popular success in this period with her critique of a 'post-feminist' media discourse that, she argued, was ideological and illusory and constituent in a wider patriarchal 'backlash' against second-wave feminism and its achievements. In Faludi's analysis, this 'backlash' sought to turn back the clock, reversing feminist gains in the spheres of employment, reproductive rights and personal relationships, thus pushing women back into 'traditional' feminine roles. For Faludi, the media were especially culpable in this assault, by blaming feminism for increasing the likelihood of poverty, childlessness and of a life without marriage for women – in short, the media accused feminism of offering women a 'lesser life' (Faludi, 1992: 17).

As Walby has argued (1997: 164), Faludi's idea of a 'backlash' is at least partially borne out by developments in Britain during the 1980s and 1990s. Walby points, for example, to the rise of campaigns against abortion and against rights for gays and lesbians, as well as the emergence of a reactionary Puritanism among some fundamentalist religious groups. John Major's (failed) 'Back to Basics' moral crusade of 1993–4 could also be seen as evidence of a 'backlash' through its focus on 'traditional' forms of family life and sexual relationship. Despite these developments, however, Walby argues that there is little evidence to support the claim that women were being pushed back into 'traditional' roles by a scheming establishment. Indeed, aspects of women's autonomy undoubtedly increased, exemplified by some women's growing access to high-status employment. Certainly, some state initiatives hindered women's autonomy in the sphere of work and confined many women to part-time work and poor employment conditions. But this did not necessarily amount to a wholesale campaign geared to a revival of 'traditional' gender roles. The policies of the Thatcher and Major governments, therefore, did not add up to the kind of systematic, 'backlash' perceived by Faludi. Instead, Walby argues that both governments pursued a project of 'public patriarchy', intensifying women's exploitation in the *public* (rather than the private) sphere (Walby, 1997; 164–5).

Also interesting is Walby's suggestion that patriarchal pressure in the public sphere has produced greater inequalities between women, identifiable in terms of divisions of class and 'race' (Walby, 1997: 164–5). Dimensions of class and 'race' have, she argues, ensured differential access to things such as higher-level occupations, good pay, job security, pension schemes and childcare. Essentially, then, Walby argues (1997: 165) that patriarchy is dynamic in its form and represents something much more complex and variable than 'post-feminist' authors such as Faludi have acknowledged.

Post-Fordism, post-feminism and the 'New Woman'

This chapter has surveyed various interpretations of recent economic and cultural change in advanced industrial societies, exploring these with specific reference to developments in Britain during the 1980s and 1990s. It has also drawn on popular and academic literature to consider the impact of such developments on women's economic and cultural experience. I have argued that, although post-Fordist flexibility in the realm of production certainly impacted on patterns of class and gender relations, any assumption that it engendered greater economic equality is grossly misleading. I have also outlined the rise of 'post-feminist' perspectives – though any notion that feminist politics had become 'redundant' has been vigorously contested. But how does all this enhance our understanding of the development of women's magazines during this period?

When considering the emergence of new, glossy women's magazines during the 1980s and 1990s, they cannot be explained as the straightforward products of a contemporary 'mood' or general 'feeling' about British femininity that can be 'read off' from the texts' representations and mode of address. Instead, these magazines have to be understood in terms of their complex relation to the wider social, economic and political context. In this chapter I have outlined the economic, political and technological shifts that characterized Britain during the 1980s and 1990s. In the chapter that follows, I explore the significant impact that these shifts had within the organization and operation of the women's magazine industry.

Nevertheless, attention to changing patterns of business organization cannot, alone, account for the phenomenon of women's 'glossy' magazines. Consideration must also be given to material developments in women's lives. In the media celebration of 'post-feminist' emancipation, changes in patterns of gender relations were misunderstood and distorted. But for some women – mainly white, young and middle-class – opportunities *did* arise for an improved quality of life. And, as I will argue in Chapters 5 and 6, the attempt to address this group of relatively affluent, upwardly mobile women as a distinct market segment was a key factor in the development of 'the glossies'. Pitching themselves to a 'New Woman' who could please herself, be self-sufficient and autonomous, the glossies were constituent in the fabrication of a 'post-feminist' emancipation. Their iconography, however, was not pure mythology. Indeed, the glossies' mode of address worked so successful because it managed to connect with the life experiences of a fortunate minority of women who *were* enjoying the fruits of the commodity culture. As later chapters in this book will show, it was these women whom the magazine industry took as symbolic of femininity during the 1980s and 1990s, the glossies developing a range of techniques to address these women as a distinct 'community' of readers. Nevertheless, it must be remembered that, in doing so, the glossies also constructed some women as 'Others' who were excluded from this 'community'. In the sparkling world of the glossies, some forms of femininity were accorded greater cultural and symbolic power than others.

3

THE EMPIRES STRIKE BACK

From Fordism to post-Fordism in the British magazine industry

The previous chapter established that any attempt to 'understand' women's magazines has to consider both the cultural *and* the economic conditions of their emergence. And in the case of the women's 'glossies' that emerged in Britain during the 1980s, it is clear that their rise was underpinned by a confluence of cultural and economic forces. We have already seen the importance of the economics of flexibility, the ethos of enterprise and the discourses surrounding the growth of 'post'-feminism. Building on this, much of the rest of this study will be concerned with exploring the business of women's magazines and related institutions as discursive arenas of late twentieth-century femininity – a place where the cultural meanings and repre-sentations of modern femininity are forged, fought over and understood. At the same time, however, we also have to remember that women's magazines are the products of an *industry*, with its own particular relations of production and consumption. Any attempt to understand the cultural discourses associ-ated with women's magazines, therefore, must do so with an eye to their economic context and business imperatives. As we shall see, the history of the magazine industry during the late twentieth century cannot be understood in isolation from its broader socio-economic context. In particular, this chapter focuses on how the 1980s and 1990s saw the British magazine business negotiate with both the rise of post-Fordist industrial flexibility and the growing hegemony of ideologies of free-market enterprise. In the case of the latter, we will see in coming chapters how – for the British magazine industry at least – the 1980s 'enterprise ethos' was not simply a chimera of abstract ideas, but was translated into very real economic and cultural *practices* that completely reconfigured women's magazines as cultural forms.

The rise and fall of Fordism in British magazine production

Fordist methods of production, as we saw in Chapter 2, are frequently associated with large-scale, assembly-line manufacturing in a factory context. But this is not always the case. This style of production, for example, was not always typical of the early organizational structures of the British magazine industry – nor, for that matter, of many other culture industries such as the record industry and book publishing in Britain. Yet, early on in their histories, these industries can still be seen as developing a decidedly Fordist character. During the first half of the nineteenth century, for example, the industrial-ization of British magazine publishing was relatively slow, but by the 1890s a range of new technologies was being widely introduced to processes of paper production, typesetting and printing. The initial expense of new technologies has meant that (as with newspaper publishing) the ability to invest in fixed capital has always been a key factor in patterns of ownership and control in the magazine industry. Traditionally, the magnitude of such investments also demanded a Fordist-style search for economies of scale through a drive towards ever larger print runs (Ballaster *et al.*, 1991: 80–1). This became possible during the late nineteenth century through a combination of factors. While the abolition of taxes on paper and periodicals in 1853 kick-started the development of the magazine industry, growth was sustained by a steady increase in potential readership as a result of population growth, greater literacy, increased leisure time and growing levels of disposable income. Growing readership, in turn, attracted advertisers. Keen to promote sales of consumer goods, advertisers were especially attracted by magazines' ability to make products appear enticing through improved techniques of photographic reproduction, and by the 1880s it was common to find magazines carrying (as many do today) editorial and advertising in equal measure (Ballaster *et al.*, 1991: 81–2; Davis, 1995: 7).

By the end of the First World War, a small coterie of owners had come to dominate British magazine publishing. Many of these were set to hold their command over the industry into the twenty-first century. For example, the late nineteenth century saw the rise of Newnes, Harmsworth and Pearson as industry giants, and then in 1958–61 the three combined to form the largest British publishing company of the twentieth century – IPC. Founded in 1869, the Dundee-based publishing company, D. C. Thomson, also became a highly successful player in the magazine market. In addition, the boldly titled National Magazine Company was taken over by the American publishing tycoon, William Randolph Hearst, in 1911, and was used to publish British editions of magazines already successful in North America. These trends towards the national and international consolidation of business interests allowed a significant accumulation of capital through new economic benefits. Larger circulations, for example, allowed magazines to both raise their adver-tising rates and reduce their production costs, while international ownership allowed for the greater syndication of copy. Moreover, magazine publishers – like other media producers – assembled increasingly standardized ranges of products, aiming to appeal to the widest (and thereby largest) possible readership (Curran and Seaton, 1991: 50–2). The industrial development of magazine production also impacted upon the organizational structure of the business. As with the newspaper industry, aspects of magazine production increasingly became akin to a factory – though (in contrast to newspaper publishing) processes of magazine production were not drawn together at a single location.[1]

From the late nineteenth century, a formal division of labour took shape in British magazine publishing. On one hand, there were the publishing houses themselves. On the other, there were a host of independent production firms on which the publishers relied – typesetters, printers, repro-houses and so on (Driver and Gillespie, 1992: 149–50). The close industrial relationship between the different sectors of production meant that most businesses tended to be concentrated around London or other big cities, though print operations were invariably some distance from the publishers' offices (Driver and Gillespie, 1993a: 57). Compared to newspaper production, the publication of a magazine requires more preparation – or longer 'lead times' in industry parlance – and as a consequence the proximity of printer to publisher was generally less important. Nevertheless, in true Fordist fashion, some magazine publishers (IPC for example) consolidated their structures through the development of large, in-house printing divisions. But by 1945 most magazine publishers had decided that it was inefficient to rely on printers located in expensive, prime city sites, and instead switched to cheaper printing operations based in city outskirts and suburbs (Driver and Gillespie, 1993a: 57).[2]

In this system of production, jobs in publishing, pre-press and printing were also tightly defined. As processes of production became more mechanized during the 1950s and 1960s, areas of employment and their responsibilities became more firmly demarcated (Davis, 1995: 171). Similar divisions of labour also took place in the publishing houses. Located in purpose-built, city centre offices (invariably in central London), publishers were increasingly segmented into specialized departments – editorial, advertising, sales, accounts and circulation. These departments, meanwhile, were overseen by new layers of executive management that included managing editors, editors, deputy editors, associate editors, production editors, art editors, picture editors, features editors, news editors, cookery editors and so on (Davis, 1995: 16–21). In turn, these divisions of labour also required new management systems and bureaucratized work routines. The content of magazines was normally planned at conferences or 'think-tanks', sometimes attended only by heads of departments who then passed decisions down to other members of staff. Predetermined, long-term production schedules also became common, as publishers fixed their sights on the regular production of standardized commodities with mass circulations and a high volume of advertising (Davis, 1995: 40).

This was the system of business organization that dominated British magazine production until the late 1970s. By this time, however, the magazine industry (along with many other sectors of British business) was finding that a new economic environment was making these Fordist systems of production increasingly moribund. Particularly important was the fracture of the magazine industry's assumptions of market predictability. In 1977 a Royal Commission on the Press noted that British magazine publishing was in trouble as mass-market magazines – especially in the women's consumer, general interest and television listings markets – experienced a sharp drop in circulation. IPC, for example, found that while its popular woman's weekly title, *Woman*, had sold up to 3.2 million copies a month during the 1960s, its circulation had plunged to around 1.5 million. Tumbling sales were experienced throughout the magazine industry (Royal Commission on the Press, 1977: Tables 8–11). The combination of a general economic recession and growing competition from other media (especially television) seemed to have impacted severely on magazine circulation. The magazine market seemed to be becoming more volatile and increasingly fragmented, readers appearing to be less interested in the standardized magazine formats that had been the industry's backbone. Moreover, dwindling sales and growing competition for advertising from other media also meant that advertising revenue was ebbing, forcing many magazines to introduce higher cover prices that made them even less attractive to potential buyers.

Fearing that the market for magazines (especially that for women's titles) might all but disappear, publishers desperately sought to cut costs. All levels of production, therefore, saw a concerted drive to eliminate practices deemed wasteful. Despite being among the most labour-intensive areas of the magazine industry, the pre-press and printing sectors were the first targets. There was a general feeling among publishers that the pre-press and print unions – the National Graphical Association (NGA) and the Society of Graphical and Allied Trades (SoGAT) – had too much power and were maintaining unfeasibly high wage rates for their members. High wages had been more acceptable to management in the prosperous years of the 1950s, but the bleak economic climate of the late 1970s prompted a tougher stance (Seymour-Ure, 1991: 23). As circulations and advertising revenues fell, the large, vertically integrated publishing houses (IPC, for example) struggled with their production costs, but in the short term they could only survive by raising magazine cover prices. In the longer term, however, management were determined to reduce costs by breaking the unions (Driver and Gillespie, 1992: 150–1).

Margaret Thatcher's Conservative government broadly endorsed the publishers' strategy. In the terms of the government's neo-liberal ideologies – implemented in the Department of Employment by James Prior and Norman Tebbit – the trade unions were perceived as subverting the free market, demanding artificially high wages that restricted industrial development and productivity. The government also argued that unions priced workers out of jobs, creating a barrier to a more flexible, competitive and dynamic economy. In an 'enterprise economy', it was argued, there could be no place for trade unions that wielded such influence and the government introduced legislation designed to curb their power (Hayes, 1994: 65). Notable here was the Trade Union Reform Bill, spurred by a bitter miners' strike and piloted through the

Commons in 1984 by Norman Tebbit. This Bill made unions liable for damages incurred during a strike, unless a majority vote for strike action had been secured in advance by a secret ballot of members. It also required unions to hold secret ballots, not only for the election of leaders but also prior to affiliating to political parties (Sked and Cook, 1990: 452). In conjunction with earlier legislation that had outlawed secondary picketing, this Bill can be seen as a concerted attempt to demolish British trade unionism. It was, however, a strategy that met limited popular opposition. As Sked and Cook have observed, during the mid-1980s the British electorate seemed resigned to high levels of unemployment, government spending cuts and a more coercive state apparatus, believing these to be the only means of saving a nation in decline (Sked and Cook, 1990: 436–7).

Nevertheless, workers at the sharp end of these economic policies often sought to resist. In the world of magazine publishing, for example, workers in the pre-press and print sectors stood firm against employers' attempts to restructure the industry. This was a stand-off that provided one of the first occasions in which the new union legislation could be tested. Industrial action in the pre-press and print sectors initially affected only newspaper production but, as Driver and Gillespie observe (1992: 151), strikes by print workers in Stockport (1983) and Wapping (1986) had long-term effects on the whole of the print industry. These disputes focused on employers' efforts to introduce new technologies as a way of offsetting rising production costs. Greater use of technological innovation, employers claimed, would permit lower numbers of staff and increased levels of productivity – though many in the labour force perceived this as an attempt to lay off workers, reduce wages and break the bargaining power of the unions. The disputes were angry and protracted, but ultimately it was the employers (buttressed by the authority of the new, anti-union legislation) who were victorious. And – in what many commentators dubbed 'the Wapping Revolution' – the introduction of cost-cutting technology and new employment practices heralded a wholesale reconfiguration of the British newspaper industry (Seymour-Ure, 1991: 23).

In retrospect, debate exists as to the precise significance of the 'Wapping Revolution' in the history of British newspaper publishing (see Bromley, 1996: 237–8). There can be no doubt, however, that the Wapping dispute threw into stark relief the issue of new technologies and employment practices in the pre-press and print sectors. And, after the employers had triumphed, there arose a new climate of de-collectivized industrial relations in which the print unions were significantly weakened and marginalized. Nor were these consequences confined to the newspaper industry. Magazine publishing was also transformed by the fall-out from the Wapping Revolution. By the early 1990s the management of all the major magazine houses (and the smaller ones too) had ceased to recognize not only production workers' unions, but also those of editorial staff (i.e. the National Union of Journalists). This ended the long-standing 'house agreements' that had not only recognized the unions' place in collective bargaining over employment terms, but had also secured unions the right to consultation in matters of workers' health and safety and had guaranteed the individual members' entitlement to union representation in disciplinary procedures (Gall, 1998: 151). These changes amounted to a major reconfiguration in labour relations, but in hindsight they can be seen as even more significant. The transformations in the realm of employment practice were indicative of the profound shift in the organizational structure of British magazine publishing as the industry stumbled from the age of Fordism into a new post- (or neo-) Fordist era (Gall, 1998: 151–61).

Towards a post-Fordist magazine industry

The drive towards post- and neo-Fordist-style production processes within British magazine publishing first registered in pre-press working practice. In an attempt to streamline and rationalize the pre-press sector, new technologies were adopted in the form of word processors and computer-based publishing systems. Further advances came with the introduction of new, more complex 'mainframe' systems such as Atex. These made it possible for journalists to input their text directly, removing the time-consuming system of 'double-keying' by which typesetters had been responsible for the input of copy. The print unions were initially concerned about the change, but by the end of the 1980s journalists' direct input of text had become standard practice (Driver and Gillespie, 1992: 152). The computer-based desk-top publishing (dtp) systems of the 1980s were not capable of meeting the high standards demanded in magazine production, but the decade saw the industry gradually deploy dtp technology in a way that incrementally eroded the boundaries between the publishing house, the typesetters, the repro-house and the printer. However, as Driver and Gillespie observe (1992: 154–5), the use of computers varied between different publishing houses – and sometimes even between different magazine titles produced by the same publisher. Publishers were cautious in their adoption of the new technology and, conscious that new equipment might quickly become obsolete, erred towards small-scale investments whenever possible.

Nevertheless, the introduction of dtp technology ultimately transformed the traditional networks of production within magazine publishing offices. From their computer terminals, magazine journalists could pass copy to sub-editors and art departments, where computer programs could be used to lay out the pages, with gaps left for the later insertion of pictures. Pages and picture transparencies were then sent (on computer disk, or through a telecommunications line) to the repro-house where they were downloaded. After pictures and text were merged through the use of high-resolution digital scanners, an image setter would then produce film separations from which a proof copy of the magazine could be made for the publisher's approval before the film was finally sent to the printers. In this new system of production, therefore, the responsibility for typesetting was effectively removed from the pre-press sector and placed in the hands of the publisher (Driver and Gillespie, 1992: 156). Change also registered in the repro-sector of magazine production. As publishers increasingly favoured pre-press systems that could accept pages in digital format (either on disk or on-line), small scale repro-houses were compelled to make significant capital investments in digital scanning technologies. To make this cost-effective, however, new employment patterns were also required and three-shift working became commonplace. Some repro-houses, meanwhile, combined to form larger pre-press businesses, hoping to cover the costs of new technology through economies of scale. Inevitably, however, some parts of the pre-press sector were badly affected by the changes. Typesetting, for example, faced large job losses during the 1980s and early 1990s, while several large pre-press companies announced their closure or entered receivership (Driver and Gillespie, 1992: 156–7).

In the wake of the Wapping dispute, industrial relations in the magazine print sector were also significantly transformed. In an effort to reduce printing costs (which, on average, accounted for 50 per cent of magazine publishing costs), the magazine publishers Maxwell, Reed/IPC and Murdoch sold off their colour-printing companies – the British Printing Corporation, Odhams and Bemrose (Driver and Gillespie, 1992: 151). This effectively freed the publishers from the power of the print unions and enabled them to abandon long-term contracts with specific printers. At the same time the major publishers also developed active print- and paper-buying departments, helping them secure discounts on bulk orders for paper and allowing them to bargain for cheaper print deals (Driver and Gillespie, 1993a: 58).

The cost-cutting drive also altered the geographic location of magazine production. Traditionally, magazine publishers had preferred printing to take place close to central London, the city regarded as the major British magazine market.[3] The 1980s, however, saw print operations shift towards more suburban locations as publishers engaged in a 'complex balancing act between the cost of print, the time sensitivity of the magazine and the distribution of consumer demand' (Driver and Gillespie, 1993a: 58–9). Though this shift had significant ramifications for some news and current affairs driven publications, the impact on women's monthly magazines was relatively slight. With copy produced usually three or four months in advance, women's magazines have never been especially time-sensitive and so the distance of printers from London has been a factor of less importance compared to issues of quality and economy. As a consequence, many women's monthly magazine titles began to be printed outside the traditional hundred-mile radius of London – *Elle*, for example, was printed in Plymouth, while *Cosmopolitan* and *Marie Claire* were both printed in Yorkshire (Driver and Gillespie, 1993a: 58–9).

Despite its expense, London remained the focal point of magazine production. Given the cost-cutting climate, this might seem strange – especially given that other publishing industries (the book trade, for example) were increasingly locating to more economic environs. But a location in the capital was especially important for magazine publishers for three key reasons. First, London remained the centre of the journalist labour market and a shift further afield might have presented publishers with problems in terms of staff recruitment and retention. Moreover, any commercial gain made through a move might have been outweighed by the costs of staff relocation (Driver and Gillespie, 1993a: 55–6). Second, as Jeremy Tunstall (1971: 11–12) noted in the case of newspaper journalism, London is where the stories are. In the case of women's magazines, for example, the city hosts events such as London Fashion Week, film premieres, book launches and numerous important fixtures in the diaries of fashion and consumer journalists. Close proximity to these events is essential, since much magazine journalism relies on networking with formal and informal contacts – connections that would be difficult to maintain outside London. In the case of fashion journalists, for example, Angela McRobbie (1998: 152–61) has observed that effective links with other fashion-related industries are essential if a journalist is to maintain regular employment. Finally, London is also the centre of a nexus of services on which magazine publishers depend – from press cutting and picture libraries to graphic designers and artists, advertising agencies and so on. Moreover, as Frank Mort observes, for most creative media workers, London represented:

> a focal point for de-luxe markets and . . . a cultural entrepôt [which] provided these individuals with the economic rationale for living and working in the capital. . . . [F]or the journalists, designers and other personalities who made up this loose alliance, the metropolis was also a focus of creative inspiration.
>
> (Mort, 1996: 149–50)

Though the publishing houses remained centred in London, they were not exempt from the search for cost effectiveness. During the 1980s and 1990s, magazine publishers' cost-cutting measures were especially focused on journalists' working practices. These decades, for example, saw dramatic changes in the working conditions of magazine journalists, while the position of the main journalists' union – the National Union of Journalists (NUJ) – became increasingly marginal within the industry, many publishers ceasing to recognize it altogether. Gregor Gall (1998) explains these events as a consequence of the changes in magazine journalists' working practices that followed the introduction of new technology. According to Gall, magazine publishers' introduction of this technology had undermined the collective organization of print workers, but as a consequence had put journalists in a strategic position within the production process (Gall, 1998: 153). Now able to halt or disrupt production processes, journalists seemed to be in a strong bargaining position. Employers responded by attempting to undermine the union's existing power, and by preventing them from establishing a foothold in new areas of development. As a consequence, the 1980s saw the NUJ slip into decline and there followed a deterioration in magazine journalists' terms and conditions of employment as, by various means, publishing houses gradually withdrew agreements on starting salaries, overtime, casual labour, holiday and redundancy pay, the working week and allowances (Gall, 1998: 154).

In addition, Gall observes, a two-tier system of journalism was introduced. At the top, employers offered senior journalists 'executive contracts' with higher pay (Gall, 1998: 154–6). This meant that some magazine journalists – including chief subeditors and section heads – took up managerial roles and become senior members of production teams, employers hoping they would then deter colleagues from industrial action. At the bottom, some full-time and permanent journalists remained on contracts similar to those negotiated under collective bargaining. Others, however, remained working for their companies, though they were 'forced' into freelance status. Overall, many newly appointed employees found (and still find) themselves employed on contracts vastly inferior to those of their predecessors. The pay structures of many journalists were also affected, with a greater emphasis on *individual* performance. Increasingly divided into separate groups, with different terms and conditions of work, journalists found it more difficult to organize collectively (Gall, 1998: 156).

Angela McRobbie's research (1998: 160) on fashion journalism suggests that such changes were pronounced within the magazine industry. McRobbie notes that major women's magazines such as *Marie Claire* depend on a surprisingly small core of full-time staff, assisted by contract workers who are employed under a variety of terms. For McRobbie, this has generated a new 'freelance culture' within women's magazine publishing – a culture with distinct forms of social relations in the workplace. In tandem with the deterioration of their contracts and working conditions, for example, freelance staff have become increasingly immersed in informal survival strategies of team-work and subcontracting in order 'to get the job done' (McRobbie, 1998: 160).

At the same time, magazine journalists have also become increasingly multiskilled. Indeed, the 1980s and 1990s saw a steady 'reversal' of the traditional, Fordist-style management divisions within magazine publishing. For instance, not only did magazine journalists take on the double-keying role of the typesetter, they also increasingly operated as technicians, researchers and so on. In addition, as McRobbie (1998: 160) notes, it became the norm for many permanent staff (both part- and full-time) to take on additional freelance work. It was not unusual, for example, for a fashion editor to be employed on a three-day contract for one magazine and to do freelance work for other titles during the remainder of the week. Numerous full-time staff worked in a similar way, McRobbie finding that staff worked in a variety of freelance roles – filing copy for foreign newspapers, proofing material for radio and television programmes and working as a consultant for a design company (McRobbie, 1998: 160). Effectively, then, many magazine journalists had become – to use a term coined by Stephenson and Mory (1990) – 'generic media workers'.

The trans-national trend and the distribution revolution

From the early 1980s the push towards post-Fordism within the British magazine industry was unmistakable, as publishing houses steadily adopted company structures that were more diverse, increasingly de-centralized and less bureaucratic. It was hoped that these new forms of business organization – in conjunction with greater use of new technologies and new systems of work practice and labour relations – would deliver greater profits through the promotion of flexibility, internal competition, innovation and a greater emphasis on design and quality.

Developments at the East Midlands Allied Press (EMAP) exemplified these shifts. During the 1980s EMAP expanded by establishing semi-autonomous satellite companies that were managed under a broad divisional structure and that specialized in specific business markets (Driver and Gillespie, 1993b: 188). IPC also adopted a more de-centralized form of business organization. For example, ancillary services that IPC had formerly undertaken in-house were increasingly contracted to outside firms, a move that brought numerous job losses in both management and the labour force (Driver and Gillespie, 1993b: 188). Even more significant, however, was IPC's decision to transform its magazine titles – previously grouped together as a single corporate entity – into competitive 'mini-profit centres'. As a result, IPC magazines was rearranged into four distinct sectors to handle different ranges and genres of magazines – the IPC Weeklies Group, the Southbank Publishing Group, the Holborn Group and the Specialist and Leisure Group (Norton, 1993: 246). The rationale behind this shift towards a variety of company sectors was that it would allow publishers to focus more effectively on the 'lifestyle' attitudes, aspirations and preferences of specific groups of readers. Large publishing companies, therefore, moved away from the production of 'mass' titles – making their profits through economies of scale – to 'niche' titles that achieved success through zeroing in on specific market segments (Driver and Gillespie, 1993b: 188).[4]

The 1980s also saw major magazine publishers diversify their interests into other business sectors, particularly the information, communication, leisure and entertainment industries. In the early 1980s, for example, EMAP attempted to acquire the franchise for Anglia Independent Television – though this particular bid was ultimately rejected. IPC's parent company, Reed, was more successful with its investments in on-line media and satellite broadcasting. This cross-media diversification widened potential audiences for IPC and EMAP's products, enabling them to 'cross-subsidize' risky business ventures – magazines, for example – with investments in new media markets. While some of these moves were relatively straightforward investments by the major publishers, others involved the creation of independently owned and controlled divisional or satellite companies (Driver and Gillespie, 1993b: 195–6).

By the 1990s, all the larger publishing groups were seeking to consolidate their economic positions through revamping their systems of business organization and diversifying their industrial base.[5] In particular, the financial clout of the British magazine industry's 'Big Four' – the National Magazine Company, IPC, EMAP and Condé Nast – allowed moves into lucrative cross-media agreements. Of the 'Big Four', EMAP was most active in expanding its business interests beyond the realm of magazine publishing. By the late 1990s EMAP's stated corporate objective was 'to create one of the world's most highly rated media businesses' (Max-Lino and Poissonnier, 1999: 175), and in addition to operating three core media businesses – in consumer magazines, radio and TV – the company was striving to develop interests in on-line and e-commerce. IPC was also making similar moves. Indeed, by the end of the 1990s, IPC saw little future in magazine publishing per se, instead expanding into television, digital 'media brands' for the Internet and other new media forms. Underlining this shift of direction, IPC even changed its name to IPC Media in 2000. While magazines still remained a significant part of IPC's output, they were clearly now regarded as just one component of IPC's multi-faceted media business (Teather, 2000: 18). In July 2001 AOL Time Warner of the US paid £1.15bn for IPC Media.

Diversification and cross-media agreements also helped the 'Big Four' expand their financial interests across international markets. EMAP was particularly active, and by the late 1990s had made significant acquisitions of media companies in the US, Australia and France (Max-Lino and Poissonnier, 1999: 171).[6] Indeed, during the 1980s and 1990s international expansion was a marked trend within the magazine industry as a whole. The British market, for example, saw the arrival of several foreign magazine publishers, including the French publishing group Hachette in 1985 with *Elle*, the German publishers Gruner and Jahr (G & J) in 1986 with *Prima*, together with their rivals Bauer in 1988 with *Best*. The Spanish parent company of *Hola!* magazine also pitched camp in Britain with the launch of a British version – *Hello!* – in 1988. In turn, British publishers increasingly sought to expand overseas. Some publishers established satellite companies abroad, to oversee the launch and development of British titles in foreign markets. Others entered into joint venture or franchise agreements with local publishers, such as IPC and Groupe Marie Claire with *Avantages*, the French edition of IPC's *Essentials*. Each strategy had its own advantages. Satellite companies were adept at tailoring titles to a new market and were well placed to draw on the expertise of local journalists and marketers. Franchise agreements with publishers in other countries, meanwhile, were potentially hugely lucrative. The profits possible from a successful international magazine were immense, publishers finding that such titles were extremely successful in attracting advertisers keen to promote the growing number of internationally marketed consumer goods (Driver and Gillespie, 1993b: 196–7).

The search for increased profitability also extended to processes of distribution. For the publisher, the time-scale of magazine distribution is hugely significant, since profits can only be made when titles are stocked on retailers' shelves. During the 1980s and 1990s, therefore, publishers sought to boost the speed and efficiency of distribution. Traditionally, distribution had been the responsibility of the publisher, who delivered copies of magazines to wholesalers, who in turn supplied them to retailers. In this arrangement retailers initially received the magazines under a 'firm sale' agreement that made them liable for any copies left unsold. From the early 1970s, however, the increasing popularity of 'sale or return' agreements allowed retailers to buy magazines on credit from the wholesaler and to return any unsold copies. The unsold magazines were then sorted by hand into piles of individual titles and, ultimately, the wholesaler would pay the publisher according to the number of copies sold. It was a laborious process, but the shift into 'sale or return' agreements prompted both wholesalers and retailers to be more ambitious in their ordering of titles (Labovitch, 1985: 26–7).

During the 1970s magazine publishers further refined the distribution chain by introducing the distributor as a mediator between themselves, the wholesaler and the retailer. In this system, the distributor had the responsibility for supplying magazines to the wholesaler, where they would be packed and labelled as the wholesaler canvassed orders from retailers. The distributor's role was also to arrange transport for the magazines with road and rail haulage companies, to locate suitable sales outlets and to help target titles towards the market with greater effectiveness. The wholesaler, however, remained responsible for calculating sales. As before, the process was time-consuming, distributors waiting up to three months to receive the unsold copies of a single magazine issue. And the publisher was only paid after the distributor had deducted a variety of costs incurred during the process. *Media Week*, then, was probably close to the mark when, in 1985, it estimated that this complex system often left magazine publishers with only 45 per cent of the cover price of each sale, with unsold copies bringing no revenue at all (Labovitch, 1985: 27).

As a consequence, the wholesale trade during the mid-1980s pioneered a more efficient 'affidavit' system of calculating returns. This was a cheaper method of counting unsold copies since it did not require them to be transported back to the distributor or publisher. Instead, the wholesale sorting officer was required to fill out an affidavit form showing the total number of unsold copies and this was then forwarded to the distributor for payment. Copies of unsold magazines were then destroyed within the week. The fierceness of industry competition, however, meant that many publishers were understandably fearful of the possibilities for corruption and error within this system and many went so far as to pay for whole editions of unsold magazines to be returned to them for double-checking (Labovitch, 1985: 27). In view of these problems, diversification into the field of distribution became a logical step for the larger magazine companies.

Independent distributors continued to survive, but they faced increasing competition. IPC's Marketforce, for instance, became one of the largest distribution concerns, distributing not only all of IPC's own titles but also titles for a range of smaller publishers. Britain's leading distributor, COMAG (a joint venture between the National Magazine Company and Condé Nast) also moved into the distribution of third-party titles, as did EMAP's Frontline and the BBC's magazine division. The financial benefits for publishers involved in magazine distribution were considerable. Substantial revenues could be gained by distributing the magazines of smaller companies, and smaller companies were keen to use the muscle of large publishers to achieve sales (Bland, 1989: 19).

Combined with strategies of internationalization and diversification, therefore, British magazine publishers' move into magazine distribution signified a drive towards the economies of scope. And, across the board, the 1980s and 1990s saw distribution companies strive to improve their business efficiency. In an attempt to enhance their appeal to third-party publishers, for example, many distributors began to move into the realms of magazine marketing and advertising. In doing so, they made growing use of complex market research tools such as ACORN (a residential classification system, discussed more fully in the following chapter) (Labovitch, 1985: 28), together with increasingly sophisticated electronic data interchange (EDI) networks (Braithwaite, 1998: 102). The latter was an inter-organizational computer network which offered distribution companies greater efficiency through its ability to streamline systems of order processing and payment, as well as offering a more accurate system of sales tracking (Blackett, 1993: v). Overall, compared to the traditional system of wholesaler distribution, the new systems' greater focus on the targeting and marketing of magazine titles appealed more to publishers who were becoming increasingly concerned with 'staying close' to their customers. Better able to co-ordinate between circulation departments and retailers, the new system of distribution was also an asset in publishers' promotional efforts. During the early 1980s, for example, COMAG successfully improved their marketing strategies through the introduction of a computerized marketing system which helped them identify locations where the readers of a particular magazine were likely to live, adjusting their distribution to better match these readers' 'purchasing potential' (Lee, 1985: 21).

The services offered by distributors were further enhanced by the introduction of electronic data processing (EDP) technologies into the retail news trade. A combination of EDP technologies based on bar-coding – specifically, electronic point of sale (EPoS) tills and electronic funds at point of sale (EFTPoS) facilities – allowed chains of retail newsagents to obtain instant records of items sold. This permitted more efficient and effective systems of stock management, as well as providing more detailed information on individual customers paying by credit card or cheque (du Gay, 1996: 106–7). The benefits this information offered to distributors were huge and they clamoured for all publishers to introduce bar-coding on their products as swiftly as possible.

Bar-coding allowed a magazine's edition number, issue date and price to be instantaneously identified and recorded in a central database, this information allowing retailers and distributors to keep a close eye on the performance of each title. Bar-coding could also provide data on supply, return and sales more quickly and accurately than the traditional manual systems (Rand, 1991: iv). Smaller publishers, however, were initially resistant to demands for the introduction of bar-coding, pointing to the expense of putting such a system into operation (*Magazine News*, 1989b: 9). For bigger publishers, however, the advantages of bar-coding were irresistible and IPC was the first of the 'Big Four' to embrace the practice. Working in conjunction with the major news-agents chains John Menzies and W. H. Smith, IPC developed an electronic bar-coding system for its products and by 1988 computer-to-computer links existed between the publisher and the major retail chains, a facility that greatly accelerated the processing of credit claims and provided IPC with details of unsold magazines at a speed far quicker than any wholesaler could hope to match (*Magazine News*, 1989a: 10).

The ultimate catalyst for the implementation of bar-coding in the British magazine industry was pressure from supermarket chains such as Tesco and Sainsbury.[7] During the 1960s, Thomson magazines had negotiated an exclusive contract with some British supermarkets for the in-store sale of their lucrative women's titles *Family Circle* and *Living*. By the 1980s, however, Thomson had grown into an international business conglomerate and its British subsidiaries had come to represent 'bottom-line figures on a multi-national balance sheet' (Garth, 1988: 37). In 1988, therefore, Thomson sold its consumer magazine interests to IPC, effectively providing them with a much desired 'Trojan horse for the supermarkets' (Garth, 1988: 37). By 1989, the opportunity to sell magazines in supermarkets was so appealing to publishers that Tesco was able to insist that, for its own convenience, all magazines on its shelves must carry a bar-code, and other supermarket chains followed suit. By 1990 newsagent chains such as John Menzies and W. H. Smith had taken the same stance, insisting on bar-coding for all magazine titles they stocked (Dignam, 1989: 1; Blackett, 1990: 13).

At the same time, major wholesalers were also recognizing the ability of bar-coding to speed magazine distribution and the collation of sales data, John Menzies Wholesale and W. H. Smith News both gradually adjusting their wholesale systems to accommodate bar-code scanning. As a consequence, wholesale procedures were revolutionized. The laborious and error-prone system of checking every copy of a magazine against the quantities claimed by retailers' affidavit notes disappeared. Instead, bar-coded magazines could be passed swiftly across a scanning beam, allowing the quick and accurate identification of the title. This, wholesalers claimed, vastly improved systems of ordering and distribution and allowed the development of much more effective systems of trend analysis (Coyle, 1991: iii; *Magazine News*, 1989a: 10).

Markets, management and magazines

Overall, the 1980s and 1990s were a period of profound reconfiguration and adjustment within the British magazine industry. The Fordist structures of publishing, printing and distribution that had traditionally characterized the magazine industry seemed increasingly ill-suited to the emerging economic, political and cultural climate. In their place, publishers sought business structures and distribution processes that were more cost-effective through their greater flexibility, more effective use of technological innovation and enhanced responsiveness to consumer demand. As we have seen, many of these changes centred on the computerization of production processes, a trend that brought unemployment to a range of industry sectors. Simultaneously, a cost-cutting drive within magazine publishing led to smaller core organizations that were more specialized and increasingly focused on specific market niches, while many tasks (especially in the sphere of magazine journalism) were increasingly subcontracted. Moreover, spurred on by contemporary political rhetoric that promoted ideologies of free-market 'entrepreneurialism', occupations within the magazine industry became more multifaceted and multiskilled. Organizational structures also became more 'organic'.[8]

In the magazine industry's shift towards 'post-Fordist' business practices, many sectors of production were de-centralized. Nevertheless, it is impossible to ignore concurrent moves towards more centralized processes of decision-making in some areas of publishing activity. As we have seen, for example, most large publishers developed and consolidated their in-house distribution departments, believing that these could function as the 'eyes and ears' of a more market-led business (Barrell and Braithwaite, 1988: 131). Greater centralization also took place in the spheres of typesetting (which moved towards vertical integration) and paper and print buying, where better discounts could be achieved through bulk orders. The financial operation of magazines, meanwhile, also remained under central control (Driver and Gillespie, 1993b: 199). Driver and Gillespie (1993b: 199), therefore, are justified in their argument that we should not over-emphasize moves towards 'flexibility' within the magazine industry during this period. Certainly, there were elements of a 'post-Fordist' style of restructuring within the industry, but shifts towards greater centralization were also in evidence. And, while company structures such as those that developed at EMAP could be labelled 'post-Fordist' fairly easily, others – for example, those adopted at IPC – could, at best, be described only as 'neo-Fordist'. As Driver and Gillespie maintain, straightforward notions of 'post-Fordism' do not do justice to the complex diversity of transformations that took place within the magazine industry as it adapted to the changing business environment of the 1980s and 1990s (Driver and Gillespie, 1993b: 199).

Nonetheless, it is clear that in order to maintain their profitability, magazine publishers sought more flexible, responsive and innovative forms of production and business organization. There was, however, also an important cultural dimension to these economic transformations. As Paul du Gay argues (1997a), to be meaningful for the people involved, economic practices must be translated into 'cultural' discourse. For example, du Gay (1997a: 309–10) sees the motif of 'the customer' as looming large in much managerial discourse of the late twentieth century. According to du Gay, 'the customer' has become 'an overriding imperative' in many industries, used to justify a range of organizational reforms and transformations as the internal life of many firms has become centred on this notion of an enterprising and consuming subject.

This notion of the 'customer' as a discursive device is useful in the analysis of the relationship between the magazine industry and its two primary 'customers' – the advertiser and the reader. In particular, du Gay's ideas can be used to understand how magazine publishers and related industries made organizational and technological change *meaningful* for their workforce. The 'modernization' and 'professionalization' of business practice could be justified as an attempt to adapt to 'the customer's demands' – publishers citing 'customer need' as a rationale in their transformation of labour relations. The erosion of long-term contracts with journalists, the pre-press sector and wholesale companies also meant that the magazine industry was increasingly predicated on customer/supplier business relationships, while the introduction of satellite companies and 'mini-profit centres' meant that interactions between employees and departments *within* individual publishing firms could be conducted through the discourse of 'the customer'. The process exemplifies du Gay's (1996) argument that employees of the same company can literally become 'customers' for each other, conceiving of one another as 'customers' in their daily working practices as the boundaries between 'worker', 'manager' and 'customer' become increasingly difficult to distinguish and there is a blurring of the boundaries separating '"inside" and the "outside" of organizational life' (1997a: 311).

According to du Gay, the focus of the contemporary business ethos on 'the customer' encourages subjects within organizations to internalize and behave in ways that correspond to ideologies of free enterprise and market competitiveness (du Gay, 1996). Within 'customer-oriented' working environments, du Gay claims, workers are encouraged to become 'enterprising individuals', investing more of their sense of self in their work. In the context of the magazine industry, this is exemplified by the responses of wholesale employees to the bar-coding of magazine titles. Initially, some magazine sorters perceived bar-coding as a strategy of managerial surveillance, but employers argued that bar-coding allowed a more effective response to the needs of the 'customer' (in this case the publisher) (*Magazine News*, 1989a). Bar-coding, it was claimed, could also increase levels of job satisfaction for manual sorters, as they were now able to sift through greater numbers of magazines and could be assured that the risk of human error had been eradicated. In addition, the sorter could now be conceived more prestigiously, as an 'information processor' who supplied the customer with a constant stream of essential sales information (*Magazine News*, 1989a).

Far from being abstract economic theories, therefore, concepts of post-Fordist flexibility and the ethos of 'enterprise' were tangible forces throughout the British magazine industry during the 1980s and 1990s. These processes, moreover, were not purely 'economic', but were inseparable from the realm of 'culture'. The 'economic' and the 'cultural' spheres are mutually constitutive and the transformation of production processes and business practices found their corollary in a range of concomitant social and cultural changes. As we shall see in Chapter 4, for example, many of the industrial shifts in women's magazine publishing during the 1980s and 1990s were intrinsically tied to changing discourses around the nature of contemporary femininity. The profound shifts in notions of femininity, however, were not smoothly accommodated within the magazine industry. Instead, as we shall see, magazine publishers' recognition of change in women's identities and lifestyles came only as a grudging response to shifting practices in the field of advertising.

4

WHO'S THAT GIRL?

Advertising, market research and the
female consumer in the 1980s

Magazine publishing does not exist in isolation from other commercial institutions of cultural production. Allied especially closely is the advertising industry. Advertising has been central to the business of women's magazines since the 1890s, when the 'ladies' papers' realized the potential profits to be gained through the subsidy of cover prices by advertising revenues (Ballaster *et al.*, 1991: 115). Prior to World War Two, however, British advertisers saw women's magazines as relatively unimportant to the business of marketing compared to, say, newspapers and general interest publications. By the 1950s this had changed. The expansion of mass consumer markets, especially those oriented around women's expenditure, brought a significant increase in women's magazines' share of total advertising expenditure (Elliott, 1962: 209).[1] Janice Winship (1987: 38) has observed that this close relationship between the magazine business and advertisers has always placed magazine producers in a double bind. Women's magazines have to appeal to their readers in order to maintain a high circulation, yet since no magazine can make a profit on its cover price alone it is 'the wooing of advertisers which is . . . pivotal in the competitive search for revenue' (Winship, 1987: 38).

This chapter explores this relationship in relation to the success of the 'glossy' women's magazines of the 1980s. This success, it is argued, was constituent in a broader drive by advertising practitioners to develop new forms of 'commercial femininities' during the period. Across a wide range of marketing campaigns, the decade saw advertisers develop imagery in which women were constructed as 'enterprising consumers', a marketing strategy which emerged alongside the development of new, more 'customer-responsive', forms of organization and production within the women's magazine industry. This chapter examines the development of the business attitudes and practices that intersected in these marketing campaigns of the 1980s. Particular attention is given to the 'creative revolution' that Sean Nixon identifies as having characterized the British advertising industry from the late 1970s – a profound shift in advertisers' priorities and practices that brought a wholesale reassessment of 'what constituted an effective advert;

how advertisers addressed consumers within campaigns; and the image of the market place which underpinned campaign development' (Nixon, 1996: 76). Central to this transformation were growing attempts by advertisers to 'stay close to the customer', marked by a major reassessment and reformulation of advertising research and production as practitioners sought to keep their fingers on the pulse of a consumer market they perceived as unprecedentedly variable and fast-moving. In the context of women's magazines, these processes were accompanied not only by new techniques of consumer-focused market research, but also by a new understanding of the organizational identities of advertising practitioners themselves. These identities embraced ideologies of 'individualism' and 'creativity', advertisers understanding themselves not as 'organization men' of the Fordist era – but as sovereign subjects and dynamic figures of the 1980s 'enterprise culture'.

Global markets and the rise of international advertising

Published in 1982, Terence Nevett's history of advertising in Britain painted a somewhat gloomy picture of the industry's potential future. Pointing to recent decline in UK industrial output, high rates of inflation and unpredictable rates of economic growth, Nevett argued that as conditions became more complex, advertisers' clients would become more demanding about the way their money was spent. In order to survive, Nevett contended, advertising agencies would need an exceptionally rare blend of 'skill, flair, and imagination' (Nevett, 1982: 205). In part, Nevett was correct. During the 1980s broad patterns of economic change dictated that the advertising industry was compelled to rethink its organizational structure and practices. But, on the other hand, Nevett's prognosis was unduly pessimistic, under-estimating the ability of British advertisers to reorganize and expand along new institutional, financial and creative lines (Nixon, 1996: 78). Indeed, the 1980s saw the UK advertising industry experience an unprecedented period of expansion, a growth underpinned by a marked increase in expenditure on advertising – from 1.1 per cent to 1.6 per cent of GDP between 1980 and 1988 (Nixon, 1997a: 104).

The reasons for this dramatic change in advertisers' fortunes were complex. The change was largely brought about by a general resurgence of the British economy. Between 1979 and 1989 labour productivity in British manufac-turing rose by 4.8 per cent a year, while the 2.2 per cent growth rate in GDP achieved across that period was among the highest in the European Union (US Department of State, 1995). As we saw in the previous chapter, the driving force behind this recovery was a government-orchestrated consumer boom, with consumption rising from 62.2 per cent of GDP in 1979 to 67.5 per cent ten years later (Penn World Tables, 1992). A further factor in the renaissance of British advertising was the emergence of new areas of demand for advertisers' services. Here, Frank Mort (1996: 91) identifies the increased use of advertising by political parties and demand generated by the privatiz-ation of public utilities (beginning with the share flotation of British Telecom in 1984) as especially important. In addition, UK advertisers (spurred on by the prospect of more open European markets) increasingly became inter-national players, seeking higher volumes of sales via the worldwide (as opposed to the domestic) market. Across the board, meanwhile, businesses began to plan, co-ordinate and implement their activities on a global scale and turned to advertisers in their attempts to establish an international market profile superior to that of their competitors (Meffert and Bolz, 1993: 46–7).

As Celia Lury and Alan Warde (1997: 90) argue, such changes in market organization often provoke periods of intense business anxiety. As a response, producers invariably turn to the skills of advertisers and marketers to guide them through the volatile world of consumer demand. But during the 1980s the advertising industry itself was also affected by the push to become internationally active. Amid the shifting economic climate advertisers were, themselves, compelled to find new ways of representing their business activities to their clients. To do this, they needed to sell the ethics and logics of their agencies, promoting their businesses as research-grounded organiza-tions with the ability to understand and appeal to the attitudes and interests of consumer markets that were not only increasingly fragmented and variable, but also increasingly global.

Like other industries during the early 1980s, advertisers deliberated over the impact of globalization on their business practice and explored various strategies for operating at an international level. By 1991 all of the top thirty British agencies (except Bartle Bogle and Hegarty (BBH)) would have access to an international network, ensuring that their names would appear on a pitch list anywhere in Europe (Brierley, 1995: 73). Partly as a consequence of these moves, profits in British advertising quickly began to rise – a trend chronicled in 1994 by accountants Spicer and Pegler's annual study of British agencies' profitability. The positive aura generated by these findings was consolidated by the introduction of the price–earnings index – a new system of assessment criteria for investors interested in assessing the performance (as opposed to the capital) of advertising agencies. Whereas traditional forms of assessment criteria had made a 'publicly floated agency . . . [look] like a flimsy, low-asset company', the new system made advertising agencies look much more attractive as investment opportunities (Nixon, 1996: 78). In addition, following the de-regulation of London's financial markets in 1985 and the introduction of new accountancy regulations in the City, financial institutions increasingly purchased publicly floated agencies over and above their real capital asset values. Nevertheless, as long as price–earnings ratios remained good, the City was happy to ignore an increasing accumulation of debt within the advertising industry, as well as turning a blind eye to international agen-cies' resistance to managerial restructuring – an oversight that eventually led to a major slump in the agency sector (Brierley, 1995: 73; Nixon, 1996: 78–9).

In the downturn that ultimately hit British advertising, Saatchi and Saatchi were one of the chief casualties. During the 1980s, however, the agency had been an enviable success. Flotation as a public company delivered capital sufficient to finance international expansion and, through the acquisition of several foreign advertising and communication businesses, Saatchi and Saatchi became a major player in world advertising.

Nevertheless, while Saatchi and Saatchi were convinced that the world's advertising media could dissolve national boundaries, the agency did not see itself as a monolithic, international agency offering bland, 'global' advertising campaigns geared to homogeneous mass markets. Instead, they envisioned themselves as a 'one-stop' agency with a co-ordinated approach to international selling that gave particular recognition to the 'locally specific' character of global markets (Nixon, 1996: 79–83; Mort, 1996: 91–4).

During the 1980s many other agencies also had aspirations to tap the potential of the increasingly global nature of production and consumption. But not all followed Saatchi's move into public flotation. Bartle Bogle and Hegarty (BBH), for example, chose a different route. In an approach virtually the opposite of that adopted by Saatchi and Saatchi, BBH developed a 'small shop' (as opposed to 'one-stop shop') ethos. BBH argued that globalization in itself could not provide their customers with an improved service provision. According to BBH, the inflexibility of management structures in other multinational advertising agencies produced obstacles to 'creativity' in marketing campaigns. Instead, BBH contended that its own campaigns would be more appropriate for international advertisers, claiming that their emphasis on 'creativity' was a strategy that could promote affectivity in all markets (Nixon, 1996: 83–9; Mort, 1996: 107–13).

Saatchi and Saatchi and BBH, then, were keen to highlight the differences between their respective operations. Nevertheless, Nixon (1996: 86) observes some marked similarities between their strategies. While important differences certainly existed between their organizational forms and practices, together with their routes of expansion, Nixon finds a parallel between Saatchi and Saatchi's commitment to a 'creative global advertising' that was effective in 'local' markets, and BBH's belief in tailoring their campaigns to a non-generalized, 'local' audience (Nixon, 1996: 86). This shared emphasis on the 'local' (as opposed to the global) was designed to allay clients' fears about marketing their products via a large, multinational business in an international context. The strategies developed by both Saatchi's and BBH were designed to appeal to clients who felt uneasy about standardized marketing in a global market and who were looking for approaches that could respond to local variables such as different political and legal contexts (affecting issues such as price and communication), different distribution and retailing structures and variations in local markets and consumer behaviour (Meffert and Bolz, 1993: 49–52).

Admittedly, a few commentators continued to argue that companies should ignore national differences in their global marketing strategies.[2] Most observers, however, were not convinced by the cases made for the global economies of scale and 'global consumer convergence'. For producers who had introduced flexible production techniques to deal with the rise of 'niche' consumer markets, the idea of 'globalized' marketing was especially unattractive. For these business interests – who required relatively small volumes of production in order to gain significant cost savings (Halliburton and Hünerberg, 1993: 26–7) – the arguments against 'globalized' advertising were powerful, as were the logistical barriers to market standardization. It is, therefore, unsurprising that advertising agencies such as Saatchi and Saatchi and BBH should emphasize the flexible, dynamic and decidedly 'local' character of their business structures in their attempts to win over international clients during the 1980s. In a cultural, economic and political climate oriented around 'enterprise' and 'the customer', evidence of a special insight into localized and niche markets was fundamental to advertisers' business success.

Lust for lifestyle: the qualitative turn in market research

Advertising practitioners are involved in generating advertising imagery, co-ordinating marketing campaigns and purchasing media space. As such, they rely on an acute understanding of the consumers they are addressing (Nixon, 1996: 91). Since the early twentieth century, advertisers have sought this through techniques of 'consumer segmentation'. These have a dual function. First, they allow advertisers to generate a concept of the 'target consumer' to which marketing campaigns can be pitched. Second, processes of segmentation help advertisers convince clients that investing in the development of a media campaign is money well spent, ultimately reaching the 'right' consumer market (Tunstall, 1964: 116).

Historically, this approach to consumer marketing played a key role in the consolidation of a Fordist economic system in Britain. During the inter- and immediate post-war periods, national advertising campaigns helped generate demand sufficient to absorb the quantities of standardized goods pouring out of Fordist systems of mass production. So, while it was revolutions in technology that made the rise of mass production possible, it was the development of marketing that ensured its survival (Benton, 1987: 246). The sale of mass-produced, uniform products – including cars (e.g. Morris and Austin), medicines and toiletries (e.g. Beecham), cocoa (Rowntree) – was accompanied by the rise of mass-market research that attempted to identify particular types of consumer through an understanding of their attitudes and behaviour. But, despite an embryonic sense of different consumer categories, the marketing industry for the most part conceived consumers as belonging to mass, relatively homogeneous groups (Nixon, 1997a: 191–2). In the post-1945 period, for example, it was common to base market research on socio-economic groupings derived from the Post Master General's classificatory system. This classified people according to their social class, dividing the population into five different categories, labelled from A (at the top) to E (at the bottom).[3] Taking their cues from this approach, a variety of similar paradigms developed in the field of marketing. The most influential system of socio-economic classification, for example, was the National Readership Survey (NRS). Administered by the Joint Industry Committee for National Readership Surveys (JICNARS), this was introduced in 1956 and was subsequently adopted by many market researchers in their attempts to analyse the lifestyles, status and income of different social groups.

According to Robert Bocock (1993: 138), socio-economic approaches to consumer classification predominated within British marketing until the early 1980s. This account, however, is a little over-simplified. During the 1960s marketers were already viewing socio-economic models as misleadingly 'tidy' in their approach to consumer groups. Social gradings were certainly regarded as useful, offering a degree of reliability to market research and sometimes relating quite accurately to actual market behaviour. And by introducing variables such as age, socio-economic data could be used to create notions of target markets that were often fairly reliable (Nixon, 1996: 92; Jhally, 1990: 124). Nevertheless, socio-economic classifications were also thought to have distinct weaknesses. Such models, for example, were often criticized for offering an 'idealized' picture of a class structure whose inherent stability could provide the basis for firm, predictable patterns of consumption. For many critics, this approach concealed significant differences *within* socio-economic groups, especially variations in taste derived from people's cultural and educational background (Chisnall, 1992: 221).

During the early 1960s many British businesses were still committed to socio-economic concepts of market segmentation. Nevertheless, in some quarters at least, market research based on socio-economic data was being supplemented by that based on other types of information. Particularly influential were psychologically based models of consumer behaviour (Tunstall, 1964: 124–9). Much of the impetus for this approach came from the work of the American marketing guru, Ernest Dichter. Claiming to be applying Freudian theory to marketing through what became known as 'motivational' research (Tunstall, 1964: 128), Dichter had become a major influence in American advertising and in the 1960s he set up a consultancy business in London, offering clients an insight into 'what makes people act the way they do and on how we can motivate them' (Dichter, 1960: 15). However, while Dichter was undoubtedly an influence on British developments, Frank Mort has argued (1997: 27; 2000: 47) that 'psychological' approaches to marketing already had currency among British marketers from the late 1940s onwards – an interest further galvanized by the publication of John Hobson's *The Selection of Advertising Media* (1955) and its arguments that advertisers should concentrate on the 'atmosphere' of their messages, together with the mood and emotional responses of customers to products.

Some British advertisers were sceptical about the potential of 'motivational' or 'atmospheric' research, dismissing it as dealing in 'aesthetic intangibles' (Mort, 1997: 27). There were, however, a significant number of British agencies who attempted to produce campaigns that would appeal to the emotional and creative preferences of the public. Here, advertisers argued that socio-economic market categories alone could be unreliable and that the cultural variables of 'lifestyle' needed to be introduced (Mort, 1997: 27). During the late 1960s qualitative, attitudinal and motivational research achieved widespread acceptance among UK advertising agencies and was widely used in conjunction with data derived from socio-economic models. By the mid-1970s, qualitative research was considered orthodox by many marketers and – thought to offer 'direct, sensitive, and observable way[s] of assessing consumer reaction' (Colwell, 1990: 13)[4] – it also proved popular among clients, many readily assimilating its results into their own conceptual frameworks.

During the late 1970s and early 1980s British marketing further abandoned socio-economic modes of consumer segmentation in favour of qualitative research. New methods of qualitative marketing were informed both by popular accounts of changing patterns in contemporary cultural life and by recent academic analyses of shifts in class structure and social values. Sociological studies such as the study of *The Affluent Worker* (1968–9) by John Goldthorpe and his associates, and David Lockwood's study of *The Black-coated Worker* (1966) were particularly influential. Both studies highlighted the changing life experiences of the working class in post-war Britain, arguing that shifts in labour markets and workplace cultures had been accompanied by a wider change in workers' social attitudes and aspirations. As a consequence, it was argued, some clerks and well-paid workers had begun to hold values and world-views at odds with those of the 'traditional' working class. In contrast to the 'traditional' workers' ethos of 'us v. them' collectivity and a culture oriented around communal institutions such as the pub and the local football team, the new 'affluent worker' was perceived as being more home-centred and consumption-oriented, spending his money on family trips, cars, shopping and DIY (Bocock, 1992: 132–3; Cuff and Payne, 1981: 78–81).

This perception of a fragmentation of traditional class structures was paralleled in the world of marketing, where there was growing doubt about the usefulness of occupational status as an indicator of social standing, values and aspirations. As a consequence, there emerged a number of new approaches to market segmentation. An especially influential innovation was the Target Group Index (TGI), launched in 1968. Available on subscription to advertisers, agencies and media owners (and still much used today), the TGI attempts to describe specific target groups of consumers and their media exposure. The TGI bases its information on a yearly sample of 24,000 adults selected by a random sampling procedure known as GRID. Using a variety of research techniques (including personal interviews and self-completed questionnaires), the TGI provides information to marketers about consumption attitudes and purchasing decisions in relation to a diverse range of media forms (McDonald and King, 1996: 225–7).

New American marketing techniques were also beginning to register an influence in Britain. Most important were two systems that combined quantitative and qualitative research in their analyses of consumer 'lifestyles'. The Yankelovich Monitor (1969) and VALS 2 (Values and Life-Styles 2) (1978) both drew on extensive interview and survey data to divide people into typological consumer groups. Here, classification was on the basis of whether or not people agreed with attitude statements such as 'What I do at work is more important to me than the money I earn' – responses then divided into clusters and given labels such as 'emulators', 'sustainers', 'achievers' or 'couch potatoes'. Alternatively, clusters were personified in an evocative 'lifestyle portrait' – for example, 'Fred, the frustrated factory worker' (McDonald and King, 1996: 161).

Initially, British market researchers were suspicious of 'lifestyle clustering' and what they saw as its lack of specificity and 'unscientific' stress on subjectivity. During the 1970s, however, the TGI began to apply methods of 'lifestyle' research developed by the Leo Burnett Agency in Chicago, with the aim of adding qualitative material to the demographic profiles constructed from their consumer surveys (McDonald and King, 1996: 161–2). Like the Yankelovich Monitor and VALS 2, TGI started to cluster consumers into 'lifestyle types' – or 'Outlook' groups – a typology that included such categories as 'the indifferent', 'pleasure seekers' and 'working-class puritans' (Chisnall, 1992: 241–2). According to the TGI, this attention to 'Outlook' provided a more 'three-dimensional' picture of consumers, offering not only information on general life aspirations, but also a more fully rounded account of people's attitudes to time, money and effort (Baker, 1984: 113).

Other segmentation techniques were also developed in Britain. ACORN (1977) and SAGACITY (1981), for example, both employed a 'geo-demographic' model – a system of consumer classification that combined information on life-cycle, income and socio-economic status. Along with the influence of American qualitative research, the rise of ACORN and SAGACITY was indicative of British marketing's growing dissatisfaction with socio-economic forms of consumer classification. ACORN enjoyed particular success, developing an ACORN Lifestyles List which classified every UK household into one of eighty-one 'lifestyle segmentations' – including such categories as 'affluent single metropolitan dwellers' (subdivided, in turn, by age and gender); 'older traditional suburban couples and families' (subdivided by length of relationship and age) and 'affluent rural couples and families' (subdivided by location of residence) (Chisnall, 1992: 242–56).

The rise of more qualitatively based, 'lifestyle' research during the 1970s and 1980s was a response to advertisers' and marketers' desire for tools that would allow them to negotiate more effectively the shifting patterns of consumer behaviour in the 'real' world. The information offered by the segmentation techniques employed in TGI, ACORN and SAGACITY attempted to meet this demand by providing accounts of consumer attitudes and behaviour that were more thorough, more three-dimensional and more 'in touch' with the vagaries of the market. The claim for, and chief selling point of, this kind of 'lifestyle' research was that it would eliminate uncertainty from the marketing process through its assiduous attention to the complex world of consumer *difference*. At the same time, however, the growing embrace of lifestyle segmentation can also be seen as a desperate search for *sameness*, as both manufacturers and advertisers struggled to find identifiable consumer 'clusters' in a market perceived as increasingly fragmented and volatile.

Close to the customer/close to the client

As the advertising industry wrestled to get close to the customer, the 1980s also saw a significant reassessment of advertisers' professional roles. The advertising industry was not only interested in capturing the hearts, minds and wallets of consumers – those of their business clients were equally important. One way of achieving this was to offer businesses an enhanced customer service – advertising agencies striving to gain a competitive edge through a personalized, 'value-added' relationship with their clients. Sean Nixon's work (1996: 104–10) demonstrates how many of the most successful agencies of the 1980s achieved this through a foregrounding of the roles of the account planner, the media buyer and creative personnel.

A relatively new figure within the advertising industry, the account planner operated as an intermediary between the client, the consumer and those involved in the agency's creative work. During the 1970s many agencies began to drop their account executives, who had traditionally prepared briefing documents and liaised with the client on behalf of the agency. It was the account planner who took their place. Often with a background in social scientific research (usually in psychology) (Brierley, 1995: 58–9), the account planner's role was as an intermediary between the agency and the client. Using mediation skills that the French communications researchers Antoine Hennion and Cécile Méadel (1993: 178) have characterized as being 'a little like free association used by psychoanalysts', the account planner's role was to develop advertising strategies through deft liaison between the client, market researchers, target consumers and the agency's creative staff. Planners were introduced as a way to assure clients that information from market research – with particular use being made of TGI, geodemographics and qualitative study groups (Brierley, 1995: 58) – was being implemented effectively throughout the advertising process. In effect, the claim made for account planners by the agencies who employed them was that their expertise allowed *all* aspects of a marketing campaign to be literally 'mapped out' in advance –

the production, circulation *and* consumption of the proposed advertisement (Nixon, 1996: 110). Cautious clients could thus be won over by the exclusive, high-class service offered by the planner and his ability assured them that they would be getting a high-quality, 'individualized' advertising campaign.

The same period also saw the media buyer become more integral to the advertising process. Formerly, the role of media buyers had been to obtain the greatest amount of media coverage for an advertisement at the most cost-effective price. But during the 1980s their role became more tactical. Increasingly their function was to combine media research and consumer information in an effort to target the 'right' consumers as efficiently as possible (Brierley, 1995: 106). The media buyer's brief was also to 'get close to the client', offering a more specialized, client-friendly service – and the 1980s saw a growing number of businesses make use of specialized media buying agencies that operated either separately or quasi-independently from a creative agency.[5]

Among advertising agencies' creative staff – or 'creatives' as they are sometimes known – a traditional esteem for intuition and individual flair was often accompanied by a disdain for what they saw as the pedestrian, number-crunching rationality of their colleagues in account planning and market research. During the 1980s, however, the work of 'creatives' increasingly drew on the insights offered by 'lifestyle'-oriented consumer research. To some extent, creative staff had always been involved in the development of brand 'personalities', intended to differentiate products from their market competitors. But during the 1980s creatives became more systematic in their attempts to 'aestheticize' the values and attitudes of specific consumer groups, sometimes going as far as to conceive a 'mythic individual' associated with specific 'loves, hates, prejudices and aspirations', as they designed and developed what they thought of as 'lifestyle' advertisements (Brierley, 1995: 143–4).

For Hennion and Méadel (1993: 185), the balance between roles such as the account planner, the media buyer and the creative cannot be viewed as a straightforward division of labour. But nor can it be seen as a set of fluid functions that overlap and freely interact. Within the 'creative industries', Hennion and Méadel argue, the relationship between these three roles is negotiated, as enterprising employees with different specialities, skills and networks link together to work in different 'local totalizations' (Hennion and Méadel, 1993: 189). No one figure, therefore, has total control of the advertising campaign. Successful advertising work is organized around the *specialization* of professionals who delegate tasks to other groups of skilled personnel who, in turn, recompose the product brief in their own way. This form of organization results in 'a game of cut-throat competition' among employees, who have to fight ruthlessly on behalf of 'their' ideas. It is, though, also an organizational form that can generate a 'close-knit solidarity' focused around a commitment to the customer and the product (Hennion and Méadel, 1993: 189).

Alongside the growing embrace of 'the customer' and 'the client' within advertising industry discourse, advertising professionals also began both to internalize and to behave in ways consistent with the dominant 1980s ideologies of 'enterprise' and 'competitiveness'. The restructuring of the organization of advertising agencies invited practitioners to become more thrusting in their professional environment and to invest more of themselves in their work, seeing their job as a purposeful vocation rather than a mere occupation. An emphasis on relative autonomy within the advertising profession, moreover, registered in a new stress on the importance of 'self-representation' and the rise of a slick, 'classy' masculine style among young, male advertising professionals. Indeed, more generally, advertisers were integral to the fabrication of new images of masculinity that placed an accent on style and the personal pleasures of consumerism – with a wave of advertising campaigns pitching a welter of consumer products and services (from Levis 501s to Brylcreem) to a 'new man' who was conceived of as a narcissistic and self-conscious consumer.[6]

Change also registered in the styles of self-presentation associated with the 'new' men in the advertising profession itself. Here, 'the dominant version of masculinity associated with the civil service' and the managerial constraints of the 'organization man' were rejected in favour of an entrepreneurial intentionality signalled in a more 'creative' style of dress (Bagguley, 1991: 152; Entwistle, 1997: 318–19; Nixon, 1997b: 103–19). The new advertising 'look' was constructed around sharp, flamboyant suits, expensive fragrances, bow-ties, waistcoats and coloured braces – all worn with an air of confident panache, both at work and in the swanky 'dos' regularly covered by the popular media (Nixon, 1997b: 103–19). Through their wardrobes, then, the advertising 'boys' of the 1980s celebrated a new entrepreneurial (as opposed to managerial) masculinity – one attuned to the ascendant business culture of vigorous individuality and ruthless 'enterprise'. Fervent self-promotion was also the order of the day, while the doctrine of the 'creative individual' was venerated both in laudatory features in the trade press and at the back-slapping awards ceremonies that increasingly punctuated the advertising industry's calendar.

In various ways, then, the 1980s saw the advertising industry reorganized and restructured around the paradigm of 'closer' customer–client relation-ships. As a consequence, the boundaries between 'advertising professional', 'client' and 'customer' became increasingly difficult to define. And, for advertising professionals too, the lines demarcating the 'inside' and 'outside' of their work lives became increasingly hard to distinguish.

There was, moreover, a pronounced sense of 'gendering' within this work culture. The 'masculine' ethos and posturing that had traditionally been features of the advertising profession were still pervasive during the 1980s. Indeed, advertising agencies themselves took on a distinctly gendered form of organizational structure. Commissioned by the IPA in 1990, for example, the report *Women in Advertising* (Baxter, 1990) noted the absence of women in managerial positions within the industry and expressed anxiety about sexual discrimination and the 'glass ceiling' barriers that blocked women's career advancement. In practice, the biggest obstacles to women's professional development in the advertising industry were the masculine codes of self-advancement nurtured within the male-dominated agency teams, with success invariably achieved through a peculiarly masculine form of boardroom 'bully-ing'; or through informal male networks involving out-of-hours socializing at pubs, restaurants and sports clubs. Women's access to the 'professional' cultures of the advertising industry, meanwhile, was further impeded by the boisterous character of the working environment – a world that gave licence to macho banter, vulgar rituals, offensive language and sexual innuendo (Mort, 1996: 116–17; Nixon, 1999).

'What do women do all day?' Feminism, femininity and the 1980s advertising industry

Although a resolutely masculine work culture remained deeply embedded within the advertising industry, advertisers' representations of women's lives were facing strong criticism from a number of quarters. Critical engagement with media representations of women had increased with the emergence of a re-energized Women's Movement in Europe and America during the late 1960s and 1970s (Myers, 1986: 82–106). Many feminist critics, for example, offered swingeing critiques of the media's stereotyping, neglect and marginal-ization of women. Advertising attracted particular censure. In the 'real' world, it was argued, women were becoming a more visible and active presence within the public realms of work and politics – but this rarely featured in advertising imagery, where stereotypes of submissive and domestic-oriented femininity remained prevalent. Among the first studies to elaborate a critical contrast between the 'real lives' of women and the 'stereotyped' world constructed in advertising were Carol Adams and Rae Laurikietis's *The Gender Trap: Messages and Images* (1977) and Josephine King and Mary Stott's *This Is Your Life?* (1977). Both books argued that advertising images of women were dangerously misleading, provoking insecurity and reinforcing gender inequalities. A more theoretically informed approach quickly followed, with the publication of Judith Williamson's highly influential study, *Decoding Advertisements* (1978). Informed by an Althusserian Marxist perspective, Williamson's analysis proffered semiotic readings of a number of high-profile advertising campaigns, highlighting the ways in which advertising texts generated meanings and connotations in which women were routinely objectified and disempowered.

Nor were feminist critiques of advertising representations confined to the academy's ivory towers. A wider upsurge of feminist activism during the 1970s included a range of moves against the advertising industry. Activist strategies included the targeting of specific advertisements and advertisers through writing letters of complaint to the Advertising Standards Authority (ASA), TV and radio stations, newspapers and consumer magazines.

Some feminists also favoured a direct action campaign in which posters and hoardings were defaced and recaptioned, while 'anti-sexism' stickers and slogans were slapped on advertisements deemed offensive. Other groups (such as AFFIRM – the feminist alliance against advertisements, articles and images that exploit women) campaigned for the censorship of offending images, arguing that advertisements objectified women and even (as AFFIRM argued) incited violence against them, since 'if men can't *have* the women they're offered, they take' (Nicholls and Moan, 1982: 69). Other feminist activists of the 1970s also challenged the media's (and especially advertising's) representations of women. Groups campaigning against sexual assault and pornography – for example, 'Women Reclaim the Night' and 'Women Against Violence Against Women' – also called for the censorship of advertising, arguing that advertisements were akin to pornography in the way they encouraged rape and sexual assault through their degrading and objectifying portrayal of women (Wallsgrove, 1982: 451). Other women's groups – for example, 'the Hackney Flashers' – turned their attention to producing images of 'real' women, creating montages which subverted the intended meanings of advertising campaigns (Myers, 1986: 88–9; Price, 1997: 98).

The advertising industry also faced opposition in institutional quarters. In May 1984, for example, the Women's Committee of the Greater London Council (GLC) persuaded London Transport to refuse to display advertisements that presented women as 'sex objects', that implied or depicted violence towards women, or that would be likely to offend women (GLC Women's Committee, 1984a; 1984b). In the same year a media working party of the Trades Union Congress (TUC) produced a pamphlet dealing with sexual stereotyping in advertising, arguing that the imagery offered by advertisers was impoverished and incompatible with the lifestyles of the consumer groups they were attempting to reach (Rawsthorn, 1984: 28).

Yet British advertisers generally resisted this growing criticism and during the 1970s, for the most part, kept feminism at arm's length. Undoubtedly, this was partly a consequence of the entrenched sexism within the industry. But commercial factors were also influential. Advertisers felt able to ignore blithely the issues and ideas raised by the Women's Movement because, as Frank Mort (1996: 114) observes, they assumed that 'feminists did not represent an influential group of consumers'. During the 1980s, however, this was set to change.

Within the advertising industry, dissatisfaction with the established conventions of targeting the women's market first surfaced among women practitioners working with 'lifestyle' methods of market research. Hoping their arguments would be treated more sympathetically by the industry, these women couched their criticisms in emphatically commercial (as opposed to 'feminist') terms, contending that to increase the effectiveness of their campaigns, advertising creatives needed to listen more carefully to the 'voice' of the 'woman consumer', getting closer to her through more extensive use of qualitative market research. As early as 1980, for example, women agents from the Leo Burnett agency were claiming that their researchers had identified not only significant socio-economic shifts, but also important attitudinal changes among British women. Increasing levels of women's employment outside the home meant, they argued, that the traditional 'domestic' or 'model-girl' roles offered by advertisers no longer 'spoke' to women. Indeed, they argued, many women consumers rejected these depictions outright, perceiving them as 'old-fashioned', 'static', 'stupid' and 'patronising' (Wolk, 1980: 27). According to Jackie Dickens, Leo Burnett's creative research director, British women wanted to see themselves in more 'realistic' situations, where they were portrayed as 'modern and active, intelligent and discriminating, independent and confident' (quoted in Wolk, 1980: 27). At the same time, however, she maintained that these situations should not be 'fantasy' ones, which made undue concessions to 'women's libbers' by totally removing women from a domestic setting since, Dickens rationalized, 'even working women cook and clean' (quoted in Wolk, 1980: 27). Burnett's sentiments were echoed at J. Walter Thompson where Judy Lannon, the director of creative research, argued that '[o]ne of the hardest things to do is to get the woman right'. In approaching the female consumer, she asserted, advertisers should be wary of stereotypes and should always ask 'What sort of person is she – what are her interests outside of the home – how do these reflect her as a person?' (quoted in Wolk, 1980: 28). One answer, Lannon suggested, might be to focus on the emotional qualities of 'the product' rather then the 'woman' consumer.

By 1983 a plethora of articles in the advertising and marketing trade press were also addressing a perceived fragmentation of the 'women's market'. For example, Liz Fallaw, planning and account director at Dorlands, argued that advertisers could no longer 'regard "women" as a uniform "market"'. As she explained, while there was:

> a market in pet owners, some of whom are women, or in people interested in losing weight, many of whom are women, or in DIY, where an increasing number of women are active, women *as such* do not constitute a homogeneous market.
>
> (quoted in Nuttall, 1983: 22)

From this perspective, then, advertisers who talked about marketing to 'women' would struggle to reach their target consumers. '[It is] a bit like saying "All Russians are backward"', Fallaw claimed, 'It's stupid' (quoted in Nuttall, 1983: 22). In *Campaign* magazine, meanwhile, David O'Reilly also urged advertisers to 'face the facts' about the realities of women's lives. Citing statistical data on social trends, he suggested that marketers and advertisers needed to become 'more acute and subtle' in their approaches to women consumers, using market research techniques to 'take advantage of greater segmentation among women' through developing 'fresh' attitudes to products and advertisements (O'Reilly, 1983: 38). In a similar vein, the pages of *Campaign* saw Harold Lind (an economic consultant) and Philip Wisson (the Managing Director of Attwood Index) entreat advertisers and researchers to use 'rather more initiative . . . in their search for the . . . female market'. Although conventional marketing wisdom had been to treat women as a mass market of 'housewives', Lind and Wisson argued that this category no longer described 'women' because: 'like the category "love" . . . ["women"] is a many splendoured thing. For a real understanding of marketing to women, we have to separate women as housewives from women in their personal capacity' (Lind and Wisson, 1984: 73). From this perspective, then, the future of market research lay in techniques that used ever more accurate systems of market segmentation. 'Before very long', Lind and Wisson predicted, 'the whole concept of marketing to women will have disappeared, to be replaced by techniques for marketing to the particular sectors of women that the nature of the product requires' (Lind and Wisson, 1984: 73).

As I argued in Chapter 2, changes in the lives of women were not simply a figment of the 'lifestyle' marketer's imagination. Since 1945 there *had* been major shifts in British women's social and economic roles, women steadily moving into the workforce to take up occupations from which they were previously excluded. However, the advertising and marketing trade press presented and commented upon statistics confirming major shifts in the social and economic roles of British women with some astonishment. In an article in *Marketing*, for example, David O' Reilly (1983: 29) presented his readers with some sobering facts about the real lives of British women. Between 1951 and 1981 the percentage of women in the workforce increased from 31 per cent to 43 per cent, partly as a consequence of changes in family structure and the growing social acceptability of working mothers.[7] By 1981, meanwhile, women's earnings amounted to (on average) 75 per cent of men's earnings, an increase of 12 per cent over ten years, while a third of working women were responsible for providing up to 50 per cent of the family income. It was inevitable, therefore, that changes in women's relationships to the workforce would result in new dynamics of purchasing power, patterns and demands (O'Reilly, 1983: 29).

O'Reilly (1983: 29) also offered his readers some significant examples of changes in women's consumer activity. The increased presence of women in paid employment, for example, made women significant customers for the financial sector, and in 1983 they made up about half of current account and deposit account holders in Britain. In addition, women's use of credit facilities and loans was on the increase, as was their purchase of insurance policies. Between 1978 and 1983 credit card ownership amongst women had increased by 29 per cent, and there was evidence to suggest that women were beginning to use these credit cards more frequently (O'Reilly, 1983: 28–30). Another growth area in women's consumption was the car market, and between 1974 and 1983 there was an increase of 42.7 per cent in the number of women holding current driving licences. Between 1981 and 1982 women purchased 21.2 per cent of all new privately owned cars, with a particular impact on the smaller car market. Women had also become greater users of business services such as airlines and hotels during this period (O'Reilly, 1983: 30).

The sea-changes in the working patterns of women, O'Reilly (1983: 30) observed, had also resulted in shifts in women's leisure patterns. Women participated to a greater extent in the purchase of alcohol, both in pubs and the supermarket. According to survey statistics produced by IPC magazines in 1983, women were particularly important decision-makers in the purchase of fifteen out of nineteen drinks mentioned. Their decisions were crucial in all stages of the purchasing process for liqueurs, sherry, wines, bottled water, aperitifs, vermouth, mixers and perries. At home, O'Reilly claimed, women were also engaged to a greater extent in the traditionally 'masculine' pursuits of gardening, decorating and minor electrical repairs (O'Reilly, 1983: 30).

The growing impact of qualitatively oriented, 'lifestyle' market research obliged British advertisers to give closer attention to these changes in women's lives. Even if they were hostile to the feminist movement, advertisers had to concede that 'women' could no longer be considered an all-inclusive market category. For instance, while traditional (socio-economic) market categorizations had placed women in the same class as the head of household, marketers increasingly recognized that this approach might not offer a 'realistic' picture of contemporary femininity. Indeed, industry anxiety mounted as the possibility arose that a lucrative market of millions of class B and C1 women might have been entirely overlooked – this important market segment vanishing into the less commercially attractive C2 group of skilled, manual workers simply because the women had been categorized according to their husbands' occupations (Lind and Wisson, 1984: 73).

Perhaps paradoxically, the quickest responses to the shifting social, economic and cultural contours of women's lives came from those consumer industries that had traditionally targeted women in terms of their domestic roles. For example, convenience foods such as McCain's oven chips, Birds Eye Walls' 'Menu Master' range of ready-made meals and Homepride's Cook-In-Sauces were all marketed in campaigns that addressed women in a way that acknowledged their working lives and depicted them as integral members of the family rather than mere servers or providers. The cosmetics industry also responded to the diversification of women's lives. Long-lasting ranges of make-up such as Max Factor's Colourfast were marketed towards working women who had little time to spare during their hectic schedules, while suntan lotions graded according to different skin types and two-in-one deodorants/perfumes such as Limara and Impulse were pitched towards 'busy women' with little time to spend on themselves (Nuttall, 1983: 22–4).

71

In contrast, industries that had customarily appealed to a male market were slower to acknowledge women's growing buying power. Corporate advertising and advertising for financial and business services, for example, initially did little to appeal to women or to research their consumer interests (O'Reilly, 1983: 30; Rawsthorn, 1984: 28). Nevertheless, a few industries that had traditionally appealed to men as their primary customers *did* initiate marketing campaigns geared to women. For example, after market research suggested that women were increasingly making decisions about home decoration, ICI Paints launched Dulux Natural Whites – a paint range targeted at women. Kitchen appliances were also reinvented as timesaving gadgets for busy working women. Marketing campaigns for microwave ovens, multi-wash washing machines, slow cookers and particularly food processors (such as the Magimix) abandoned conventional sales strategies that had presumed wives would persuade their husbands to purchase the products for them. Instead, new campaigns were targeted directly at women (Nuttall, 1983: 22–4). Car manufacturers, too, began to zero in on women as a consumer market in their own right. Sometimes, however, their attempts were woefully passé and were greeted with ridicule from both consumers and women advertising executives. Audi, for example, depicted a fur-coated, glamorous woman driver in their sales campaign for a car intended as an everyday 'run-about'. The Volkswagen Polo, meanwhile, was marketed as 'Safe enough to let your wife out on the road in' and Volvo – who actually had a sizeable market of women for their smaller cars – adopted the slogan 'To father, a son' (Nuttall, 1983: 22).

Though initially slow, the reconfiguration of representations of women in British advertising campaigns quickly picked up pace. By the mid-1980s, advertisers and marketers were even proclaiming the concept of 'the housewife' to be a 'dirty word in adland' (Burchill, 1986: 40). Yet, advertising and marketing practitioners were still deploring the lack of imagination in their industries' attempts to target women's markets. There was almost universal agreement that the 'housewife eulogising over soap powder or washing-up liquid' was a redundant concept, but a new stereotype of the 'briefcase-brandishing business-woman' seemed hardly more convincing (Hodson, 1985: 77). Negative consumer responses to advertising targeted at women were a topic of hot debate. Advertisers were quick to justify their use of stereotypes, arguing that in the marketing of mass products recourse to representations of 'the average' were inevitable – even if, to some observers, these seemed unduly contrived. Shrewder industry opinion, however, was well aware that a successful marketing campaign needed not simply to recognize the shifts that were transforming women's socio-economic experiences. Account also needed to be given to the changing ways that women engaged with advertising texts (Hodson, 1985; O'Reilly, 1983; Rawsthorn, 1984).

One of the first marketing studies to suggest that the changing conditions of women's lives might be accompanied by a different attitude towards advertising was produced by the Research Business in 1983. Basing their arguments on qualitative research data, the Research Business identified a range of attitudes to advertising among women consumers. Women aged between thirty-five and fifty-five, they claimed, saw advertising as a 'hidden persuader' of which they had to be wary. These women also tended to be 'unsophisticated' in their understanding of 'how ads work', showing relatively little awareness of the various codes and conventions deployed in the construction of 'brand' image. In contrast, younger respondents – who had grown up with media as an integral part of their lives – were found to be more confident and discriminating in their judgements about advertising and had less fear of its 'effects'. They also displayed more of an understanding of how advertising created 'moods' and 'feelings' around products, these women seeing themselves as detached critics of advertising with an awareness of its underlying motives (O'Reilly, 1983: 34).

Similar variations in 'advertising literacy' were identified in research produced by the AB marketing group in 1985. Focus groups conducted with a range of professional women suggested they applied their work skills in their approach to advertising, looking at advertisements with a 'professional eye'. Indeed, these women were often scornful of advertisers' attempts at producing 'acceptable' images of women in business. The women, however, did appreciate advertisements they felt had some creative merit, praising those that were '[h]ighly visual' and that made 'full use of good photography and art direction' (Hodson, 1985: 79). An advertisement for Sharwood's Curry Powder, for instance, was singled out for its unusual and interesting presentation in the way it emphasized the visual and artistic qualities involved in making a good curry powder (as opposed to the finished dish). A campaign for Clinique Cosmetics was also admired for its combination of attractive packaging and clever photography. Overall, it seemed professional women responded best to advertisements that seemed skilfully crafted, using effective photography and thoughtful art direction. They especially appreciated 'understated' visuals, regarding busy, overly laboured images as 'alien' and aimed at women other than themselves (Hodson, 1985: 79). Professional women, it appeared, were a discerning and elusive market. Advertisers, it seemed clear, had to rethink their strategies in order to appeal to these women's more complex and demanding consumer attitudes.

Desperately seeking Susan: advertising, media buying and the quest for women's markets

Generally, the 1980s saw British marketers increasingly adopt concepts of 'lifestyle segmentation' as they struggled to adapt to the fragmentation of the 'women's market'. As early as 1983, for example, the Social Futures Group of the Henley Centre for Forecasting (in conjunction with the advertising agency Wasey Campbell-Ewald) had 'discovered' a group of women who had an 'underestimated inclination to spend money on themselves'. Dubbed 'the

Divorcynics', these women took 'a jaundiced view of advertising and marketing methods after the break-up of their marriages' and regarded 'brand choice as increasingly trivial and value for money as increasingly important'. Finding that few product categories were unaffected by these (transitory but 'real') emotions, the report concluded that marketers should add 'a new dimension to their thinking', giving more attention to issues of life-cycle (Mason, 1983: 41).

A more extensive and better-publicized piece of market research was McCann-Erickson's 'Woman Study' of 1985. A 'sister' report to a successful 'Man Study' of the previous year (Restall, 1985: 26–8), McCann-Erickson's ambitious research sought to provide a full account of people's attitudes, beliefs, wants, needs, personalities and behaviour. Both studies segmented men and women into various 'lifestyle' groups, using a typology of eight 'psychological and lifestyle' clusters – and, in an attempt to breathe life into these categories, an illustrator interpreted their lifestyle characteristics into 'gentle and witty drawings of animals'.

The eight 'lifestyle' clusters of McCann-Erickson's 'Woman Study' were divided into four motivational pairs. One pair of lifestyles – dubbed 'the Avant Guardian' and 'the Lady Righteous' – were motivated primarily by ideals or opinions. Another – 'the Lively Lady' and 'the New Un-Romantic' – were characterized by their self-awareness and independence of spirit. The 'Hopeful Seeker' and 'the Lack-A-Daisy', meanwhile, were driven by their questing personalities. And, finally, 'the Blinkered' and 'the Down-Trodden' were denoted primarily by their lack of involvement (Restall, 1985: 27). Out of the eight clusters, the first two pairs were described as 'their own person' and as 'leaders of opinion in their separate ways', while the subsequent pairs were 'followers' (Restall, 1985: 27). Overall, the various clusters were defined in terms of 'Key Attitude Statements' – for example, 'The most important thing is believing in God'; 'Women do not have a separate identity these days'; and 'I don't care to buy new products'. The clusters were also provided with distinguishing synopses of their lifestyles – for example, 'Into many modern trends (health foods and so on)'; 'Admires effective people, tries to mirror their attitudes'; and 'I'm always under pressure'. Finally, the report offered lists of typical brands consumed by these lifestyle groups – *'Daily Mail'*, 'Wimpy', 'Littlewoods', 'National Giro' and so on. Six of the eight lifestyle clusters of McCann-Erickson's report had counterparts in the earlier 'Man Study'. Of the two clusters identified as peculiar to women, 'the New Un-Romantic' was characterized by her world-weary lack of interest in the opposite sex, while 'the Down-Trodden' was portrayed as 'typically female' – with 'somewhat traditional doormat-like attitudes' (Restall, 1985: 26–8).

The chief claim made for the 'Woman Study' was that its insights into women's attitudes to consumption would enable advertisers to address each 'lifestyle cluster' more effectively, while marketers would be better able to identify potential gaps in the market. 'Lifestyle' information, McCann-

Erickson argued, had become an invaluable resource in advertisers' attempts to target specific consumer groups as 'a segment of womanhood in the UK'. Moreover, the company elaborated, this lifestyle research would put advertisers in the best possible position to help women 'make the best of what [they] are' (Restall, 1985: 28).

By the late 1980s lifestyle research was a key tool in advertisers' attempts to address women consumers. In 1987, for example, Damian O'Malley, joint deputy managing director of the Gold Greenlees Trott agency, declared that concepts of lifestyle segmentation had been an unqualified success, enabling advertisers to finally 'captivate the modern woman'. For O'Malley, it was an assertive 'anger' that had emerged as one of the key characteristics of the modern woman – embodied in marketing campaigns such as that for Black Magic chocolates (where a forlorn man attempted to 'regain the favours of his dominatrix') and that for Boots cosmetics (which oozed 'with opulent and sensational colour' on models who were 'zany and vulpine, not vapid and consumptive') (O'Malley, 1987: 55). O'Malley acknowledged that none of these campaigns pretended to 'show women "as they really are"', but he insisted that they were a positive step forward, abandoning the patronizing tone traditionally taken in advertisements aimed at women (1987: 55).

O'Malley's views were shared by many within the advertising industry. Some women advertisers, however, contested the idea that existing 'lifestyle' marketing techniques had made much of a difference to campaigns targeted at women. Kay Scorah, planning director at the Miller and Leeves agency, was particularly incensed by the smugness and sexism of the advertising industry, and by advertisers' assumptions that they had now found a 'solution' to the 'woman problem'. Citing focus group research conducted in Newcastle, Scorah argued that the only reason young women no longer termed advertising 'offensive' was 'because they don't even realize it was them we were trying to offend' (Scorah, 1990: 14). Showing a selection of advertisements to a range of focus groups of young women, Scorah found them to be highly media literate, many suspecting that the advert's representations of women had been produced by a 'lech-in-Levis for his mates' (Scorah, 1990: 14). From this, Scorah concluded that young women were adept at deconstructing advertising images that were often ham-fisted in their approach, Scorah chastising advertisers for resting arrogantly on their laurels while their campaigns still failed to 'touch the mind or the feelings of the character of women' (Scorah, 1990: 14).

Developing effective representations of the 'woman consumer' was just one part of the problem facing advertisers in the 1980s. Another important consideration was finding an appropriate media environment in which advertisements for women could be placed. As we have seen, the right choice of media vehicle for 'lifestyle' campaigns was becoming increasingly important throughout the advertising industry. In purchasing space for advertisements, media buyers were becoming keenly aware of the importance of market position and timing in their efforts to 'get close to the customer'

(Barrell and Braithwaite, 1988: 118). And, in express relation to women, a study by Lind and Wisson highlighted the way in which particular media vehicles were more suited to specific consumer groups. Channel 4, Lind and Wisson claimed, was a medium especially suited to campaigns geared to self-supporting women under the age of forty-five – these women being light viewers of ITV compared to housewives of a similar age. Judged against housewives, self-supporting women were also lighter readers of daily newspapers, though older women in this group expressed a preference for the *Daily Telegraph* and Sunday newspapers were popular with all age groups (Lind and Wisson, 1984: 73). Women's magazines – particularly the mass weeklies such as *Woman's Own* and *Woman's Weekly* – were also popular among self-supporting women over the age of forty-five. In contrast, younger self-supporting women felt ill-served by magazines – thus suggesting that the market segmentation techniques deployed in the magazine industry were lagging some way behind those being developed by advertisers.

Within the magazine industry a degree of prejudice lingered against the use of 'lifestyle' research techniques in marketing. As late as 1983, for example, the Centre for Business Research produced a report on the women's monthly magazine market that argued that 'highly qualitative and psychologically oriented' research techniques were best avoided. This, the report claimed, was because these techniques were 'subject to fluctuations and changes in their subject matter, e.g. people's attitudes and feelings change' (Carr *et al.*, 1983: 29). Publishers, it was argued, should steer away from such unscientific methods, instead basing their analyses on 'safer' systems of segmentation grounded on the demographics of age and class.

On the other hand, advertisers hoping to target the 'Divorcynic' market expressed dismay in the trade press at what they perceived as a distinct lack of media options for their products. Marketing consultant Sian Johnson, for instance, saw the lack of 'lifestyle' media geared to the 'Divorcynic' as the major obstacle barring access to this market and she implored magazine pub-lishers to rethink their strategies of market segmentation. The 'Divorcynic', she explained, was no longer interested in the magazines she had read in her youth and did not feel addressed by titles such as *Good Housekeeping, Homes and Gardens* and *Woman and Home*. What the 'Divorcynic' needed, Johnson claimed, was a new magazine for self-supporting women, a magazine whose impact could equal that of *Cosmopolitan* during the 1970s (Mason, 1983: 44). Other advertisers seeking the buying power of the professional or executive woman also identified a glaring lack of available media vehicles. Women's magazine publishers, it was felt, still refused to accept that since the 1960s the life experiences of many women had changed (Hodson, 1985: 77). To many, it seemed that magazines such as *Woman, Cosmopolitan* and *Vogue* were all proving incapable of reaching the buying power of professional and executive women and publishers were implored to adopt new media and marketing strategies as a response to the growing diversification of women's lives.

Within the trade press a common complaint was that existing women's magazines failed to appeal to professional women. Freelance journalist Pat Campbell-Lyons (1983: 45), for example, argued that the 'women's magazine empire, presided over mainly by men, is stuck in a rut'. For Campbell-Lyons, many titles were 'still obsessed with the stereotyped image of women – that they live for home, babies, cooking, clothes and sex' (Campbell-Lyons, 1983: 45). In place of this, she called for a new type of women's magazine that catered for the contemporary woman:

> Apart from working, they want to read intelligent material. An explosive magazine, full of variety. Articles on politics, psychology, world affairs. Keep the serials and features on home and gardening, but play them down. We are all tired of reading the same old stuff, putting us where the men think we belong – in the home.
>
> (1983: 45)

In these terms, magazine producers – like advertisers – needed to rethink their marketing strategies by listening to women. The issue was not simply that women were reading fewer magazines in preference to other media. Women were still interested in reading magazines – just not the ones on offer.

In this context (and fearing a loss of advertising revenue to Channel 4 and other television companies) magazine executives scurried to make a case for their medium. Women's magazines, they insisted, *were* specialist vehicles – not through their 'limited interests', but through 'their mood, environment and their ambience' (d'Arcy, 1982: 39). Such claims provoked scathing responses among many advertisers. For example, Barry Snellgrove, account director for McCormick Intermarco-Farner, argued that television was a more glamorous and exciting medium than women's magazines, with 'specialist' TV channels like Channel 4 providing an avenue to niche markets that was far more economical than that offered by magazines with shrinking circulations. In a similar vein, Cameron Piper, media buyer at Saatchi and Saatchi, announced that the heyday of magazine advertising was long gone and that it should only be used as a secondary adjunct to television campaigns (d'Arcy, 1982: 42).

Other advertisers, however, were more optimistic about the future of women's magazines as an advertising medium. In fact, in some quarters, it was felt that women's magazines had potential to be an ideal 'lifestyle' medium. But, if this potential were to be realized, publishers had to be less nervous of change and more willing to move away from their formulaic and outdated approach to design and editorial content. Successful adaptation would also require the magazine industry to re-evaluate the assumptions it had traditionally made about its readers: assumptions that were based on increasingly outmoded methods of market research.

As we have already seen, during the 1980s new strategies of marketing to women were taking shape within British advertising. The roles of the account planner, the media buyer and the 'creatives' were crucial to this process – though these, in turn, relied on the new ideas and approaches being employed by market researchers. Qualitatively based, 'lifestyle' research was increasingly seen as the best way of investigating markets that were perceived as becoming more variable and fragmented. Marketing geared to women had been initially slow to draw on these methods, but they had become increasingly popular as advertisers acknowledged that 'women' could no longer be addressed as a homogeneous market. Instead, advertisers needed to draw on new styles of market research, and develop new modes of representation, that could respond to the growing diversity in women's life experiences and attitudes. This new approach in advertising to women was driven, ultimately, by economic contingencies and the search for profit. In the dynamics of the new campaigns, however, there were important dimensions of interaction between economic calculation and cultural expertise. By themselves, economic evaluations would indicate that mass-market advertising was still the cheapest method of reaching the target consumer. The cultural insights offered by 'lifestyle' research, however, suggested that more nuanced campaigns that 'got closer to the customer' had become the most effective strategy in modern advertising – and it was this style of marketing that was increasingly adopted in campaigns aimed at women consumers. Additionally, changes in audiences' 'media literacy' dictated a more sophisticated approach to advertisements' content and mode of address. In particular, a greater level of 'media competence' among younger women was perceived as necessitating a more creative approach in campaigns geared to this market.

It was these new research methods and advertising practices, then, that began to transform the world of women's magazines. At the beginning of the 1980s the women's magazine industry was still relatively untouched by notions of lifestyle markets and consumer segmentation. As we shall see in the next chapter, however, this was set to change. Gradually, the magazine industry responded to the shifting configuration of consumer culture by refashioning its products to meet advertisers' desires for new media environments appropriate to emerging perceptions of women's lifestyles, aspirations and attitudes. And, within this process of reconfiguration, one set of representations became especially influential – the image of the enterprising woman consumer.

5

SERIOUSLY GLAMOROUS OR GLAMOROUSLY SERIOUS?

Working out the 'working woman'

In the previous chapter I explored shifts in the market research methods and practices of the 1980s advertising industry. The next two chapters examine the impact of concepts of 'lifestyle markets' and 'consumer segmentation' on the women's magazine industry. Faced with advertisers' desires for media environments that would be suited to new understandings of women's lifestyles, aspirations and attitudes, the magazine industry was compelled to respond. However, in the early 1980s, the large magazine publishing companies operated through rigid organizational and managerial structures that were not sympathetic to change. Indeed, despite the hunger of advertisers for new media vehicles for young women, the early 1980s saw only one attempt from the 'Big Four' to launch a new 'lifestyle' magazine with IPC's *Options* in 1982.

One independent publisher, however, thought the women's magazine market of the early 1980s was ripe for exploitation. Drawing on the results of lifestyle market research, Audrey Slaughter's Wintour publications developed a glossy title for a 'New Woman', which was launched in 1984. *Working Woman* was a glossy 'sister' edition to the popular US title of the same name, and targeted a reader who was defined by her young, professional lifestyle. Despite strong support from advertising agencies, however, *Working Woman* failed to win over its target readership. Its appearance on the news stands, however, provides us with some insight into magazine publishing of this period. Whilst many publishers and advertisers liked the idea of target markets made up of young, professional, middle-class women, the *culturalization* of the research data was problematic. How was this 'New Woman' to be represented in a magazine? Moreover, how could an image of an independently minded woman be projected in a way that would be agreeable to both advertisers and readers?

Magazines and market research

As we saw in Chapter 4, media buyers have become increasingly prominent figures in the advertising industry since the 1980s. Media buyers aim to buy the most effective space for advertising campaigns, and are faced with making difficult choices between a diverse range of media. The media buyers' main criterion for selection of advertising space is the effectiveness of the media vehicle in delivering the advertisement to the target audience. There may also be other supplementary criteria to consider, including budget, the appropriateness of the media environment for the creative treatment of the campaign, and the media used by competitor brands (Randall, 1993: 152). Market research specialists and professional organizations therefore produce a large number of media market reports for the media buyer. These are intended to help the media buyer achieve maximum value for their expenditure, and assist them by analysing data about the 'reach' of different media into specific market segments (Chisnall, 1992: 218).

The advertising industry has traditionally included the circulation statistics of individual titles in their calculations about whether or not to buy space in women's magazines. Advertisers, advertising agencies and advertising media owners therefore fund a professional body, the Audit Bureau of Circulations (ABC), to collect and collate circulation figures. ABC provides independently audited total circulation figures for the consumer press, applying standardized and uniform methods of circulation audit, net sales figures, circulation variances and distribution. Because of demand from advertisers, ABC now produces qualitative and geographical data. During the 1980s, however, ABC measurements were purely quantitative, and therefore not suited to the purposes of media buyers who were increasingly basing their decisions upon the qualitative information provided by 'lifestyle' market research (Audit Bureau of Circulations, 1999: Chisnall, 1992: 237).

The statistics on magazine readerships produced by the National Readership Survey (NRS) were, however, considered by advertisers to be of more use than the ABC. The NRS was also easy to use in conjunction with geodemographic and 'lifestyle' research offered by the Target Group Index (TGI), TGI 'Outlook', ACORN and SAGACITY (Political and Economic Planning, 1980). The NRS is still widely used by media buyers, and bases its findings on a stratified random sample of 27,000 adult interviews over twelve months, selecting readers according to A to E socio-economic classifications. The NRS attempts to identify 'types' of consumers, and to point to the attraction of specific consumer 'types' to particular publications. Research techniques employed by the NRS involve asking respondents to look at a set of pictures of magazine covers, and to put these pictures in piles based upon whether they remember reading or looking at that title in the last year. Whether respondents looked at a magazine for two minutes, or read one for two hours, these figures are all recorded within the readership socio-economic grading statistics of the NRS (Chisnall, 1992: 218).[1]

Despite the availability of NRS data on magazines, and its congruence with 'lifestyle' market research, the ratio between the amount of magazine advertising purchased and the amount bought in other sectors of the advertising market went into decline from the early 1970s onwards. Between 1965 and 1975 the total share of advertising revenue received by magazines fell from 29 to 24 per cent – a trend that continued into the 1980s (Driver and Gillespie, 1993b: 186). Profits from the 1980s advertising 'boom' did not fall directly into the pockets of magazine publishers. Between 1985 and 1988, for example, there was a 57.9 per cent increase in spending on consumer magazines by advertisers. This must, however, be compared to a 66.3 per cent increase in total advertising expenditure in the UK and to a growth in the overall number of consumer magazines during this period (Jordan and Sons, 1990: 17; Direct Marketing Association (US), 1997). Big advertisers were also increasingly lured away from magazines to television, attracted by the commercial channels' claims to offer 'audience selectivity' and 'programme environment[s]' (New, 1983: 7). By 1983, the larger magazine publishers had realized that they had been complacent about marketing their magazines to advertisers. They were therefore forced to find methods of getting closer to the needs of their advertising clients, and to rethink their sales pitches.

Given the close relationship between magazine publishing and advertising, it is unsurprising that many of the large publishing houses of the 1980s produced research data to supplement the ABC and the NRS. This data was usually produced by a professional research organization to ensure that the results would be considered 'objective' by potential clients (Chisnall, 1992: 237: Barrell and Braithwaite, 1988: 119–20). IPC led the way in this field, providing advertisers with services that pre-tested and post-tested advertisements in their magazines in attempts to evaluate their effectiveness. Groups of publishers also sometimes got together to employ professional research organizations to argue the case for magazines, as compared to other media, in market reports (Barrell and Braithwaite, 1988: 119–20).[2]

In March 1983, IPC, the National Magazine Company and International Thomson, along with four smaller magazine publishers went one step further, launching the promotional publication, *Magazine Marketplace*, a magazine about magazines. *Magazine Marketplace* was sent to 12,000 advertisers and media, account and creative personnel in the hopes of winning back their custom. It contained research analysis, articles on magazine editing, international magazine news, and case histories (Finley, 1983: 67). Through *Magazine Marketplace*, publishers argued that magazines, and particularly women's magazines, could provide advertisers with better results for their money than television (Brooks, 1983: 11). Magazines, it was claimed, could 'brand' a product better than a television campaign, placing 'selective pressure on the right consumer' *(Campaign*, August 1983b: 7).

Many advertisers, however, remained unconvinced by the renewed promotional efforts of the magazine industry. Mike Sommers, marketing director of CPC, parent company to Hellmann's mayonnaise, claimed that their switch from magazines to television had led to a 50 per cent increase in sales over twelve months. Television had also created greater visibility for the brand, above the actual spend. Young and Rubicam's media director, John Mallows, also urged magazine publishers to stop 'droning on' about the high cost of television as compared to magazines. Moreover, Mallows claimed that he would be stuffing his ears 'with cotton wool' until magazine publishers could tell him what magazines actually had going for them (Brooks, 1983: 11).

Honey: 'Read this before you vote'

As Dick Hebdige (1988a: 171–2), Frank Mort (1996: 26–7) and Sean Nixon (1996: 132–3) have all observed, one of the big financial successes of the 1980s magazine industry was the 'style press'. Magazines such as *The Face* and *Blitz* were 'lifestyle'-oriented publications, with young, relatively wealthy readerships. They were, therefore, notably successful in attracting quality advertisers during this decade. Advertisers reputedly liked the aura of 'exclusivity' that was fostered by the 'style press', and responded positively to their (now legendary) ease at turning advertising away if it did not aesthetically blend in with the rest of the publication (Mort, 1996: 27). Indeed, advertisers began to draw upon the aesthetics of these magazines in their campaigns, using them as visual benchmarks for the execution of adver-tisements for target consumer groups.[3]

The relationship between advertisers and the women's press, however, was somewhat different and has, to date, received less scholarly attention. Whilst advertisers may have been unsure about how to imagine the lives, lifestyles and dispositions of contemporary women, they could not look to the old-fashioned aesthetics and falling sales of the women's press for answers. Given their financially perilous positions, the large women's magazine publishers were reluctant to reorganize their practices and/or to invest in new launches (Driver and Gillespie, 1993b: 185). They therefore adopted a more half-hearted strategy to generate interest in their titles, namely 'relaunching' an old 'mass-market' magazine for a newly defined 'lifestyle' market.

The most notable relaunch of a women's magazine in the 1980s was IPC's young women's non-domestic title, *Honey*, which had been on news stands since 1960.[4] Fairly popular in its heyday, *Honey*'s circulation had dwindled from a satisfactory 195,000 in 1978 to just 163,000 in 1981 (Winship, 1987: 166). By relaunching *Honey*, IPC hoped to win over new readers and advertisers to the title whilst retaining the loyalties of the old ones. It would retain the 'identity' that existing readers and advertisers liked, but 'up-date' its brand image with a more contemporary 'lifestyle mood'. In 1980, therefore, *Honey* became perfect bound[5] like its competitors (including *Company* and *Over 21*), acquired a new design, underwent a £150,000 promotional cam-paign, and was given a controversial new editor, Carol Sarler (Barrell and Braithwaite, 1988: 92).

For Sarler, *Honey* was a magazine that would combine traditional fashion

Figure 2 Cover of *Honey*, July 1983 (courtesy of IPC).

and beauty spreads with a 'more thinking' editorial, political debate and feminist arguments (Winship, 1987: 20). *Honey* would target a specialist audience, and not attempt to sell readers a 'lumpy amalgam of all the things that a few executives think are about Being a Woman' (Sarler, 1983: 40). *Honey*'s traditional formula had provided readers with 'a glossy shop window for the latest in fashion and beauty products' (Winship, 1987: 44). Sarler's *Honey*, however, juggled fashion, beauty and cookery with features on careers, women's health issues and politics; a typical edition including an interview with the actor Martin Sheen, an article on voluntary services in the

'Third World', a piece on 'safe' sun-tanning, and an interview with a successful career woman (i.e. the Radio One disc jockey, Janice Long) (July 1983).

Some advertising that appeared in *Honey* seemed very comfortable with its new 'mood'. Canon cameras, for example, advertised their 'Sure Shot' camera in *Honey* in early 1983, providing full detail of its technical features, and describing it as the camera 'professionals take on holiday'. Louis Marcel also placed a campaign for 'Strip Wax' in *Honey* that offered a 'photo-story' of one young woman's summer activities. None of these activities involved a male partner, and the message seemed to be that there were more important things for a young woman to do than deal with problematic boyfriends and body hair (waxing, presumably, providing a medium-term solution to the latter).

The address of other advertisements, however, seemed awkward alongside the new *Honey* 'mood'. Immac hair remover, for example, advertised a 'feminine way to remove unwanted hair' and depicted (literally) a Tarzan and Jane scenario. The Canned Salmon bureau advertised Pink Salmon through *Honey*, and offered its readers an image of a pinnied housewife who hoped to 'give the family a really special treat'. The Pronuptia store depicted a bride in a long white gown being gazed at adoringly by a handsome groom, and claimed that brides in Pronuptia gowns would 'always be remembered'.

As Sarler (1983: 36) later argued, the incongruity of such advertisements with the rest of *Honey*'s editorial mix was a product of IPC's continued insistence on offering advertisers a 'group buy'. The 'group buy' was a discounted package of advertising space that could be bought across a 'group' of IPC magazines. For many years, advertisers interested in mass-market campaigns had seen the 'group buy' as value for money. For IPC, the advantage of the 'group buy' was that it provided advertising revenue for their financially weaker titles (Barrell and Braithwaite, 1988: 121–2). For the new 'lifestyle' magazines such as Sarler's *Honey*, however, the 'group buy' could be equivalent to the death knell. Individual advertisements could work against the grain of the magazines' lifestyle image. The non-traditional lifestyles promoted by magazines such as *Honey* could also work against the brand image of the advertised product, and attract complaints from advertisers (Cullen, 1984: 64). Thus, as *Honey*'s sales continued to fall, Sarler's plans for *Honey* and the image of the 'ideal' reader received less and less support from IPC management. Unsurprisingly, IPC were more concerned with profit than with the possible personal and social gains to be derived from reading women's magazines.

Ultimately, the tensions between IPC and Sarler reached a head (rumour has it that this was over the anti-Conservative slant of an editorial on the General Election), and she was suddenly dismissed in September 1983. The advertising trade press lamented Sarler's departure, calling her 'one of IPC's most talented' editors *(Campaign*, 1983a: 7). IPC, however, justified their stance by pointing to *Honey*'s extremely low sales figures of 149,000 in the first six months of 1983. John Mellon, director of IPC's women's group, claimed that his decision had been 'dictated by the marketplace' (John Mellon, quoted in *Campaign*, 1983a: 7). IPC continued to attempt to revive *Honey*'s sales, but turned it back into the fashion and beauty title of old with a new slogan: 'The Magazine That Makes Fashion Sense' (*Honey*, July 1986). Readers and advertisers, however, were not won over, and *Honey* finally closed in 1986.

Options: 'For the way you want to live now'

In March 1982, IPC attempted to launch their first new glossy magazine of the 1980s, calling it *Options*. *Options*, IPC claimed, was attempting to break with the formulas of mass-market women's titles. It would therefore be launched through a new company subsidiary, Carlton Publications, that could 'focus' upon the 'lifestyle' of the *Options* reader. *Options* aimed to attract a target group of ABC1 women between the ages of twenty-five and forty-four, who made up a mere 7 per cent of the female population. It was to be an up-market publication that could fill a market 'gap', slotting in between National Magazines' *Cosmopolitan* and *Good Housekeeping* (Barrell and Braithwaite, 1988: 87).

In advance publicity for *Options*, the 'ideal' reader was described for advertisers in terms of her 'lifestyle'. Thought by IPC to be '[u]npredictable', the *Options* reader might express a preference for 'milk or martini, jazz or jacuzzi, New York or new kitchen, baby or baby grand' (McKay, 1983b: 37). Her lifestyle was 'rich' and 'varied', and would be encompassed in *Options* – a 'magazine about choice' (McKay, 1983b: 37). As Janice Winship (1983b: 47) has argued, however, the 'choice' offered by *Options* was couched in terms of 'consumer choice'.

In the first *Options* editorial, Penny Radford welcomed readers to the magazine for women who 'worked out their own attitudes for themselves, who don't want to be told how to think, dress or cook, how to arrange their homes – or their lives'. *Options* was, therefore, literally a manual for women who liked to 'make their own decisions' (*Options*, issue 1, March 1982: 3). Issue 1 included articles on women with unusual jobs, money-spinning ideas for livening up the front room ('Ever thought of using test tubes as vases?'), an interview with MP Shirley Williams and a 'refresher course' on culinary basics. However, IPC was dissatisfied with Radford's product and described it (or her?) as 'rather chilly', employing a new editor from issue 4 onwards. In the advertising trade press, *Options*' new editor Sally O'Sullivan described her 'ideal' reader as a woman who had fallen:

> off the end of *Cosmo*. . . . She had been swept up in the Superwoman myth which laid down the perfect woman, she had been through all of that. She has made her decisions now on her life and is more relaxed.
> (O'Sullivan quoted in McKay, 1983b: 37)

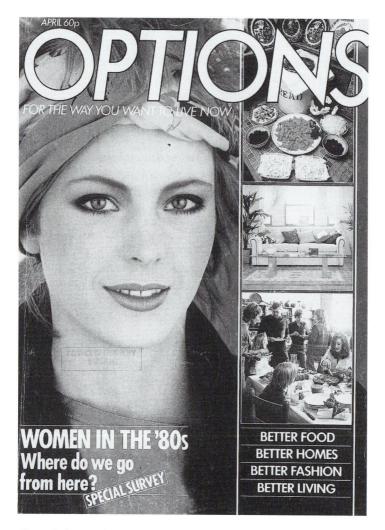

Figure 3 Cover of *Options*, April 1982 (courtesy of IPC).

The other members of *Options*' editorial staff were also, according to O'Sullivan, carefully chosen by IPC for their resemblance to the 'ideal' *Options* reader (McKay, 1983b: 37).

Despite a one million pound spend on publicizing *Options*, the initial responses of advertisers and readers were disappointing for IPC (Barrell and Braithwaite, 1988: 88; McKay, 1983a: 7). Whilst the pre-publicity material had promised a visually interesting, intelligent and provocative magazine, *Options* was criticized for being 'busy to no general effect, confusing and unchallenging' (McKay, 1983b: 37). IPC claimed that the editorial of *Options* was geared towards a new 'lifestyle' segment of young women. Advertisers, however, were not impressed and thought that the content of *Options* was too broadly defined. *Options*, therefore, was widely thought to be a clever 'marketing idea', but not a magazine that truly addressed a 'lifestyle' market (McKay, 1983b: 38).

Sally O'Sullivan defended *Options* against the critics, and claimed that they were being unrealistic if they expected IPC to produce a 'niche' publication akin to 'the *Guardian* women's pages. There just aren't enough of those readers' (O'Sullivan, quoted in McKay, 1983b: 37). The advertising trade press replied that advertisers had not been anticipating a magazine that would target fashion-conscious feminists (e.g. '*Spare Rib* with lipstick'). They had, however, been expecting editorial that would deal with 'mainstream subjects and problems from a woman's perspective' (McKay, 1983b: 37).

Criticisms of the *Options* editorial mix were short-lived. *Options* gained sufficient advertising from those advertisers who entered into a 'group buy' at IPC. It also attracted those media buyers who could not find more appropriate magazine environments for reaching young women. Whilst the sales of *Options* in the first six months of publication were lower than those projected, IPC invested a further £200,000 on promotions, and gave it a 'second push', with a major television advertising campaign (McKay, 1983a: 7). Within a couple of years, *Options* had become one of the most successful women's magazine launches of the 1980s, with satisfactory circulation figures of 236,000 by 1987. However, according to the NRS, *Options*' readership profile was vastly different from that originally targeted, with one third of readers under the age of twenty-four, and only 28 per cent in the target age catchment group (Barrell and Braithwaite, 1988: 82). *Options*, therefore, did not 'fill' its target 'gap' in the magazine market or attract a particularly 'new' type of readership. Instead, the NRS figures suggested that *Options* was a surprise success with pre-existent target groups of domestic magazine readers, who were buying it as an alternative to National Magazines' thriving domestic monthly, *Good Housekeeping* (Barrell and Braithwaite, 1988: 82).

The *Working Woman* work-out

The size of the IPC conglomerate was undoubtedly a significant factor in the eventual success of *Options*. IPC was able to launch the magazine on an extravagant publicity budget, and could make the long-term investments often required to win over both advertisers and readers. IPC also had a support structure with ancillary departments, such as advertising, accounts, paper-buying and distribution. As Joan Barrell and Brian Braithwaite (1988: 100) have observed, however, the publishing of magazines has also 'always had an attraction for amateurs and dilettantes' who dream of owning their own successful title. Because there are so few restrictions involved in setting up publishing businesses, entrepreneurs seem to think they need only a title, a *raison d'être*, and an editor before they can launch onto the market. Magazine publishing, however, is a notoriously risky business, and is, according to Barrell and Braithwaite (1988: 91–100), 'littered with the wrecks of some abject failures which have been launched with plenty of money and goodwill' (Barrell and Braithwaite, 1988: 91–100). Indeed, many entrepreneurial publishers have found their dream of fame and fortune has turned into a nightmare of bankruptcy.

Publishing entrepreneurs can obtain the initial capital investments they require, and fend off many of the difficulties inherent in the launch of a new title, by entering into a title franchise arrangement with a foreign publishing company. This method of launching magazines was increasingly popular in 1980s Britain. New magazines could be promoted by drawing upon the existing reputation of the title, the reputation of the franchise publisher, and evidence that the title could attract readers overseas (Barrell and Braithwaite, 1988: 97). The franchiser often provided the 'host' publisher with advertising opportunities, financial backing for the launch, an established brand image, and sometimes some of the content for the magazine itself (Bunting, 1997: 52).

In an ideal world, the large magazine publisher would not enter into this form of agreement with a 'host' publisher. Instead, they would simply sell an identical but translated version of their magazine to advertisers and readers across the globe. The reality, however, has been somewhat different and large publishing businesses have had to be more diverse and flexible in their scope, developing localized strategies for the development and marketing of their products (Driver and Gillespie, 1993b: 197). The aspirations of magazine publishers to expand into international markets are, unfortunately, scuppered by the realities of cultural diversity. Marketing advocates of the 'globalization' thesis often represent the market as a 'preference structure [which] gets pressed into homogenized commonality' (Robins, 1997: 29). Magazine publishers, however, have been forced to compromise between their aspirations to expand and the existing social and historical realities, creating what Kevin Robins (1997: 29) has termed a 'global–local nexus'.

Until the mid-1980s, expansion into international markets was not a popular business tactic with women's magazine publishers in Europe, and only large US companies with saturated domestic markets investigated its opportunities (Bunting, 1997: 58). Before 1984 then, *Cosmopolitan*, *Vogue* and *Harpers and Queen* were the only monthly women's glossy titles in the UK that had their roots elsewhere, being produced by British subsidiaries of their American parent companies. *Working Woman* magazine, however, was launched onto the British market in 1984, originating in a complex international franchise arrangement between an established North American publisher, Hal Publications, and a small independent British publisher, Wintour Publications. In the US, *Working Woman* was already a very successful, 'lifestyle' research driven magazine, aiming at a market of 'professional women'. The new British edition of *Working Woman*, however, was keen to stress that it would not simply duplicate the lifestyle address of its sister publication, and claimed it would be 'localized' for British 'career women' (*Campaign*, 1983c: 7).

Hal Publications met up with a number of large British publishing companies in an attempt to interest them in the launch of a UK licensed local edition of *Working Woman*, but did not meet with immediate success (Barrell and Braithwaite, 1988: 82). Indeed, *Working Woman* (UK) would not have appeared at all had it not been for the persistence of its editor, creator and eventual part-owner, Audrey Slaughter, who spent almost a year seeking financial backing for a British edition.[6] After several potential backers pulled out of the project, Slaughter eventually secured a small capital investment of £700,000 (McKay, 1984: 34). Twenty per cent of *Working Woman* (UK) was owned by Hal Publications. The rest of the capital was raised from ICFC, part of the government-promoted scheme Investors in Industry, and from a range of private backers that included Slaughter herself and her friends *(Campaign, 1984: 4)*.

The launch of *Working Woman* was widely welcomed by the advertising industry, which is evidenced by the extensive coverage the magazine received in the industry's trade publications. Slaughter claimed to have identified a 'lifestyle' group of 'New Women' in the highly desirable and affluent AB women's market that consisted of:

> women who actually like working, who have discovered a job can be both absorbing and worthwhile, who feel their own salary is some-thing to be treasured and who, although defining themselves through their jobs, are not excluding men from their lives. On the contrary, they choose their man because his company is indispensable, not because he has a healthy pay cheque or important status – surely more flattering to men? They are feminists with acceptable faces.
>
> (Slaughter, 1984: 77–8)

Slaughter explained that the target working woman might still want a husband and children. However, better educational opportunities, economic independence and experience of travel meant that she would not accept that 'her only ultimate destination is marriage and motherhood' (Slaughter, 1984: 77). For advertisers, the prospect of a new up-market women's magazine that would deliver this high-spending woman to them was very attractive (Cooper, 1984: 15). *Working Woman* added to its appeal for advertisers by employing 'lifestyle' techniques of market research to provide evidence of the existence of their target reader. They engaged advertising agency Leo Burnett (well known for their innovative lifestyle methods of research), who confirmed the existence of *Working Woman*'s target group by analysing TGI figures. The potential *Working Woman* reader was, according to Leo Burnett, an

Figure 4 Cover of *Working Women*, October 1984 (courtesy of Wintour Publications).

advertiser's dream: 'up-market, on a continuing career path and with earnings of £12,000 and above'. Moreover, 'a lot of the target group' was thought to work in advertising (McKay, 1984: 35).

Despite the pre-launch enthusiasm in the advertising trade press, the reception for issue 1 of *Working Woman* was cool. *Campaign* surveyed female advertising executives after the magazine's launch, commenting upon a 'less than rapturous welcome' from this key section of the magazine's target readership. *Working Woman* was criticized for being humourless, 'a bit intense and heavy going' and lacking in 'fun' (Cooper, 1984: 15). Some commentators were also concerned that there appeared to be some confusion about the 'lifestyle' of 'the working woman' within the magazine's editorial. Features about 'getting a foot on the first-time property ownership ladder', and 'cop-out' cookery, were uncomfortably placed next to articles on building your own fine art collection, business travel, salaries, investments and company profiles (*Working Woman*, issue 1, October 1984). Judie Lannon, research director at advertising agency JWT, declared that the magazine was not about any working women that she knew, suggesting that its articles cohered only because they were about 'becoming a successful business woman by working very hard' (Cooper, 1984: 15).

An article in *Campaign* which appeared just after *Working Woman*'s launch commented that many advertisers seemed confused about how to 'speak' to the magazines' target readership. Indeed, many of the advertisements were thought to be 'incongruous':

> Sanpro ads seemed strangely out of place ... as did Jasper Conran's maternity dress (even though the model carried a briefcase). But the ad which caused most comment was that for Cathay Pacific airlines, which depicted a man in the passenger seat holding up the world with his little finger aided by the 'effortless charm of our Oriental hostesses'.
>
> (Cooper, 1984: 15)

By 1985, *Working Woman* had run into financial difficulties resulting from poor sales and a lack of advertising. Hal Publications pulled out of *Working Woman* in March 1986, putting the company into receivership (Jivani, 1986: 6). In the spring of 1986, the business entrepreneur, Peter Cadbury, stepped in to 'save' the magazine. Photographs of Slaughter and Cadbury appeared on the editorial page of Cadbury's first issue, but they seemed an unlikely pairing, Cadbury's patriarchal 'businessman' image being uncomfortable within the pages of a magazine about successful, independent women. Indeed, differences in opinion about the lifestyle 'mood' of *Working Woman* quickly led to Audrey Slaughter's decision to resign as editor (Payne, 1986: 12).

Unmoved by this, Cadbury claimed that the editorial tone of Slaughter's *Working Woman* had been 'boring', and said that the magazine needed to be 're-positioned, re-launched and re-built' (Payne, 1986: 13). He employed a new editor for the title, Pandora Wodehouse, who publicly expressed a very different understanding of the *Working Woman* than her predecessor. 'Since I am not a feminist – dreadful word – there will be more men featured with more articles written from the male viewpoint', Wodehouse announced, 'I can't think of a single woman who doesn't like men. We all know we can live without them, as they can live without us, but who wants to?' (*Campaign*, 1986a: 6)

Cadbury also appointed Marina Leopardi as the new advertising director for *Working Woman*. Leopardi confidently predicted a circulation increase to 50,000 ABC1 women within a short space of time, stating that 'the readers we think we can get are not actually buyers of other magazines' (Edwards, 1986: 18). The creative advertising agency, Ted Bates, was also taken on by Cadbury to help stimulate advertising interest in the magazine (Payne, 1986: 13). Adopting 'psychographic' methods of lifestyle market research, Ted Bates deduced that the size of the target readership for *Working Woman* was not as vast as originally predicted. 'Feminists' and 'strivers' were, apparently, already readers of *Working Woman*. The only other potential 'lifestyle' groups worth targeting were the perplexing 'latent strivers' (i.e. 'those who don't know exactly what they want, but are certain that it isn't what they already have') and the non-readers of women's magazines (Edwards, 1986: 17). The results of this market research, coupled with financial difficulties, led to Cadbury's withdrawal from the *Working Woman* rescue in September of 1986 (*Campaign*, 1986b: 6). After a brief purchase of the title by Preston Publications, the magazine finally folded in January of 1987 leaving eighty-six creditors and staff suing for breach of contract (*Campaign*, 1987c: 6).

The advertising trade press hotly debated the collapse of *Working Woman*. Some practitioners centred on the magazine's characterization of its 'ideal' woman reader, and argued that the editorial mix was inappropriate for its market. Carol Sarler was particularly scathing, insisting that *Working Woman*: 'didn't ever address the reality of women working. A real feminist would not read *WW*. It's a pre-feminist magazine, locked in the time . . . when the only way you could make it was to pretend you weren't a woman' (Edwards, 1986: 18). Other commentators believed that *Working Woman* was much too focused upon selling space to advertisers at the expense of developing a magazine for a target reader. According to magazine editor Sally Brampton, for example, women's magazine publishing could not be 'a question of ABC1s; it's a question of an attitude of mind' (Brampton, quoted in Edwards, 1986: 13).

Despite *Working Woman*'s spectacular failure, many in the advertising industry continued to maintain that there was still an unfilled gap in the market for a 'lifestyle' women's magazine title. Kirsty Hutton, associate media director of SSC&B Lintas argued that there was 'a shortage of media to reach the late twenties/early thirties woman who is not just interested in her home'. It is difficult, Hutton moaned, to find 'human being titles'. Steve de Saulles, media manager of Wight Collins Rutherford Scott also believed that a 'market gap' was there, maintaining that '[t]here *is* room in women's magazines for something that isn't *Cosmo* or *Woman's Own*' (quoted in Edwards, 1986: 18).

The rise and fall of the *Working Woman*

The demise of *Working Woman* can offer some insight into the business of women's magazine publishing during the early 1980s. Moreover, it can provide us with an understanding of the various elements that need to fuse together if a women's magazine launch is to be commercially successful. If we compare *Working Woman*'s launch to that of the more profitable *Options*, we can see that *Options'* footing at IPC gave it considerable advantages. IPC could make substantial capital investment in *Options*, and could spend large amounts on the publicity that is essential for attracting advertisers and readers to a title. IPC could also entice advertisers by announcing substantial investment in *Options'* launch, and could plough much of this budget back into IPC by placing advertisements for *Options* within other IPC magazines (Barrell and Braithwaite, 1988: 98). IPC could also easily carry the costs of *Options* within its existing structure, as it already possessed effective accounting, advertising and central production departments, as well as office space, telephone exchanges and so on. It was easy for IPC, therefore, to absorb *Options* into their existing organization, enabling them to spend relatively small amounts of money on hiring editorial staff and on advertising (Barrell and Braithwaite, 1988: 98–9).

Wintour Publications, on the other hand, faced immediate expenditure on commercial premises, an entire staff and office machinery before *Working Woman*'s launch. They also had to invest significant amounts of money in advertising to potential advertisers and retailers in the trade press (which have notoriously high page rates) and on market research to support their rationale (Barrell and Braithwaite, 1988: 98–9). For independent publishers, therefore, the launch of a new magazine does not come cheaply. The small size of Wintour Publications did bring with it some advantages, allowing them to move fairly quickly with their idea. They did not have to engage in any long-term discussions about the implications of the magazine for the finances of their other business interests, which doubtless occurred at IPC with *Options*. They were also, initially, in a better position to appeal to 'lifestyle'-oriented advertisers who were seeking suitable specialist environments for their campaigns for young, professional women. IPC was well known amongst advertisers for its unwieldy organizational structure, indiscriminate approach to advertising, and for its history of mass-market publications. The smallness of Wintour Publications, on the other hand, could be used to signify to advertisers the 'distinctiveness' of their magazine environment, and their ability to focus upon the 'lifestyle' of a 'New Woman'.

So, if *Working Woman* was not entirely doomed as a business venture from the start, why did it go into such a rapid decline? Were advertisers and market researchers wrong to identify 'new' lifestyle groups of women? Or did Slaughter, Wodehouse and their colleagues never really manage to incorporate the results of lifestyle market research into the address of the magazine they produced, and thus fail to 'speak' to these target groups? There were almost certainly some misjudgements from both sides. First, in the early days of *Working Woman* there was an assumption amongst many advertisers and market researchers that sales of existing women's magazines were falling because women were bored with their traditional editorial mixes. Some therefore hailed *Working Woman* as the 'solution' for reaching young, professional women, and presumed that significant quantities of this target group would be desperate to read a magazine with a non-traditional editorial formula. This may not have been the case at all, and indeed if it was, *Working Woman* was clearly not the answer.

Second, if there were groups of women who were seeking a more up-to-date women's magazine in the early 1980s, there seems to have been a failure of *Working Woman* itself to target this group convincingly through its magazine format. Whilst *Working Woman* moved away from traditional magazine formulas, it also moved away from the long-standing editorial mix of home, leisure and pleasure related features to an emphasis on 'work'. As Janice Winship has noted (1987: 48–9), introducing 'realism' is a 'risky business' where women's magazines are concerned. This is because, Winship argues (1987: 48–9), even if women's magazine readers are bored by the existing titles on the market, 'realism' is 'commonly seen as anathema to entertainment and pleasure'. Therefore, a magazine that focuses its editorial around the often dull and un-pleasurable realm of 'work' is a risky venture altogether.

In the following chapter, therefore, I offer an account of the launches of more prosperous glossy women's publications of the 1980s and early 1990s. As we shall see, all the new launches I discuss were, like *Working Woman*, the products of transnational business agreements. Like *Working Women*, these new titles also attempted to move away from traditional images of femininity and mass-market magazine formulas, hoping to target socio-economic groups similar to those of *Working Woman*. Like *Working Woman*, these titles were also the products of extensive 'lifestyle' market research into the lives of women. This research also suggested that the world of work might be a crucial component of the lives of women readers. The new launches, however, all remembered that *Working Woman* had failed. The new glossies therefore adopted a 'lifestyle' orientation which suggested that 'work' might not be the first thing on a woman's mind when she settled down after a hard day at the office to read a women's magazine.

6

'WHAT WOMEN WANT UNDER THE COVERS'

New markets and the 'new woman' in the 1980s

In a 1985 article in *Campaign* magazine, the media director of Aspect Advertising, Richard Eyre (1985: 41), was unusually complimentary about the recent activities of the magazine business. The sophistication and variety of a new 'breed of individualistic magazines' for women particularly struck him (1985: 41). It was time, Eyre declared, for advertisers to realize the full potential of the women's magazine medium, because:

> the variety of magazines available allows communication with a wide range of women, distinguishable in terms of age, class, and a whole range of other discriminators, but in addition, because of their much debated 'relationship' with the medium, also in terms of their attitudes.
>
> (Eyre, 1985: 39)

Eyre (1985: 9) was also complimentary about the forms of market research recently employed by the magazine industry, which had, in his opinion, helped the magazine editor to develop a clearer image of her target readers. Magazine editorials were no longer targeted at women of a particular age or social class, because editors had recognized that 'the difference between a reader of *Cosmopolitan* and *Working Woman* is as much a function of attitude' (Eyre, 1985: 39).

Eyre's article identified an important shift in the business of women's magazines in the 1980s. In the latter part of the decade, British news stands heaved under the weight of new ranges of thriving women's weekly and monthly titles. In the pages of the new monthly glossies for young women, a variety of 'lifestyle' depictions were offered to readers and advertisers. However, taking heed of the market failure of *Working Woman*, all the new glossies steered clear of addressing young women as *working* women. Whilst work was understood to be a part of the make-up of the identity of the 'New Woman', it was seen to be a risky lifestyle orientation for a women's magazine.

As I argued in Chapter 5, 'work' introduced an element of 'realism' to the content of women's magazines, and it is likely that many young working women found this unpalatable in a medium they associated with 'fantasy' and 'pleasure'.

The new glossy titles discussed in this chapter were all products of joint venture acquisitions made by UK publishers with overseas magazine publishers. This chapter therefore begins by examining the 'international' contours of the 1980s magazine industry, focusing in particular on the impact of what became known in the business as the 'German Invasion'. The 'German Invasion' – namely the successful launches of domestic weekly and monthly titles by large German publishers – was, I argue, the catalyst for the launches of three glossies in the late 1980s: *Elle* (UK), *Marie Claire* (UK) and *New Woman* (UK). All three were titles already available in other countries, and the British versions were the products of complex international business arrangements. The concepts for these new glossies also derived from market research, which was constructing transnational target groups of women with similar attitudes, aspirations and 'lifestyles'.

Elle (UK), *Marie Claire* (UK) and *New Woman* (UK) ultimately proved successful in reaching many of their target readers and advertisers, and in so doing they altered the landscape of glossy women's magazine publishing. As I will show in the final part of this chapter, the success of these three new glossies challenged the sales of women's magazines that had previously dominated the glossy market, particularly National Magazines' *Cosmopolitan* (UK), *Company* and *She*. Not to be outdone, National Magazines were compelled to up-date the lifestyle 'moods' of these titles, and to redefine their target readerships in the context of increasingly uncertain trading conditions. In doing so they attempted to project new images of the 'lifestyles' of young, professional women that would appeal to readers and advertisers alike. Their quest was to produce some stable and marketable icons of youthful femininity, but this was not an easy task. Not only did they face the difficulty of understanding the proliferation of identities and consumption patterns adopted by young women in their everyday lives, but they also had to translate these convincingly into a magazine format.

'The eagle has landed . . .'

In Brian Braithwaite's (1989: 28) retrospective of a decade of British magazine publishing, he claimed that the 'runaway success' of the 1980s was 'the German realisation that the British [magazine] market held undreamt-of riches'. Braithwaite was referring to the post-1986 expansion of Germany's biggest publishers, Bauer and Gruner and Jahr (G & J), into the domestic weekly and monthly markets. This move had astonished IPC and National Magazines, who had long conceded defeat in this sector and turned their attentions elsewhere (Braithwaite, 1989: 28). G & J's monthly *Prima* (launched

1986), accompanied by the weeklies *Best* (launched 1987) and Bauer's *Bella* (launched 1988), however, all flourished and consequently altered the face of British magazine publishing.

German publishers were strategically well placed to initiate these magazine launches in Britain and, almost simultaneously, across Europe (Scott, 1989: 62). The German magazine market had been thriving for some time – partly because of government regulation of commercial television in the post-war period, which had provided publishers with a relatively 'captive' audience. German publishers were therefore prosperous and, because of anti-monopoly legislation and high taxation at home, had explored avenues for expansion through international investments (Scott, 1989: 62). By the 1980s, the lower end of the German magazine market was almost saturated with profitable titles, but there were few high-quality magazines available. German publishers therefore sought to develop the quality sector at home, and to export their knowledge about the lower end of the magazine market abroad (Scott, 1989: 62).

G & J's *Prima* and *Best* were designed to compete with IPC's mass-market domestic weeklies. Both magazines included sections on practical ideas, beauty, home-crafts, gardening, childcare and cookery, and targeted women in the B, C1 and C2 socio-economic categories. Their target age groups were different, *Prima* seeking women between the ages of twenty to forty-four, and *Best* coveting younger readers between the ages of twenty and twenty-four. The lifestyle 'mood' of the *Prima* woman was 'practically minded', whilst the *Best* woman was thought to enjoy reading about 'all areas of their lives'. Bauer's *Bella* imagined similar target readers to those of *Best*, but emphasized 'real life drama' in its features (Barrell and Braithwaite, 1988: 97). Like their British counterparts, German publishers aimed at profits from economies of scale. However, instead of pandering to the whims of prospective advertisers like IPC, German publishers were more focused on developing their editorial content to suit their readers, and hoped to build brand loyalty through an emphasis on 'areas of interest', quality features, and value for money (Howard, 1989: 46). In *Campaign* in 1987, Henning Lauer of Bauer highlighted the difference in strategy between British and German publishers, arguing that:

> [y]ou cannot advertise something which you do not have. First you establish circulation, then you go for the advertisers. That is what we do in Germany. When we are established – say 500,000 sales – then we start. We begin with modest rates and move up – or down.
>
> (Lauer quoted in McKee, 1987: 34)

The German publishers made substantial long-term financial investments in the launches of these titles (figures as high as £10 million were estimated for the start-up of *Prima*, for example). *Prima*'s publishing executive, Rolf Paltzer, also astounded British publishers by claiming that he would be happy to wait seven years to see a return on investments (Barrell and Braithwaite, 1988: 98). Both G & J and Bauer demonstrated their commitment to entering the British market by setting up company subsidiaries in the UK. This was financially demanding for their companies, and higher risk than an export, licensing or joint venture arrangement, and suggested that they intended to be around for the long term (Hafstrand, 1995: 2–4).

There was little advance warning or advertising before the arrivals of *Prima*, *Best* and *Bella* on the news stands. Their launches, however, were accompanied by significant PR campaigns on television and in the press. Advertising was notably sparse in all early issues of these titles, and the editorial tone deviated from the 'gossip' and 'chat' of IPC's traditional weekly titles such as *Woman* and *Woman's Own*. Moreover, the royal family and minor celebrities (staple figures in the IPC women's weekly) were nowhere to be found (Barrell and Braithwaite, 1988: 99).

After the launches of *Prima*, *Best* and *Bella*, Young and Rubicam carried out focus group research in an attempt to evaluate the success of the three German titles in 'speaking' to their target readerships (Howard, 1989: 50). *Bella*, *Best* and *Prima*, they found, scored well with young women who Young and Rubicam identified as 'aspirers' and 'succeeders'. IPC's *Woman's Own* and *Woman's Realm*, on the other hand, scored highly with less affluent 'lifestyle' groups, and particularly appealed to 'the resigned poor', who were older and possibly widowed (Howard, 1989: 50). By 1988, *Bella*, *Best* and *Prima* were proving fierce competition for indigenous titles, forcing circulation of IPC's weekly titles *Woman* and *Woman's Own* down by a quarter from their 1983 figures. German publishers, the advertising trade press suggested, had cast a fresh eye over the British magazine market, and had identified market niches that were ripe for the picking (McKay, 1987: 25). The trade press was also unsympathetic to IPC, claiming that it had foolishly allowed itself to fall victim to 'the ostrich effect' (Fraser, 1989: 19).

In 1989, Bauer's *Bella* further surprised IPC by offering advertisers a 'pan-European' advertisement rate card. This enabled media buyers to buy discounted 'packages' of space, and to place advertisements in four '*Bella*-esque' titles, namely *Bella* and *Tina* in Germany, *Maxi* in France, and *Bella* in the UK. Bauer's managing director, Konrad Wiederholz, explained the rationale for the 'Euro-discount' as an inevitable consequence of the European market, which was:

> already a reality in 1989 for many internationally operating companies. Already we have seen advertising agencies actively involving themselves with European partners and we are now structuring ourselves to the requirements that this market now demands.
>
> (Wiederholz quoted in Howard, 1989: 50)

Target manufacturers for the European rate card included international corporations such as L'Oreal, Vichy, Gillette, Nestlé and Heinz. IPC were dispirited by Bauer's actions; they had traditionally sold advertising space at discounted prices across their weekly titles, and offered this to media buyers as their unique selling point (Howard, 1989: 50). Bauer's move was, however, welcomed in the trade press by media buyers such as Nick Henley of McCann-Erickson, who commented approvingly on the flexibility Bauer's scheme gave him (Henley cited in Howard, 1989: 50).

It was the aggressive business tactics of the German publishers that ultimately compelled the older publishing houses (and particularly IPC) to re-evaluate their production and marketing strategies. IPC were rightly concerned that German publishers would crowd out their core market by employing high promotional budgets, low cover prices, quality editorial content, colour printing, reduced advertising volumes, and long-term business plans (Cumberpatch, 1988a: 25). In 1988, IPC's chief executive, John Mellon, therefore announced in the trade press that he no longer held any illusions about IPC's position in the magazine market. Under Mellon, IPC embarked upon a period of dramatic cost-cutting and rationalization. IPC's circulation department, for example, was computerized, and the functions of warehouses and some in-house departments, such as advertising sales, were contracted outside. In 1984–5, IPC had directly employed 2,600 people. By 1988, however, that figure stood at just 1,600 (Cumberpatch, 1988a: 29).

Under Mellon, IPC also fought back against the German publishers' designs on the domestic weekly market by launching 'me-too' titles. The success of *Prima* was therefore counter-balanced with IPC's launch of the practical 'how-to' monthly *Essentials* (1988), which was sold as a 'collectable' title with an expensive free binder and hole-punched editorial. Fortunately for IPC, *Essentials* was greeted positively by advertisers and readers, and by 1988 its circulation had reached a respectable 800,000 copies per month. Attempting to gain a foothold in Europe, and not wishing the traffic from European publishers to remain one-way, by late 1988 IPC had successfully exported *Essentials* to Italy, France and French Canada (Cumberpatch, 1988a: 29). In 1989, IPC also launched the weekly title *Me*, which it positioned against *Best* (Braithwaite, 1989: 29). *Me* proved to be an outstanding commercial success for IPC, with a circulation of over one million copies by the end of 1989.

'Setting the style': the launch of British *Elle*

Whilst German publishers had designs on the domestic magazine market in Britain, other European publishers had eyes for the glossy market. In 1985 came the launch of a monthly British edition of the weekly French magazine, *Elle*, by the international media group News International, in association with French multimedia company Hachette. This move transformed the face of glossy women's magazine publishing in Britain, declaring war on the circulation figures and advertising revenues of many established glossy titles – particularly those published by National Magazines (Cumberpatch, 1988a: 29; Cova, Rad-Serecht and Weil, 1993: 478).

The partnership of News International and Hachette was a product of Hachette's international business strategy that was forged in the early 1980s (Hafstrand, 1995: 3; Usherwood, 1997: 181).[1] Until this point, Hachette had been a middle-class family business with a coherent but narrow range of ventures. Hachette had published *Elle* in France since 1945, and developed the magazine for the Japanese market in 1969. In 1980, however, Hachette was taken over by Matra, a conglomerate known for activities in industrial arms and motor vehicle manufacturing (Hafstrand, 1995: 7; Kronlund, 1991: 617). Matra's director, Jean-Luc Lagardère, was ambitious to develop Matra into a multimedia multinational group, and transformed the fortunes of Hachette within a couple of years. This medium-sized French publisher, therefore, soon became one of the world's largest multimedia companies, operating in more than forty countries. By 1991, Hachette not only produced magazines, but also television programmes, films, and books. It also became a leading magazine distributor, and owned a powerful international press empire (Hafstrand, 1995: 7; Kronlund, 1991: 619).

Elle Europe oversaw *Elle*'s European expansion, which was co-ordinated from central Hachette headquarters in France. Elle Europe offered their partners, such as News International, the benefits of extensive magazine publishing knowledge, supervising the contents of each edition of the magazine and providing quantitative indicators of sales, readership, advertising turnover and so on. Furthermore, they trained the local teams of each new magazine to embrace the 'concept' and 'style' of *Elle*. This was an extensive course, undertaken for two or three months in Paris before gaining the joint venture contract and autonomy in the realm of production (Cova, Rad-Serecht and Weil, 1993: 481). In return, Hachette's joint venture partners assisted with local knowledge about the practicalities of launching magazines in different countries, and usually provided Hachette with a developed magazine distribution network (Cova, Rad-Serecht and Weil, 1993: 478).

Hachette strongly believed in the commercial importance of developing a strong brand identity for *Elle* across the world, and *Elle*'s recognizable logo and stylish cover lines were therefore common to all editions of the magazine. Elle Europe also reserved control over the style of graphic design and the content of features and fashion pages that graced each interior (Cova, Rad-Serecht and Weil, 1993: 481). Replication also enabled Hachette to keep magazine production costs at a minimum. Indeed, Elle Europe held and circulated many cover photographs, articles and illustrations to their partner publishers from a common pool. Some editorial and news pages were, however, written by the local *Elle* team, ensuring the 'localization' of *Elle* for readerships in different national markets (see Usherwood, 1997).

The driving forces behind Hachette's expansion of *Elle* were the shifting needs of advertisers, many of whom were keen to market transnational products across Europe. Hachette shrewdly employed a Parisian company, Interdeco, to offer specialist advice to media buyers, and to sell space across the various editions of the magazine. By the end of the 1980s, 30 per cent of the advertising in each edition of *Elle* was duplicated across European versions (Cova, Rad-Serecht and Weil, 1993: 483–4). Interdeco, however, was not starry-eyed about attracting major advertisers, and also informed small, locally based advertising agencies about local editions of *Elle*, and helped them to contact and negotiate for space with local head offices (Cova, Rad-Serecht and Weil, 1993: 483–4).

Elle made itself particularly attractive for large advertisers by producing extensive 'lifestyle' market research into its target readerships. The results of this market research persuaded advertisers to buy space across international editions, and demonstrated that *Elle* could reach desirable 'lifestyle' target groups living across Europe. Elle Europe's market researchers declared that European lifestyles were 'evolving' and converging, although different countries had reached different levels of 'maturity' (Cova, Rad-Serecht and Weil, 1993: 482). Moreover, they claimed to have identified two principal segments in the European population: those slow to react to change and attached to national or regional traditions; and those highly responsive to change who shared the same lifestyles, if not nationalities, with others in their segment. Drawing on these findings, Elle Europe identified what it termed three axes of 'socio-cultural advance'. The primary axis was that of 'individuality', that contrasted 'socio-cultural advance' with 'socio-cultural backwardness'. The second axis measured 'roots and networking', exploring the capacity of target groups to move from 'attachment to the familiar' to 'communication with new peoples'. The final axis measured 'reconciliation', indicating the level at which individuals were capable of 'integrating intellectuality and rationality with sensitivity, emotion and intuition' (cited in Cova, Rad-Serecht and Weil, 1993: 482).

Elle Europe's market research claimed that 24 per cent of European women belonged to the 'socio-cultural advance' group, and they attempted to imagine and target readers from this European population segment. 'Socio-culturally advanced' women were desirable target markets partly because of their open-minded attitudes, but more importantly for advertisers, they had high purchasing power. Most of these 'socio-culturally advanced' women were from privileged social categories, many of them having benefited from higher education. *Elle*, therefore, offered advertisers a title with a strong vision of its 'lifestyle' target group and a vehicle for reaching a quality, high-spending, international readership (Cova, Rad-Serecht and Weil, 1993: 483).

There was some anxiety at Hachette/News International about whether the French connotations of *Elle* should be played up or played down in the publicity for its British launch. From the coverage of *Elle* in the advertising trade press, it is clear that its publishers wanted to show that British *Elle* would be a 'localized' version of the magazine, and not a mere translation of French *Elle*. British *Elle,* it was stressed, would be a 'cousin, rather than a "clone"' of the original (Rawsthorn, 1985: 34; Polan, 1986: 64). Advertisers, however, had apparently viewed French *Elle* as 'a bible to the business' for some years, and British *Elle* were therefore keen to be associated with it (Mower, 1985: 13). In the trade press, therefore, Sally Brampton, editor of British *Elle*, summarized her vision of the magazine's mode of address in remarkably vague terms: 'We will borrow the mood of French *Elle*, the life, the freshness, to use a corny phrase the *joie de vivre*', Brampton claimed, 'but we will interpret, not translate' (Brampton in Rawsthorn, 1985: 34).

Attempts to localize *Elle* for the British market were particularly visible in the launch strategy for the magazine, and a preview edition and questionnaire were attached to a News International weekly newspaper. The *Sunday Times* was thought to attract women readers with a similar 'lifestyle' profile to *Elle*'s target readership (Mower, 1985: 13). After a few changes because of this research, issue 1 of British *Elle* appeared on the newsagents' shelves in October 1995. The cover featured the face of Yasmin Parveneh, a well-known model whose celebrity was due to the rarity of her success as an international model of Anglo-Asian descent and to a much publicized relationship with Simon Le Bon of the pop group Duran Duran. British *Elle* included articles on where to find French 'café society' in London, a preview of fashions for spring 1986, an interview with pop star Brian Ferry and family, a list of restaurant critic Egon Ronay's '25 Special Restaurants', a designer knitting pattern, and fifty pages of fashion coverage that were uninterrupted by advertising (Rawsthorn, 1985: 34).

Also appearing in issue 1 of *Elle* was a co-authored article by editor Sally Brampton and the author and journalist Tony Parsons (1985: 14–16). This offered a definition of who the ideal *Elle* reader was, by describing who she was *not*. Brampton pitched the reader of *Elle* against the popular stereotype of the British 'Sloane Ranger', known widely in the UK through the publication of Peter York and Ann Barr's best-seller of the period, *The Official Sloane Ranger Handbook* (1982). Chastizing the Sloane Ranger for her 'utter reliability', Brampton claimed that she was one of the 'the worst possible manifestations' of the British class system that valued breeding as opposed to 'talent and ability'. Parsons agreed, arguing that the 'Sloane Ranger' was a purveyor of 'chinless chic': 'afraid of foreigners, fish knives and, especially, foreigners with fish knives', the 'Sloane' attempted to 'propagate the class system as a career move' (Brampton and Parsons, 1985: 16).

There was evidence from market research that *Elle* rapidly developed a strong 'identity' in the minds of both target readers and advertisers. For both groups, the connotations of the 'transnational brand' appealed, and focus groups conducted a year after the magazine's launch indicated that the pre-existence of the *Elle* brand name was advantageous, connoting European-ness, stylishness and adventurousness (Brooks, 1986: 6). Advertisers too

Figure 5 Cover of *Elle*, November 1985 (courtesy of EMAP/Hachette).

enjoyed the international links of the magazine and big names such as Lancôme, Palmolive and American Express were soon to be found gracing the pages of *Elle* UK, and other editions (Davie, 1988: 2). British advertisers also turned to *Elle*, including mainstream retailers such as Miss Selfridge and Next, and manufacturers of travel accessories and cars (Brooks, 1986: 6). By September of 1986 *Elle* had achieved a moderate monthly circulation of 217,342, and the NRS suggested that it had cracked the ABC1 women's market coveted by other publishers.

Marie Claire: oui or non?

In 1988, IPC announced that it intended to launch a British edition of *Elle*'s French competitor, the fashion title *Marie Claire*. This came as little surprise to the UK publishing industry, as *Marie Claire*'s French parent company, Groupe Marie Claire (of which the cosmetics company L'Oreal owned a 49 per cent share) were known to be keen to expand internationally. In 1982, Groupe Marie Claire had produced the first successful transnational edition of *Marie Claire* in Japan (Cova, Rad-Serecht and Weil, 1993: 484). They had followed this with entry into many less-developed magazine markets in Spain, Italy, Greece and Turkey, employing licensing agreements which allowed publishers to use the *Marie Claire* brand name and editorial formula (Hafstrand, 1995: 3). In some more developed magazine markets (e.g. the UK and the Netherlands), Groupe Marie Claire had opted for a joint venture arrangement with respectable local publishers that was similar to that adopted by Elle Europe (Yates, 1988: 8). In 1987, therefore, Groupe Marie Claire entered discussion with IPC (who were seeking to produce more fashion-focused publications for women) about a British edition of *Marie Claire* (Cumberpatch, 1988b: 22). By September 1988, IPC had set up a satellite company, European Magazines, to launch and publish *Marie Claire* (UK). *Marie Claire* (UK) was supported by a £1.9 million PR campaign timed to coincide with its first five issues, and offered advertisers an enticing launch discount (Nathanson, 1988a: 23).

Like Elle Europe, Groupe Marie Claire in Paris offered IPC the benefits of its experience in transnational publishing. Employing a team of specialists based at its headquarters, they made sure that every aspect of *Marie Claire* complied with its brand image. Their executive fashion editor, for example, ensured that the fashion coverage met exacting standards across international editions. The features editor safeguarded a consistency of journalistic tone throughout different magazines. Some employees made sure that the weight and quality of the paper were comparable. Others were responsible for checking the quality of cover, typeface, layout, colour schemes, content, design and logo (Yates, 1988: 8).

In the advertising trade press, Groupe Marie Claire's international development manager Laurence Hembert claimed that the expansion of *Marie Claire* to the UK was chiefly a reaction to the needs of the large, international advertising clients (Scott, 1989: 62). Most major advertisers, she pointed out:

> particularly in the cosmetics area, are targeting their products at the same sector of women in every country. So it is useful for them to advertise in a magazine with the same style and title. They can be sure they will get similar standards of editorial and technical quality.
>
> (Hembert quoted in Scott, 1989: 62)

Moreover, Hembert argued, the internationalization of *Marie Claire* was a logical development in relation to the 'consumer convergence' of women readers across the world. According to Groupe Marie Claire's market research, women had 'grown closer in terms of interests and lifestyle' in recent years (Hembert quoted in Scott, 1989: 62).

The British advertising and marketing trade press viewed *Marie Claire* as a 'me-too' to *Elle*. *Marie Claire*'s stated socio-demographic target group, however, was ABC1 women between the ages of twenty to thirty-four, which was the younger end of *Elle*'s target market (Miller Freeman Information Services, 1988). *Marie Claire*'s launch editor, Glenda Bailey, declared that the magazine would be totally different from other titles, luring disenchanted magazine readers through an identification of their 'mood' and 'a unique breadth of content which covers every single aspect of a woman's life' (Cumberpatch, 1988b: 23). Like *Elle*, however, the focus of the editorial would be fashion. This would take up around 40 per cent of each issue and offer readers a 'look' that was 'confident [and] calm'. Although Bailey sensed that her ideal reader was aged between twenty-five and thirty-five, *Marie Claire*, she claimed, would define women by their attitude rather than age, and by focusing around 'how people live their lives' (Cumberpatch, 1988b: 23). *Marie Claire*'s first UK issue thus offered features on women in Saudi Arabia, an article on women's attitudes to rape and rapists and a piece on treatments for cellulite, as well as fifty pages of continuous fashion coverage.

The response to *Marie Claire* from industry commentators was generally positive, and reader research after *Marie Claire*'s launch indicated that the 'French-ness' of the title appealed to its stated target audience. Twenty-five per cent of readers that were surveyed also claimed to know the title from France *(Media Week*, 1988: 4). Advertisers also liked the French connotations of *Marie Claire*. Ex-magazine editor, Joyce Hopkirk, for example, congratulated *Marie Claire* in the pages of *Campaign* for its 'stylishness'. 'Being seen carrying a magazine like this', Hopkirk purred, 'with its sophisticated French image, flatters your self esteem and boosts self image' (Hopkirk, 1988: 24). By 1990, *Marie Claire* had achieved respectable circulation figures of 195,119, and was thought by Hachette/News International to be responsible for the falling circulation figures of *Elle* during the same period (O'Kelly, 1991).

Despite the positive circulation figures, IPC heavily promoted *Marie Claire* to both readers and advertisers during its first year. Within the advertising trade press an advertising campaign for *Marie Claire*, 'Oui/Non', juxtaposed images that were in tune with the magazine's ethos with images that were not. A typical 'Oui' image, for example, depicted a young woman standing in profile next to a rustic whitewashed shed wall. Dressed in a black cloche hat and jacket, with face barely visible, she gazed straight ahead, seemingly unaware of the presence of the camera lens. This was contrasted against the 'Non' image of a heavily made up model in a studio setting. Dressed in a pill box hat, large earrings, and a scarf which seemed to be flowing upwards due to

Figure 6 Cover of *Marie Claire*, September 1988 (courtesy of IPC).

the efforts of a wind machine, the woman tilted her head sideways whilst seductively gazing at a (presumably male) photographer. 'Non' *Marie Claire*, therefore, was 'fabricated', lacked subtlety and was self-obsessed. 'Oui' *Marie Claire*, on the other hand, was natural, relaxed and self-absorbed. The 'Oui/ Non' campaign also echoed the 'Who is *Marie Claire*?' advertisements for potential readers that appeared on television, in the press and on bill-boards *(Media Week*, 1988: 4).

New Woman: 'a new attitude . . . a new magazine . . . a new market'

Following its success with *Elle*, News International announced its intention to launch a British edition of a successful American title, *New Woman*, in 1988. In the US, *New Woman* was significant competition for *Cosmopolitan*, attracting sales of between 1.2 million and 1.4 million copies every month *(Campaign*, 1988d: 20). Thought by its publishers to contain 'the sort of content that translates to women around the world', the editorial emphasis of *New Woman* (UK) would, according to editor Frankie McGowan, be on the key word – 'You' (Hopkirk, 1988: 22). Typical readers would be employed in a wide variety of occupations, but their lives would not be dominated by work. Moreover, the *New Woman* reader would be 'neither a dimbo, nor a couch potato looking at TV round the clock' (McGowan, quoted in Nathanson, 1988b: 24).

New Woman's promotional budget was £3 million and was orchestrated by Arc Advertising and John Billett in the national press and on television (Nathanson, 1988b: 24). Much of this budget was reinvested into News International, as features on, and advertisements for, *New Woman* appeared in Murdoch newspapers including *Today*, *The Times* and the *Sunday Times* *(Campaign*, 1988b: 21). Double-page advertisements in the media and advertising trade press guaranteed readerships of 225,000 per issue. The title represented, so the advertisements claimed, 'a new attitude . . . a new magazine . . . a new market'. Names of top advertisers already 'sold on her' were publicized, including British Gas, Givenchy, Royal Mail International and United Biscuits (*New Woman* Advertisement, *Campaign,* March 1988).

Other advertisements for *New Woman* described it as a title for a 'lifestyle' target market previously identified by advertisers themselves. Some *New Woman* advertisements consisted merely of trade press and newspaper 'clippings' quoting advertisers' own attempts to describe the affluent and 'post-feminist' lifestyle of their target groups (*New Woman* Advertisement, *Campaign*, April 1988). A national television advertising campaign coincided with the launch of issue 1, which reached newsagents' shelves in July 1988. The campaign aimed carefully to define the *New Woman* for prospective readers, concluding with the end line: '*New Woman* – the magazine for women with a mind of their own' (Garrett, 1988: 8).

In the first issue of *New Woman*, Frankie McGowan's editorial attempted to define the 'lifestyle' of the ideal *New Woman* reader. Unlike other magazines, McGowan said that her 'New Woman' would be up-dated, 'softer' and 'more feminine' (*New Woman*, issue 1, August 1988: 3). 'We have come a long way', McGowan explained:

> since we were force-fed the illusion of that finger-snapping, high-flying executive in her power-suit pushing her way up the corporate ladder while running the ideal home, perfect children and lover,

fitting in aerobics classes on the side. No longer are we afraid to say she was a figment of the media's imagination and nothing to do with the real us – women, married or single, who are daily balancing home, husband or lover, children, friends and jobs. Realistic enough to know that sometimes we can't have it all, but optimistic enough to give it our best shot.

(New Woman, issue 1, August 1988: 3)

The first issue of *New Woman* (UK) included features on the shifting ground of married relationships in contemporary Britain, a 'pop-psychology' quiz called 'How Selfish Should You Be?', an article on the 'vulnerable, self-critical and insecure inside' of confident women, an extract from a new Fay Weldon novel, recipes for 'fish in a flash', and a feature on how to detect 'the danger signals' and 'stress-proof' your life (*New Woman*, issue 1, August 1988). Unlike sister publication *Elle*, and competitor *Marie Claire*, *New Woman* was a 'wordy, emotive read', with little visual excitement and low-key design and illustration (Durden, 1988: 30).[2] Fashion made up a very small proportion of the overall editorial, taking up approximately 15 per cent of the content of the magazine.

The responses of advertisers and marketers to *New Woman* were reportedly varied. Many agencies thought that the magazine was 'disappointing', and lacking in 'any significant point of difference from its competitors' (Mayes, 1988: 2). Some, indeed, could not actually 'see the *New Woman* woman', whilst others were convinced that the title would 'be a real put-off for readers' (Mayes, 1988: 2). However, according to McCann-Erickson's 'Magazine Monitor' which carried out focus group research on women's responses to *New Woman*, 63 per cent of women surveyed claimed they would buy the magazine. Sixty-two per cent of women said that *New Woman* would be an *addition* to their current magazine purchases, whilst 22 per cent of those surveyed claimed they would buy it every month. Furthermore, ahead of the television and press advertising campaign, 15 per cent of women claimed that they had already heard of *New Woman*. This statistic was, McCann-Erickson surmised, a result of an extensive PR campaign for *New Woman* in other News International titles (Mayes, 1988: 2). In September 1988, an independent audit for *New Woman* found it to have achieved a circulation figure of 441,132, well ahead of the other major monthly summer launch, *Marie Claire* (*Campaign*, 1988c: 26). By April 1989, *New Woman* had settled on an average circulation of 320,780. The NRS found that more than a fifth of *New Woman*'s readers read no other monthly magazine, whilst 10 per cent had never bought a women's title (*Campaign*, 1989: 25).

An examination of *New Woman*'s NRS profile of the period reveals that it was very successful in differentiating itself from other new competition in the glossy magazine market. *New Woman*'s readership profile was slightly younger and more 'down-market' than its nearest competitor, *Marie Claire*.

Figure 7 Cover of *New Woman*, August 1988 (courtesy of EMAP Consumer Magazines).

New Woman attracted 52 per cent of its readership from the ABC1 social grades, whilst *Marie Claire*'s profile was higher at about 65 per cent ABC1 readership. Thirty-six per cent of *New Woman*'s readers were estimated to be in the fifteen to twenty-four age group as compared to 42 per cent of *Marie Claire*'s readers. Twenty-seven per cent of *New Woman*'s readers were aged between twenty-five and thirty-four as compared to 22 per cent of *Marie Claire*'s. *Elle*'s social grade readership profile was also higher than that of *New Woman*, reaching 69 per cent ABC1. NRS statistics revealed, however, that despite a target market of women 'to the age of 44', *Elle* was, like *New Woman*, attracting a younger readership than *Marie Claire*. Indeed, by 1989, over half of *Elle*'s readers occupied the fifteen to twenty-four age group (source: NRS 1989).

According to the NRS, the readerships of *New Woman* and *Marie Claire* were similar in terms of marital status and patterns of employment (source: NRS, 1989). Fifty-three per cent of *New Woman*'s readership was thought to be married, with 54 per cent of the total readership estimated to be in full-time employment. In contrast, 45 per cent of *Marie Claire*'s readership were married, with 47 per cent of the total readership estimated to be working full-time. A smaller proportion (37 per cent) of *Elle*'s readers was thought to be married, and over half of *Elle*'s readers (57 per cent) were in full-time employment. Again, it is worth considering the impact that the younger readership profile may have had on these figures, as a large proportion of *Elle*'s readership described themselves to the NRS as 'single'.

Cosmopolitan: 'a problem of misconception'?

The success of *New Woman*, *Marie Claire* and *Elle* in attracting a young, relatively affluent female readership was viewed by many in the magazine industry as a threat to more established glossy titles. National Magazines' long-running, successful young women's title *Cosmopolitan* was thought to be particularly challenged by the appearance of *New Woman*. Indeed *Cosmopolitan*'s editor, Linda Kelsey, engaged in a rather undignified slanging match with Frankie McGowan in the pages of *Campaign*, claiming that *New Woman* was a 'blatant rip-off' and 'clone' of the *Cosmopolitan* formula (*Campaign*, 1988b: 21).

Cosmopolitan (UK) had been launched in 1972 by the Hearst Corporation's British venture, National Magazines. Like its long-running and highly successful American sister edition, *Cosmopolitan* (UK) aimed at a '*Cosmo Girl*' with interests neatly summarized by Janice Winship (1987: 112) as 'domestic work', 'beauty work' and 'sex work'. *Cosmopolitan* (UK) proved to be tremendously successful. Indeed, in its heyday during the mid-1970s *Cosmopolitan* regularly achieved circulation figures of around 440,000 – well above those of its competitors such as *Over 21* and *Honey*. Like other women's magazines, however, *Cosmopolitan*'s circulation figures began to dwindle in the late 1970s and, whilst it remained the glossy market leader, by 1984 circulation had fallen to 387,000 (Winship, 1987: 166).

During the first six months of 1987, *Cosmopolitan*'s circulation went into further decline, reaching an unprecedented low of 375,894 (*Media Week*, 1987: 23). In the pages of *Campaign*, Anthea Gerrie (1987: 45) argued that the reduced circulation was due to *Cosmopolitan*'s: 'seventies image that radically needs to unload the concept that there is no life without a man, a concept that's unfashionable for our times – remember the "independent, free-thinking woman?"' (Gerrie, 1987: 45). An article on the '*Cosmo* Girl' that appeared in *Media Week* (1987a: 22–3) agreed that the magazine's outdated image of femininity might be at the root of its problems. Interviewed in this article, *Cosmopolitan*'s editor, Linda Kelsey refuted this by claiming that no 'stereotype' could adequately describe the '*Cosmo* Girl'. *Cosmopolitan*'s 'real-life, flesh and blood readers' included, according to Kelsey:

> Marijit Kang, a 21-year-old from Wolverhampton who never went to college and worked for a local dress manufacturer before being made redundant . . . [and] Ermine Evans, 26, Cambridge graduate and gilt-edged securities saleswoman at Citicorp Scrimgeour Vickers.
> (Kelsey, quoted in *Media Week*, 1987: 22)

Evans and Kang were 'wildly different women – along with all *Cosmo* readers', Kelsey argued (quoted in *Media Week*, 1987: 22). However, both women had demonstrated their commitment to the '*Cosmo*' ethos, entering and winning talent competitions within the magazine, and thus demonstrating their 'ambition and drive to succeed' (Kelsey, quoted in *Media Week*, 1987: 22).

Industry observers, however, seemed unconvinced about *Cosmopolitan*, and claimed to be unable to find an image of women's 'real lives' in the pages of the magazine itself. Kirsty Hutton of SSC&B Lintas, for example, thought the target *Cosmopolitan* reader was 'probably working, but . . . not necessarily a glossy high powered career girl', and she might be 'down to earth about her life and expectations' (Hutton, quoted in *Media Week*, 1987: 23). On the other hand, Judy Rumbold, fashion editor of the *Guardian* thought that the '*Cosmo* reader remains forever the good-time girl with red nails and no knickers' (Rumbold, quoted in *Media Week*, 1987: 22). By 1987, *Cosmopolitan*'s publisher, Ross Young, had decided that *Cosmopolitan* was not differentiating itself fully enough from the 'New Woman' competition. Whilst reader research had not been essential for *Cosmopolitan* in the past, he argued, it was time to face up to the fact that *Cosmopolitan* would not continue to achieve sales on the basis of its title's kudos alone. Young therefore instigated a 'major investment programme' for *Cosmopolitan,* and in association with the Henley Centre for Forecasting and Taylor Nelson Monitor, National Magazines attempted to generate a new understanding of the 'lifestyles' of young women (Brooks, 1988: 29).

National Magazines began its search for the '*Cosmo* Girl' by commissioning a study of shifts in spending, work and childbearing trends in Britain. This alerted them, for example, to the fact that there were 29 per cent fewer births for every 1,000 women in the UK when measured against 1971 figures. Their study also found that, during the same period, the numbers of three- and four-year-old children placed in some form of childcare had soared by 76 per cent. Significantly, greater proportions of young women were also entering further and higher education. Consequently, the earning potential of women under the age of thirty-five was found to have increased by nearly a quarter over the previous twenty-seven years *(Campaign*, 1987a: 29).

The results of *Cosmopolitan*'s research prompted them to redesign and reorient the magazine both to differentiate it from other titles on the market, and to make it more 'in tune' with the lifestyles and aspirations of affluent target readers (Brooks, 1988: 29). A more luxurious feel was given to the magazine through the introduction of heavier paper and extra pages of fashion editorial. Taking stimulus from *Elle*, the amount of type per page in *Cosmopolitan* was also decreased, and the number of colour pages was doubled to give the magazine a more 'designed' feel. More expressive, 'individual'-looking models began to appear on the *Cosmopolitan* cover. Coverlines, found to be all-important in terms of impulse purchases of magazines at news stands, were given more punch and 'spice' *(Campaign*, 1987a: 29).

National Magazines also attempted to rethink the ways in which *Cosmopolitan* could beat its 'New Woman' competitors by better meeting the needs of potential advertisers. 'Advertorial' supplements became regular features of the magazine, and space was created for greater amounts of classified advertising (Cumberpatch, 1988a: 29; Syedain, 1992: 21).[3] Also introduced were 0891 telephone lines for sponsored competitions, and *Cosmopolitan* spin-offs, such as the agony aunt ('Why are you in love with a bastard?'), and at a cost to the caller of 36–48 pence per minute, must have been highly lucrative. Other sources of additional revenue for *Cosmopolitan* came from a range of new reader offers, and from the launch of new ranges of brand-related products such as catalogues, books, tapes, diaries, calendars and sponsored exhibitions (Syedain, 1992: 21).

In August 1989, publisher Ross Young left *Cosmopolitan* unexpectedly, and Simon Kippin, former publisher of *Company*, was promoted to the position (Atkinson, 1989: 20). During the same period, Marcelle d'Argy Smith replaced editor Linda Kelsey. Both Kippin and d'Argy Smith expressed their concern about the impact of the new glossies on *Cosmopolitan*'s circulation figures, Kippin estimating that they had lost over 10,000 readers to recent magazine launches (Kippin quoted in Atkinson, 1989: 20). In the national newspapers, d'Argy Smith offered her own narrative about *Cosmopolitan*'s declining circulation, emphasizing the 'problem of misconception' in the minds of young women. Drawing on their knowledge of *Cosmopolitan*'s past, d'Argy Smith claimed, young women perceived *Cosmopolitan* to be a magazine oriented around 'sex'. This was not, however, the 'reality' of *Cosmopolitan*, said d'Argy Smith, and *Cosmopolitan* had shifted from 'sex' to 'relationships' some time ago. Moreover, d'Argy Smith declared, 'sex' was not a particularly stimulating topic for editorial, as it was 'actually pretty finite unless you have individuality' (d'Argy Smith quoted in Diamond, 1990).

Figure 8 Cover of *Cosmopolitan*, May 1992 (*Cosmopolitan*/copyright National Magazine Company).

Whether *Cosmopolitan* suffered from a misconception in the minds of advertisers and readers, or from content that readers found less than enticing, d'Argy Smith tightened up the editorial focus of the magazine. Most notable here was an introduction to the magazine of a new body, health and fitness section, 'Zest', and extension of popular psychology to all areas of the magazine, most notably the career pages ('Career Agony'). D'Argy Smith's editorial strategy was very successful with readers, and by December 1991 *Cosmopolitan* had reached circulation figures of 472,480. This was an increase of 10.7 per cent on figures from the previous six months. In addition, *Cosmopolitan* gained substantial ground over its nearest rival, beating *New Woman* by a staggering 234,244 readers. *Cosmopolitan* also fought off competition from IPC's *Marie Claire*, which was still only a moderately successful publication with figures of 222,671 (Syedain, 1992: 21).[4]

Company, She and the 'religion of the brand'

The reorientation of *Cosmopolitan* was part of a broader strategy at National Magazines that focused its business activities around what is known as 'branding' *(Marketing*, 1993: viii). Magazine branding is the recognition that the title of a magazine can be valuable as a piece of *intellectual* property that can be rated as an asset. It is a remarkably intangible process in that brands are constructed by the '"character", culture and image that a title represents to readers' (Bunting, 1997: 55). Careful marketing and editorial policies are employed with the aims of reinforcing the brand identity of the magazine, and thus differentiating it from the competition. Branding has to be particularly attentive to the relationships and identifications built up between readers and their magazines. Thus branding a magazine is a process of getting closer to the relationship between the reader and the magazine, and of placing a financial value on the strength of this relationship. The idea of branding is that it encourages reader loyalty by distinguishing individual titles from their competitors. It also encourages more defined 'lifestyle' readership profiles that can be used to sell advertising space to advertisers. Valuation of titles is a difficult process, mainly because the life-span of a title is uncertain. The premise of branding, however, is that well-known titles such as *Cosmopolitan* are believed to have value *in themselves* above that of an unbranded equivalent (Bunting, 1997: 56).

The British magazine industry of the late 1980s witnessed a trend towards valuing magazines as 'brands'. Different publishers, however, chose to value their brands in different ways. IPC and EMAP, for example, valued only those brands in their accounts that they had acquired, choosing not to provide a financial value to those titles that they themselves had built up (Bunting, 1997: 56). National Magazines, on the other hand, placed 'a near religious emphasis on clear branding'. With the aim of building circulations and advertising revenues, brand identities at National Magazines were articulated, exploited and developed *(Marketing*, 1993: viii).

The logic behind the branding policy of National Magazines was that it would enhance the appeal of its magazines for advertisers in an increasingly 'cluttered' market. According to the managing director of National Magazines, Terry Mansfield, the growth in the British magazine market overall was driving down advertising rates, and therefore profits (Richmond, 1989: 40). The solution was to 'brand' magazine titles in an attempt to convince advertisers that the space purchased would give their advertisements 'added value'. 'Branding' was also more popular at National Magazines than at IPC or EMAP because National Magazines was a private company and its turn-over was not regularly scrutinized by shareholders. This meant that National Magazines could take a more long-term view of investments than other publishers, and that it could keep any plans for expansion under wraps (Richmond, 1989: 42).

In practice, National Magazines' commitment to branding meant that they went back to their traditional 'core' titles like *Cosmopolitan* and rethought them in relation to their place in the contemporary glossy magazine market *(Marketing*, 1993: viii). The image of the magazine market that they developed was much more 'lifestyle'-segmented, and National Magazines hoped that this view of the women's market would cohere with the requirements of adver-tisers. It was also hoped that branding would help to stimulate circulation figures for the National Magazines' portfolio, particularly amongst the groups of young, professional women which the new glossies seemed to be reaching. In the case of *Cosmopolitan*, the strategy of National Magazines was a success. Between 1989 and 1992, *Cosmopolitan*'s circulation grew by more than 10 per cent, signalling that it had increased its attractiveness to readers. *Cosmopolitan*'s penetration of the ABC1 target market also remained high, at around 64 per cent, which was an added attraction for advertisers (Source: NRS 1989; NRS 1992).

Cosmopolitan's sister publication, *Company* (launched in 1978), also underwent changes in attempts to differentiate its brand image from others on the glossy magazine shelves. Originally targeted at the eighteen to twenty-four ABC1 group, and aiming to attract women who were not yet committed to a family lifestyle, the first issues of *Company* had achieved circulation figures of over 300,000 (Braithwaite, 1994: 114). Yet by February 1988, figures for the magazine were at an all-time low, standing at just 164,000 *(Campaign*, 1988a: 24). In 1989, therefore, National Magazines appointed a new editor for *Company*, Mandi Norwood, in the hopes of reorienting the magazine around reader 'need and . . . demand'. Norwood hoped to distin-guish *Company* for its competitors, by making the editorial more 'straight talking in an intimate way, like a good friend' as well as 'quirky, informative, reassuring, [and] sensitive' (Norwood quoted in Coles, 1995: 14). Fashion, careers, money, sex and relationships became parts of Norwood's recipe for the magazine, because, she maintained, 'those ingredients encompass every area of our readers' lives' (Norwood quoted in Coles, 1995: 14). By 1995, *Company*'s circulation figures had increased by 40 per cent to 305,000. This made *Company* one of National Magazines' biggest circulation success stories on the young women's market, with 120,000 of its new readers under the age of thirty-four (Coles, 1995: 14). Like *Cosmopolitan*, *Company* also maintained a 70 per cent overall penetration of target groups in the ABC1 socio-economic groupings, making it hugely appealing to advertisers.

Norwood's strategy for *Company* caused some controversy in the national newspapers of the period, which argued that *Company*'s repositioning involved nothing more than using salacious articles and cover lines on 'sex' to sell the magazine (see Coles, 1995: 14; Cook, 1992: 27; Jeal, 1992: 52).[5] Norwood counteracted this by pointing out that *Company* contained fewer pages about 'sex' than about fashion. Echoing d'Argy Smith, Norwood also argued that many of the articles presumed by journalists to be about 'sex' were actually about 'relationships', although she conceded that '"sex" appeals to our market' (Norwood quoted in Coles, 1995: 14).

Perhaps the most drastic reorientation and rebranding of a National Magazines' title occurred in the case of its domestic title *She*, which had been published since 1955. The original rationale behind *She* was that it would offer a slightly quirky formula of cartoons, features, royal stories and photo features that would appeal to readers in their late thirties and early forties (Barrell and Braithwaite, 1988: 96). At its peak during the early 1970s, *She* regularly achieved circulation figures in the region of 330,000 (Brooks, 1985: 8). However, by the early 1980s, *She*'s popularity was on the wane, and circulation figures had fallen to 200,879 by the first half of 1989 (Richmond, 1989: 42).

With new editor Joyce Hopkirk at the helm, National Magazines decided to relaunch *She* as a glossy, non-domestic title, and to redefine its target market around ABC1 women, aged twenty-five to forty-four. In addition, the ideal 'lifestyle' market within this age group was defined as: '"jugglers" because they juggle home, husband, job and personal lifestyle' (Warren quoted in *Campaign*, 1987b: 2). *She*'s 'woman as juggler' approach, however, failed to stem declining sales statistics for the magazine. After a short spell when Joyce Hopkirk was made editor-in-chief of the magazine and Sally O'Sullivan editor, National Magazines again attempted to focus *She* more sharply. Linda Kelsey was employed as editor and tried to orient it to target a more specific 'lifestyle' group: 'the mother of the 90s' (Advertisement for *She*, *Campaign*, January 1990). In order to attract her, the new *She* became a glossy monthly, with more editorial pages, more colour and better-quality paper. It also introduced new editorial elements to 'speak' to its readership, including what Kelsey described as an 'agony column with a difference', examining relationship problems from the perspective of both partners. A substantial new section on bringing up children was also introduced – 'You and Your Child'.

The impact of *She*'s reorientation on its NRS readership profile was certainly striking. The number of readers in the fifteen to forty-four age groups rose by 10 per cent, and the proportion of these in full- and part-time employment also increased. *She* also slightly improved its ABC1 social grade penetration from 58 per cent in 1989 to 60 per cent by 1992. The combination of these enabled *She* to survive in the contemporary women's magazine market, albeit in a form almost unrecognizable when compared to that of ten years previously. The readership figures and 'lifestyle' focus of the new *She* also proved popular with both established and new groups of advertisers, and attracted media buyers seeking to place advertisements for a variety of products, ranging from children's wear to quality cosmetics *(Campaign*, 1990: 23).

As we have seen with the examples in this chapter, the 'New Woman' was not a universal 'lifestyle' category across the women's press during this period. What the case studies of magazines in this chapter, and of those discussed in Chapter 5, have highlighted are the differences in images of, and address to, young women's lifestyles promoted across women's magazine media. Whilst all of the magazines I have considered targeted young, relatively independent women, there was little agreement about what form of editorial address would appeal to her. *Working Woman* (discussed in Chapter 5) attempted to speak to the 'mood' of women readers by focusing around her status in the workforce. The concepts for magazines in this chapter, however, disengaged their editorial from issues relating to work, describing the 'mood' of the 'New Woman' through her attitudes to 'style', and her presumed interests in 'personality', 'individuality', 'relationships', 'sex', 'the body', 'health', 'childcare' and so on.

The 'New Woman' of the magazine industry of the 1980s and early 1990s cannot, therefore, be considered a target figure that was widely understood to be unified or coherent. As we have seen in this chapter, whilst many in the industry claimed to have identified a 'new', young, affluent and/or professional woman who was waiting at the news stand with a purse in her hand, this 'New Woman' appears to have been little more than a comforting narrative about contemporary femininity. As a broad target market, she was embraced by an industry attempting to grasp a proliferation of shifting, fragmented and multiple feminine identities adopted by women in everyday life. Indeed, these magazine industry ideations of 'New Women' are not interesting because of their coherence, but because of the ways in which they pulled their representations of femininity in a variety of different directions.

As I have argued, such feminine identities were not simply socially produced, and they also need to be understood in terms of their symbolic and economic relations to the advertising agencies and their clients. As we saw in Chapter 4, as 'clients' of the magazine industry, advertisers had some (well-founded) anxieties about the abilities of women's magazines to 'reach' women. Consequently, the publishers of women's magazines had to engage in self-promotional activity, and not only market their knowledges about femininity to their readers, but to the advertising agencies. In Chapter 7, therefore, I begin by exploring how the magazine industry presented itself to advertisers as 'in tune' with contemporary femininity. One of the ways it did this, I argue, was through claiming the status of 'cultural intermediary' to the magazine editor and members of her team.

7

'MARIE CLAIRE – C'EST MOI!'

Magazine editors, cultural intermediaries and the 'new middle class'

In their study of the business of women's magazines in Britain, Joan Barrell and Brian Braithwaite (1988: 121) have observed that one of the best selling aids for a women's magazine is the editor. The editor is not only responsible for producing a magazine that will be 'in tune' with their target readers, but also has to 'relay the real sales message' to advertisers (Barrell and Braithwaite, 1988: 121). Editors therefore need to convey a sense of the 'atmosphere' of the magazine to media buyers, which cannot be communicated through a spreadsheet of readership statistics alone. In this sense, magazine editors can be seen as intermediaries between advertisers and the target reader and they are frequently lauded in the trade press for their 'sixth sense' which enables them to understand the 'mood' of their potential readerships. Indeed, Marjorie Ferguson's interviews with women's magazine editors from the 1950s to the 1980s suggests that (1983: 128), far from seeing this 'sixth sense' as a marketing ploy, editors actually believe that they hold 'special or sacred knowledge about the nature of their particular audience and the messages it wishes to read, listen to, or watch'.

Many of the editors of glossy magazines for target groups of 'New Women' in the 1980s and early 1990s became important figures in the advertising and marketing trade press. All the major magazines, particularly the new launches, were treated to some in-depth press coverage, supplemented by intimate interviews with the magazine editor. These features provided close analyses of the magazine editor's working style, lifestyle and career trajectory, and required her to summarize the 'mood' of her ideal reader. Most frequently, the editor's claim to knowledge of her reader would be justified by an attempt to demonstrate her lifestyle 'fit', and consequent 'in tune-ness' with the tastes of the magazine's target readership.

This chapter begins by exploring how this emphasis on the lifestyle, taste and knowledge of the women's magazine editor operated as a strategy for improving the image of magazine publishing in the eyes of advertisers and other magazine publishers. This discourse of legitimation, I argue, can be linked more broadly to a rhetoric relating to a 'new' class fraction that has

118

been argued to be a product of the emergence of a 'new middle class'. I continue by examining the lifestyle strategies employed by the women's magazine industry for targeting their titles to particular 'ideal' market segments. Through developing specific modes of lifestyle address, I argue, women's magazine professionals actively generated an image of the existence of a 'new middle class' to which they could claim to belong themselves. The final section of this chapter considers evidence for the practice of 'new middle-class' modes of existence and use of compatible rhetoric by groups of middle-class women in 1980s Britain. Some women, it argues, may well have tried to incorporate 'new middle-class' aspirations into their daily lives. Indeed, magazines for the 'New Woman' may have offered means by which some middle-class women could interpret themselves as members of an existent 'new middle-class' and helped disseminate a lifestyle rhetoric associated with this formation.

Tuning in to the 'ideal reader'

As a magazine editor, Audrey Slaughter of *Working Woman* was a keen self-promoter. In numerous interviews in the advertising and marketing trade press, she stressed that her magazine was produced for women who, like her, wanted to scrutinize the lifestyles and tastes of other 'successful' women (McKay, 1984: 34). In a *Campaign* article titled 'Slaughter's plans to capture the working AB woman' (McKay, 1984: 34–5) Slaughter located the genesis of the concept of a magazine for working women in her own experience of a year spent not working: 'I found myself in a lower gear', she lamented, 'less energetic, and I found it enormously difficult to ask for an allowance from my husband' (Slaughter in McKay, 1984: 34). The article went on to detail the ins and outs of Slaughter's own working life as, asking herself 'Why . . . [women] don't set their sights higher', she sought to persuade big businessmen to part with big bucks for the magazine for the 'ambitious woman already committed to a career' (Slaughter in McKay, 1984: 34).

Campaign's article voiced some doubts from media commentators about the editorial premise of *Working Woman* and its ability to 'speak' to the target readership. Slaughter claimed, however, that she and the *Working Woman* editorial team possessed expert knowledge of the lifestyles, tastes and aspirations of their ideal readership of career women:

> All of us on the staff . . . are target audience. We'll be saying 'What do we want from a magazine?' And between us we're going to get it right. It will not be an upper class *Spare Rib*. It's not a feminist magazine. Men are not the enemy as far as this magazine is concerned.
>
> (Slaughter in McKay, 1984: 35)

If *Campaign*'s readers still found Slaughter's target audience difficult to envisage, the article was accompanied by a photograph of Slaughter in her office environment, a 'real-life' version of the 'working woman'. Indeed, in this and many similar photographs of Slaughter in industry publications, she seemed to fashion herself according to the popular stereotype of the 'career woman' that was seen in contemporaneous American image manuals for businesswomen, such as John Molloy's *Women: Dress for Success* (1980). As Joanne Entwistle has argued, the clothing adopted at this time by many professional women like Slaughter provided women with a set of fashion 'rules' that could 'promise the career woman some control over her body and self-presentation in the face of male-defined notions of female sexuality and the potential objectifying gaze in the workplace' (Entwistle, 2000: 188–9; Entwistle, 1997). The connotations of such attire accorded the wearer with authority and professionalism, but steered her away from the potential problems of appearing either too 'feminine' (and therefore silly and 'sexy') or too 'masculine' (and 'threatening').

Another prominent figure in 1980s advertising and marketing trade publications laying claim to a 'sixth sense' about the tastes of her readers was *Marie Claire* (UK)'s launch editor, Glenda Bailey. In an article in *Media Week* entitled *'Marie Claire – c'est moi!'* (Cumberpatch, 1988b: 22–3), Bailey declared that she was the obvious choice for *Marie Claire*'s UK edition, describing how she had picked up the telephone and called IPC to tell them that she was the woman for the job. Depicting the twenty-nine-year-old Bailey as a woman with a 'go-for-it' career strategy and a 'gameplan', *Media Week* detailed her long-term passion for fashion, fashion editing, and for a new fashion magazine (Cumberpatch, 1988b: 22–3). Despite the odd career knock-back (which simply demonstrated her tenacity), Bailey's success was attributed to being 'very single-minded. . . . I know exactly what I want' (Bailey in Cumberpatch, 1988b: 22).

Bailey's 'single-mindedness' was played up throughout the *Media Week* article. The 'distinctiveness' of her Derbyshire accent was commented upon, along with her bubbling enthusiasm, which 'lit [her] up like the proverbial Christmas tree', and her 'air of confidence and well-being' (Cumberpatch, 1988b: 22). A photograph of Bailey also revealed her to be the antithesis of the traditional elegant *grande dames* of fashion. As Angela McRobbie (1998: 166–71) has observed, the emphasis upon status and hierarchy prevalent amongst fashion editors of women's magazines has traditionally led them to use their personal 'stylishness' as compensation for the inferior status of fashion journalism in the journalistic world. The fashion magazine editor has therefore been epitomized by spectacular figures such as Diana Vreeland (one-time editor of American *Vogue*) with a 'signature' style (in Vreeland's case this was 'raven black hair cut into a bob and scarlet lipstick') (McRobbie, 1998: 166–71). To the industry readers of *Media Week*, however, Bailey must have appeared exceptionally ungroomed. Whilst in tasteful fashionable attire and make-up, her 'style' was understated. Bailey's face was framed by long, messy pre-Raphaelite curls, and she smiled and laughed un-self-consciously for the camera.[1]

For *Media Week*'s readers, Glenda Bailey portrayed herself as a character who was 'totally immersed' in the editorial concept (Cumberpatch, 1988b: 22). Bailey would not follow fashion (in the broadest sense of the word) for fashion's sake, and could claim to be 'in tune' with *Marie Claire*'s target market because of the lifestyle ethos and emotional proximity she professed to have with young, independently minded women like herself. Bailey, therefore, was *Marie Claire*'s ideal reader personified, declaring (should there be any doubt in the minds of advertisers) that even the *doormen* at IPC: 'think I *am Marie Claire* . . . [t]he other day, after I went past, I heard one of them say to another: "That Marie Claire, she seems to be doing all right"' (Bailey in Cumberpatch, 1988b: 23).

What these and similar interviews emphasized was the editor's 'instinctive' knowledge about appropriate methods for reaching target groups of 'New Women'. In doing so, these interviews effectively distanced the women's magazine industry from the tired and out-dated image it held amongst advertisers. In a period that, as we have seen, saw media buyers tempted away from magazines by a proliferation of new media, the women's magazine business attempted to allay the anxieties of advertising agencies by promoting its individuality and nose for taste. Through this self-promotional rhetoric, editors professed not only to be 'in tune' with their ideal reader, but also to literally personify new formations of feminine lifestyles. In their claims to be 'in touch' with their target markets, the editors of women's magazines can be seen to be emphasizing their status as cultural intermediaries – experts at making women's magazines symbolically 'meaningful' for readers. Editors were thus promoting their social position as intermediaries, or as members of a 'new middle class', as taste mappers and taste creators with the ability to identify and convert tastes into a successful magazine format.[2]

The 'new middle classes' and cultural intermediaries

Brian Longhurst and Mike Savage (1996: 281) have noted that the early 1980s witnessed a strong current of sociological analysis which pointed to the emergence and rise of 'new' social classes. It was the translation of Pierre Bourdieu's book *Distinction* (1984) and his account of the rise of a 'new petite bourgeoisie' in France, in particular, that caught the imagination of a number of British sociologists concerned with reflecting upon new forms of consumer culture (Longhurst and Savage, 1996: 279). Bourdieu's understanding of the relationship between culture and the economy in *Distinction* offers an account of how fragmented modes of consumption have developed in post-Fordist economies. Whilst writers such as Piore and Sabel (1986) have argued that the flexibility of production has emerged in *response* to the growth of specialized, niche-market consumption, Bourdieu's discussion of taste and consumption patterns suggest *why* shifts towards more specialized modes of consumption have occurred.

Bourdieu insists upon the correspondence between the production of cultural goods and the ideological production of taste (Bourdieu, 1984). The tastes that social groups are able to realize, he argues, depend upon the system of production to make appropriate cultural goods available. The consumer, he asserts, does not compel cultural producers to provide products to meet all of their needs but, conversely, cultural producers do not produce consumer taste. The process, Bourdieu claims, is more complex, as:

> every change in the system of goods induces a change in tastes. But conversely, every change in tastes resulting from a transformation of the conditions of existence and of the corresponding dispositions will tend to induce, directly or indirectly, a transformation of the field of production, by favouring the success, with the struggle constituting the field, of the producers best able to produce the needs correspond-ing to the new dispositions.
>
> (Bourdieu, 1984: 231)

Bourdieu agrees with the theorists of post-Fordism and post-industrialism that the field of capitalist production has been transformed and consolidated in the post-war era. It draws its power and profits from the production of goods, and from the production of needs and consumers. This new economic forma-tion has demanded a new social formation to enable it to function smoothly. It has therefore contributed to the production of a new social world, which 'judges people by their capacity for consumption, their "standard of living", their life-style, as much as by their capacity for production' (Bourdieu, 1984: 310).

Some sections of society have adapted particularly well to the new econ-omic formation, particularly those who have become members of the 'new petite bourgeoisie'. Many members of this group have high-level academic qualifications, but have become frustrated by the lack of prestige that is being accorded to them in the current climate where qualifications are ten a penny. Other members are those from the upper class, who for one reason or another have failed to obtain the qualifications traditionally expected of them. For this group, the 'new petite bourgeoisie' is a social position offering 'an honourable refuge' for avoiding social decline (Bourdieu, 1984: 358).

It is the efforts of the 'new petite bourgeoisie to redefine and establish their social position that engages them in what Bourdieu terms 'symbolic rehabili-tation strategies' (Bourdieu, 1984: 358). Unable to achieve success within traditional 'petit bourgeois' occupations, and unwilling to lower themselves to the inferior 'petit bourgeois' roles, this group 'endeavour to produce jobs adjusted to their ambitions rather than adjust their ambitions to fit already existing jobs' (Bourdieu, 1984: 359). Some of the most successful new occupa-tions, Bourdieu observes, have been concerned with the production of symbolic goods and services. Thus the 'new petite bourgeoisie' are a prominent social group in occupations such as 'sales, marketing, advertising, public relations, fashion, decoration and so forth', and in 'all the institutions providing symbolic goods and services' (Bourdieu, 1984: 359). Many in this social group, according to Bourdieu, are women, who find that their 'socially inculcated dispositions' towards things that are 'tasteful', 'stylish' and 'refined' can be applied in 'new middle-class' occupations (Bourdieu, 1984: 361–2).

The 'new petite bourgeoisie' is adept at legitimating its activities in the eyes of others, and it does this by promoting and selling its own symbolic authority. Indeed, according to Bourdieu (1984: 365), the 'new petite bourgeoisie' 'always sell themselves as models and as guarantors of the value of their products, and . . . sell so well because they believe in what they sell'. They deceive their customers, he argues, only so much as they deceive themselves about the legitimacy of their lifestyle, producing not only a need for the products they produce, but also an image of their 'new middle-class' lifestyle as dominant (Bourdieu, 1984: 365).

Bourdieu's 'new petite bourgeoisie' and its relationship to the 'cultural intermediary' occupations is something further taken up by the British sociologist, Mike Featherstone (1991). Featherstone argues that Thatcher's Britain witnessed the expansion of the 'new middle class' into occupations beyond that of cultural intermediary. A shift in 'power balances', he asserts, created 'new interdependencies', 'strategies' and 'alliances' between 'professional politicians, government administrators, local politicians, businessmen, financiers, dealers, investors, artists, intellectuals, educators, cultural intermediaries, and publics' (Featherstone, 1991: 47). Featherstone's emphasis, however, is on the drive of the 'new middle-class' cultural intermediary who, due to a perilous social position, seeks 'to legitimate the intellectualization of new areas of expertise such as popular music, fashion, design, holidays, sport, popular culture, etc. which increasingly are subjected to serious analysis' (Featherstone, 1991: 91).[3]

One way that the cultural intermediary seeks to legitimate the social value of 'new middle-class' cultural capital and gain influence over symbolic production, Featherstone argues, is through the promotion of their own cultural authority. This is achieved by seeking to legitimate new cultural fields and to 'undermine the traditional restricted definitions of taste provided by the established intellectuals' (Featherstone, 1991: 93). As parts of this process, new institutions and new journals are formed by those in cultural intermediary professions, and these help to promote, popularize and authenticate redefinitions of taste and attitudes to life (Featherstone, 1991: 93). The 'new middle class' also publicize their values by promoting more 'hedonistic and expressive consumption norms' than the older 'petite bourgeoisie', and they thus become both 'the perfect audience and transmitters', or 'the perfect consumer', for the symbolic products and services produced (Featherstone, 1991: 91).

Such accounts of the emergence and growth of forms of a 'new middle class' have received extensive criticism from sociologists. Longhurst and Savage (1996: 281) have pointed out, for example, that these ideas are 'rather unoriginal', and that similar ideas can be traced back to the arguments of sociologists from as early as the beginning of the twentieth century. They also note that 'there is currently considerable doubt about the supposed rise of "new middle classes" of various types', and observe that some sociologists have claimed that the established middle classes have simply matured and consolidated their professional power (Longhurst and Savage, 1996: 282). Thus, it is argued, even though the middle class is increasingly fragmented, it is overly simplistic to attempt consistently to map all of the distinctively new occupational groupings mentioned by Bourdieu, along with specific patterns of taste, onto fractions of the middle class (Longhurst and Savage, 1996: 282).

Many critics of Bourdieu have also observed that there is no substantial empirical evidence to suggest the applicability of a 'new middle class' to capitalist class structures outside of the France that he studied in the late 1960s (see, for example, Lury (1996), Nixon (1997a) and Savage *et al.* (1992)). Other commentators have been critical of Bourdieu's almost exclusive focus on class, arguing that he marginalizes 'race' and gender which must also be powerful variables in the mediation of taste and lifestyles. Beverley Skeggs (1997), for example, claims that Bourdieu fails to consider the ways in which some social positions accrue more cultural capital than others. In the network of social positions, identities can both provide and restrict access to potential forms of cultural power (see Skeggs, 1997: 10).[4]

These concerns about the actuality of the 'new middle classes' and the social structure as it is described by Bourdieu and others are clearly justifiable. However, as Anne M. Cronin (2000: 49) has convincingly argued about the advertising industry of the 1980s, the 'new middle classes' can operate as an 'imagined (although not necessarily imaginary) category' for those in media-related occupations. In this sense, whilst there might be some doubt about the actual existence of the 'new middle class' as it has been outlined by sociologists, it is present amongst some of the middle classes as a popular discourse about identity. 'New middle class-ness' is a discourse about individuality that is directed towards impressing others with an image of contemporary lifestyle. It should not, however, be understood as the self-conscious performance of identity by the individual – the performance takes place at the level of the unconscious, is literally embodied, and operates as a means of expressing 'distinction' from 'old-fashioned' lifestyles, lives and tastes.

Analysis of the rhetoric of women's magazine editors in the advertising and marketing trade press suggests that they were keen to advance an image of themselves that coheres with the discourse of the 'new middle class' and cultural intermediary. As we have seen, magazine editors including Audrey Slaughter and Glenda Bailey promoted themselves in media industry publications as experts in the taste, lives and lifestyles of young middle-class women. Their claim to expertise came from, they pronounced, the cultures they shared with their target groups of young women readers (e.g. 'All of us on the staff . . . are target audience', 'I *am Marie Claire*'). Such claims were also strengthened by the magazine editor's emphasis on her *own* strong sense of individuality, innovation, and professionalism. This ethos, magazine editors presumed, was something they shared with other cultural intermediaries working in advertising and marketing. Indeed, their rhetoric worked to legitimate the presence of women's magazine editors within the 'distinctive' space of the cultural intermediary which the advertising and marketing trade press helped to delineate and sustain. It also furthered an image of the cultural value, sophistication and contemporaneity of the magazine industry itself.

Magazines for the 'new middle classes'

The idea of the 'new middle class' and the cultural intermediary as discursive categories employed by magazine editors also suggests a useful way of thinking about the lifestyle address of some women's magazines of this period. As I have argued, one of the ways in which the women's magazine industry legitimated its expertise was through claiming that its employees shared the tastes and lifestyles of their 'ideal' readers. This belief in a shared way of life also, I want to argue, affected the lifestyle premises that were advanced in the market propositions of the women's magazines themselves. The emphasis on lifestyle targeting in magazine publishing of the 1980s was, as we saw in Chapter 5, designed to assist women's magazines to 'speak' to relatively affluent groups of young, middle-class women. In this section I maintain that the 'lifestyle' addresses that were adopted by women's magazines offered readers rhetorical devices through which they could understand and redefine themselves. I do not propose here that the lifestyles of women's magazine readers can be mapped onto magazine lifestyle representations. Nor do I suggest that we can know how magazine representations were internalized, and made sense of, by those who encountered them. I want to argue, however, that women's magazines of this period can be understood to have functioned to generate an *image* of the existence and expansion of the 'new middle classes' amongst both publishers and advertisers, and possibly amongst the readers themselves.

It is useful here to return to Bourdieu's analysis of the 'new petite bourgeoisie' and his attempts to outline the ways in which class taste is developed and embodied by this group (Bourdieu, 1984). The 'new petit bourgeois' search for distinction and validation endeavours, Bourdieu argues, to distance this stratum from older 'petit bourgeois' modes of morality and ethics. In particular, the 'new petite bourgeoisie' seeks to 'liberate' itself from a traditional 'petit bourgeois' 'morality of duty':

based on the opposition between pleasure and good, [that] induces a generalized suspicion of the 'charming and attractive', a fear of pleasure and a relation to the body made up of 'reserve', 'modesty' and 'restraint', and [which] associates every satisfaction of the forbidden impulses with guilt.

(Bourdieu, 1984: 367)

According to Bourdieu, the 'new petite bourgeoisie' seeks to replace this with 'a morality of pleasure as a duty', which brands it 'a failure, a threat to self-esteem, not to "have fun"' (Bourdieu, 1984: 367). This ethos makes the 'new petit bourgeois' the 'ideal consumer', a figure free from the moral 'constraints' and 'brakes' to consumption held by older 'petit bourgeois' groups. The drive for 'fun' compels the 'new petit bourgeois' to consume, covet the latest thing, and to be interested in following the dynamics of fashion (Bourdieu, 1984: 371). The 'new petite bourgeoisie' therefore see themselves as individuals who freely and guiltlessly indulge in consumer culture. In fact, for the 'new petit bourgeois', such easy indulgence is essential, as it is primarily through the acquisition of repertoires of goods that a sense of individuality and self-hood can be formed.

The 'morality of pleasure as a duty' observed to be a characteristic of the 'new petite bourgeoisie', Bourdieu (1984: 366) argues, explains its fascination with self-expression, bodily expression, communication with others, and 'search' for identity. The popularity of certain occupations – 'youth leaders, play leaders, tutors and monitors, radio and TV producers and presenters, magazine journalists' – is, according to Bourdieu (1984: 359), a product of 'new petit bourgeois' morality. Industries concerned with 'personal health and psychological therapy' have also grown as a result of the 'pleasure as a duty' ethic, including 'marriage guidance, sex therapy, dietetics, [and] vocational guidance' (Bourdieu, 1984: 359). Bourdieu (1984: 368) also notes a deification of bodily exercise in 'new petit bourgeois' cultures, which treat the body, he argues, 'as the psychoanalyst treats the soul, bending its ear to "listen" to a body which has to be "unknotted", liberated or, more simply, rediscovered and accepted'. Similarly, a therapeutic ethos is adopted about child-rearing which is no longer viewed as a 'training', but as a 'necessary pleasure, subjectively agreeable and objectively indispensable . . . for children and parents alike' (Bourdieu, 1984: 369).

An analysis of the lifestyle rhetorics employed by the more successful glossy women's magazines, discussed in previous chapters, shows them to be resonant with the sets of dispositions argued by Bourdieu (1984) to be characteristic of a 'new petite bourgeoisie'. This suggests that the women's magazine industry of the 1980s and 1990s was keen to promote lifestyles to advertisers and readers that were compatible with the discourse – and supposed lifestyle preferences and practices – of a 'new middle class'. We have seen, for example, that both *Elle* and *Marie Claire*'s 'ideal readers' were described in publicity as 'disenchanted' by the out-dated and patronizing tone of existing women's magazines. Many potential readers, it was suggested, were also already aware of the more 'stylish' sister editions of these magazines long available on French news stands. *Elle*'s publicity outlined the taste and disposition of *Elle*'s 'ideal reader' for 'the sheer indulgence' of fashion, 'style', '*joie de vivre*', and an 'individualistic attitude'. *Marie Claire*'s publicity also focused upon the love of its 'ideal reader' for the 'confident, calm look' of fashion, an easy relationship with 'herself' and her 'environment', and an overriding interest in 'how people live their lives'.

Other successful magazine titles offered lifestyle descriptions that were equally congruent with discourses about a 'new middle class'. We have seen that publicity for *New Woman*, for example, described its 'ideal reader' as a working woman who was almost entirely wrapped up in 'You'. *New Woman*'s readers were 'vulnerable', 'self-critical', and 'insecure inside', and consequently had a penchant for popular psychology. After their revamps, *Cosmopolitan* and *Company*'s 'ideal readers' were also described in publicity as focused on 'herself' and 'relationships', and sought the 'insights' and 'reassurances' of popular psychology. The expanded 'Zest' section of *Cosmopolitan* also emphasized the interest of its 'ideal readers' in the maintenance of body, soul and appearance. Likewise, *She*'s target readers were configured as having interests that resonated with 'new middle-class' rhetoric. They sought, it was claimed, to understand relationships between women and men, and were eager to explore the dynamics of the mother and child 'bond'.

Indeed, this analysis of 'new middle-class' discourse can also help to explain the failure of *Working Woman* with advertisers. With its lifestyle focus on a recognizably older 'petit bourgeois' discourse of conservatism, duty, hard work and reserve, *Working Woman* offered advertisers and readers a 'traditionalist' and 'out-dated' image of femininity. Potential advertisers, unsurprisingly, refused to embrace this rhetoric because it was viewed as working against the ethos and legitimation of a 'new middle-class' and cultural intermediary that they were keen to promote. As advertisers were also deemed by *Working Woman*'s market researchers to make up a large section of the target readership, it is perhaps unsurprising that circulation statistics for the title remained low. Those with 'new middle-class' aspirations would not have been 'spoken to' by *Working Woman*, and would be actively seeking to be seen to subvert its traditionalist ethos in many other aspects of their daily lives.

The 'lifestyle' orientations of the more successful titles can be read as the magazine industry's attempts to distance their titles, in the eyes of both advertisers and readers, from the 'old-fashioned' traditionalist rhetorics of mass-market women's magazines. They emphasize, instead, the ability of the magazine industry to understand new formations of femininity and to produce publications with their finger on the pulse. In these 'lifestyle' invocations, magazine producers can be seen to reiterate and relegitimate their claims to be cultural intermediaries and members of a 'new middle-class'. But their various lifestyle addresses can also be understood as attempts to offer the readers of women's magazines new ways of understanding and redefining themselves, thus encouraging them to develop a belief in – and perhaps even further legitimate – an *idea* of the existence of 'new middle-class' dispositions and tastes.

'New middle-class' rhetoric in 1980s Britain

It is, of course, hard to discern the extent to which the cultural intermediaries discussed in this chapter actually embodied and practised the 'new middle-class' lifestyle they imaged. Furthermore, it is impossible to assess the extent to which women's magazine readers practised the lifestyle, dispositions and tastes of a 'new middle-class' because of reading women's magazines. Althusserian-influenced accounts would suggest that the magazine images and narratives of 'new middle-class' femininity would constitute women readers who would relate to the world through 'new middle class' discourse. As I argued in Chapter 1, however, such explanations of the effects of women's magazines are too functionalist and simplistic. Joke Hermes's (1995) analysis of the position of women's magazines in the lives of readers has shown, for example, that women's magazines may not be that important to the women who read them. Indeed, in cases where magazines are important to readers, Hermes (1995: 41) observes that many 'give meaning to women's magazine genres in a way that to a quite remarkable extent is independent of the women's magazine text'. Thus they may use women's magazines as tools for fantasizing about an 'ideal self', whilst never putting their content into practice.

There is some interesting empirical evidence, however, which suggests that forms of consumer practices amongst middle-class groups of the 1980s were compatible with the lifestyles and dispositions said to be held by a 'new middle class'. Basing their study on an analysis of TGI consumer data, Mike Savage *et al.* (1992: 99–131) sought evidence of the fragmentation of the British middle classes. Their use of market research surveys meant that, unlike Bourdieu, Savage *et al.* could not examine tastes not expressed through patterns of spending on consumer services and products. Nevertheless, they argued that the TGI enabled them to reflect upon the principal differences in lifestyle between middle-class occupational groupings, and to trace distinctive patterns associated with age, gender, education and regional difference (Savage *et al.*, 1992: 105).

Savage *et al.* (1992: 105) found that high-income members of the British middle class engaged in 'a new culture of health and body maintenance', preferring 'individualistic' sports of the 'Californian' variety. They combined this disposition with a 'culture of extravagance' (particularly about eating and drinking), associated with excess, indulgence, and a love of 'things foreign'

(Savage *et al.*, 1992: 108). Thus immoderate eating and drinking took place in French, Chinese, Greek, Turkish and Indian restaurants, as well as on holidays abroad in 'sophisticated' Western European locations (Savage *et al.*, 1992: 106–15). Equally contradictory dispositions were apparent in this group's cultural tastes, and they embraced 'high cultural forms of art such as opera and classical music' as well as 'low' culture including 'disco dancing or stock car racing' (Savage *et al.*, 1992: 108). The extreme nature of this lifestyle ultimately led Savage *et al.* (1992: 108) to identify it as '"postmodern", where a binge in an expensive restaurant one night might be followed by a diet the next'.

Savage *et al.*'s (1992: 128) findings seem, to a large extent, to be compatible with descriptions of a 'new middle-class'. Yet they also suggest that the 'postmodern' lifestyle was more widespread in 1980s Britain than it was in Bourdieu's France, maintaining that it:

> appears to exist throughout the private sector professional middle class, not just the marginal, up and coming elements within it . . . it would seem, from our survey, that barristers, accountants and surveyors partake in the post-modern lifestyle as much as sex therapists or advertising agents.
>
> (Savage *et al.*, 1992: 128)

Longhurst and Savage (1996) have argued that occupationally driven descriptions of 'new middle-class' lifestyles and aspirations such as those offered by Savage *et al.* presume that the actions of individuals within such groups 'mirror those of wider groups' (1992: 283). Savage *et al.* (1992) overlook the possibility, Longhurst and Savage point out, that:

> some individuals within this occupational group favour the healthy lifestyle and others favour the lifestyle of excess, hence that two different cultures are being detected, not one contradictory or post-modern culture.
>
> (Longhurst and Savage, 1996: 283)

Linda McDowell's (1997) case study of professional working environments in the City of London post-1986, however, offers some support for the existence of a 'postmodern' or 'new middle-class' lifestyle orientation. Through interviews with a number of men and women in investment banks, she observes a widespread identification in this occupational group with the 'contradictory' attitudes congruent with a 'new middle-class' or 'postmodern' rhetoric.

McDowell (1997: 139) argues that there has been a significant change in forms of work in the City, characterized by a blurring of traditional distinctions between 'work' and 'leisure'. Many of her interviewees, she observes, expressed the view that work was not simply a 'duty', but 'fun'. This attitude towards work was also reflected in the changing built environment of the City, as architects designed work and leisure spaces that interconnected, combining office buildings with small parks, piazzas and cafés. Aesthetic considerations for the interiors and exteriors of new City buildings were also crucial signifiers of this new attitude towards work, as were the health clubs, pools, squash courts and medical centres provided by some City employers.

McDowell (1997: 139) also points to the relationship between bodies, personal appearance and workplace success in the City. There is, she observes, 'a greater emphasis on the cultural capital of workers, on attributes such as style and bodily form, on how they look as well as how they perform in the workplace' (McDowell, 1997: 140). The effects of this can, McDowell (1997: 140) argues, be detrimental to women's position within the workplace as it contributes to a traditional construction of women as 'for pleasure, not work', and as inferior to the 'ideal' male worker. However, this focus on the body and personal appearance is not exclusive to women employees and leads to what McDowell describes as the 'feminization' of all workers, which may ultimately challenge stereotypes about the 'ideal' City employee.

This focus on style and bodily form is not just intended to signify an attitude about work to other City employees. As McDowell (1997: 139) observes, in an occupation that is 'increasingly dependent on selling information and advice, the personal performance of workers, their ways of being and doing, are part of the service that is sold'. What women wear, and how they behave therefore, are important considerations when they interact with clients. Because of the financial nature of their services, however, City women have to walk a fine line between signifying their business acumen, and being 'feminine' and seductive (which is frequently viewed by male clients as the 'bonus' of employing a woman) (McDowell, 1997: 197–200).

Whilst McDowell's account is limited to a small group of professional women in the 1980s, my interest here is in the compatibility of her account with the various explanations of 'new middle-class' culture. Whilst I am not suggesting that McDowell's work can be used as evidence of the rise of a 'new middle class' in Britain, it clearly demonstrates that amongst some workers in the financial services sector there was an increasing imagined identification with this configuration (McDowell, 1997: 16). Thus a rhetoric about work as 'fun' was developed and promoted by this occupational group, along with a fascination for identity, presentation, physical appearance at work and bodily exercise. According to McDowell, women financiers also expressed a concern with their legitimacy in the eyes of clients and knowingly tried to incorporate a complex image of traditional ('masculine') professionalism and more liberated ('feminine') seduction. Again, this resonates with a 'new middle-class' discourse, incorporating a nostalgia for the conservatism of the City's ancestry with a fight for liberation from it. McDowell's study does not, of course, provide us with any detail about the consumer practices of this occupational group, or their penchant (or otherwise) for women's magazines. However it does suggest that women's magazines incorporating a 'new middle-class' attitude might well have offered women financiers a rhetoric of young, middle-class femininity and lifestyles which would be congruent with their own identifications.[5]

In this chapter I have attempted to show the ways in which the imagination of the social practice of a 'new middle class' played an important role in the marketing of women's magazines to advertisers. I have also suggested that such practices may have been significant in the selling of women's magazines to middle-class women readers. The editors of women's magazines had a need to demonstrate to potential advertisers their ability effectively to target and 'deliver' target markets of young, middle-class women consumers. They strove not merely to prove that they had identified the lifestyles and aspirations of these target markets, but also to confirm their own incorporation of the lifestyle practices and ideals imaged. In turn, women's magazines incorporated an imagined ideal of the market into the lifestyle assertions of the magazines they produced. This helped to generate an active image of the existence and expansion of a group of 'new middle-class' women.

I have not explored the textual strategies used by the magazine industry to target magazines to market segments of women. I have, however, assumed that the textual address designed in response to the lifestyle configurations of magazine practitioners attempted to 'speak to' sections of women who identified with a 'new middle-class' rhetoric. Whilst we cannot know how successful the textual strategies were in 'speaking' to women, it is possible to maintain that successful forms of textual address helped to develop 'new middle-class' practices and attitudes amongst groups of young, middle-class women. In effect, I am arguing that the imagination of middle-class women's lifestyles by the women's magazine industry may have had some imaginative (if not actual) basis in reality, as well as social consequences.

In the next chapter, I explore the refocusing of the format of glossy women's magazines of the late 1990s around a new target reader. This repositioning was driven, as were the initiatives around the 'New Woman' charted in this rest of this book, by calculations about shifts in the lived cultures of groups of young, middle-class women. The women's magazine industry, I argue, adopted an updated form of a 'new middle-class' feminine script. Elements of this script were already in place with images and representations of the 'New Woman' in the 1980s. However, an analysis of the new lifestyle descriptions of femininity employed by the women's magazine industry also underlines the novelty of the scripts offered by 1980s magazines for a 'New Woman', and the dynamism of magazine discourses about young, middle-class femininity.

8

DESPERATELY TWEAKING SUSAN

The business of women's magazines in the 1990s

In June 1998, Olga Craig (1998: 26) reported in the *Sunday Telegraph* on a 'quiet revolution' on the periodical shelves. Women's magazines, she observed, had 'lost their readers in droves', and women had become 'disenchanted with magazines that [. . . assume] their interests begin and end with shopping, sex and cellulite' (Craig, 1998: 26). Craig spoke to Bridget Rowe, former editor of *Woman's Own*, who argued that the women's magazine industry was burdened by a lack of innovation. If you cover up the mastheads of the leading glossy magazines, Rowe declared,

> you can't tell them apart . . . [t]hey have gone flat, they produce no surprises. From reading them you would never believe women drive cars or buy stereos or laugh. Or that they have any interest in current affairs or foreign news.
>
> (Rowe quoted in Craig, 1998: 26)

Hilary Burden, former deputy editor of *Cosmopolitan* agreed, claiming that women's glossies had 'elevated themselves to the height of absurdity' and become so 'self-obsessed' they had 'forgotten about their readers' (Burden quoted in Craig, 1998: 26). Craig concluded that the women's magazine industry was 'in the doldrums', pointing as evidence to the decline in the circulations of the top six sellers (including *Company*, *Cosmopolitan*, *Options* and *She*) from 3,452,716 to 2,098,302 in just ten years (Craig, 1998: 26).

Craig's picture of stagnation and decline was echoed widely throughout the advertising and marketing trade press of this period. Writing in *PR Week*, Stephen Armstrong noted that the 'latest fashionable mantra in media circles is to bemoan the state of women's magazines' (Armstrong, 1998). Meanwhile, a letter in *Marketing Week* declared that the women's magazine sector was 'suffering from a distinct lack of product differentiation and the introduction of pricing strategies which more closely resemble those associated with the potato futures market' (Jon Humphrey in *Marketing Week*, 1997: 36). Once again, advertising industry commentators alleged that publishers had 'lost touch' with their readers.

The slump in women's magazine circulations came as a shock to some glossy publishers. Circulations of women's magazines in the mid-1990s had suggested that the industry had achieved some stability, and titles such as *Marie Claire* and *Cosmopolitan* regularly achieved ABC figures of around 400,000. The trade press had repeatedly congratulated magazine editors on this, and had celebrated their 'emotional rapport' with readers. Women's magazine editors had continued to promote themselves in industry publications as mappers of contemporary taste, Glenda Bailey (editor of *Marie Claire*) and Mandi Norwood (editor of *Cosmopolitan*) in particular becoming personalities in a tale of power and struggle, as they competed for the top ABC position (*Marketing Week*, 1995: 5).

This chapter will explore the responses of publishers to dwindling circulations, considering their rethinks and new pitches for glossies of the mid- and late 1990s. At the heart of these developments remained the publishers' ambition to distinguish their magazines from those that had gone before, and this included breaking from many aspects of the 'New Woman' lifestyles they had so vociferously proposed in the late 1980s. Publishers of the mid- and late 1990s were therefore compelled to renew their efforts in presenting to advertisers their own 'in tune-ness' with young middle-class women, and their skills in developing innovative forms of magazine address. This time around, however, many advertisers were more sceptical and reticent about the potential of women's magazines, and demonstrated this to publishers through their preference for placing campaigns in other media. During the 1990s, therefore, the business of glossy women's magazine publishing became an increasingly perilous enterprise.

The 'Big Four' in the 1990s

The trend toward the restructuring of UK magazine publishing along post- and neo-Fordist lines (discussed in Chapter 3) was consolidated during the 1990s. At the end of the decade, the large publishing groups had strengthened their positions in the women's magazine sector – the National Magazine Company, IPC, EMAP and Condé Nast accounting for 97 per cent of all glossy magazine sales by June 2000 (Seymour Marketing, 2000a: 3–5). The size of these groups awarded them a number of financial advantages over smaller publishers. Whilst magazine publishing might still be a turbulent form of business venture, the risks incurred could be spread through diversification into other forms of media as well. The financial clout and scale of their enterprises also enabled them to enter into cross-media ownership agreements, and to continue to produce and spread their successful magazine (and other) media formulas across national and international markets (Stewart and Laird, 1994: 58–63). All the large publishing groups, therefore, saw greater rewards from the forms of organizational decentralization they had begun in the 1980s (see Bunting, 1997: 49).

The National Magazine Company was probably the most enterprising and aggressive of the 'Big Four' in its business tactics, especially in its purchase of G & J, the British arm of the German media group, Bertelsmann, in July 2000. G & J were the publishers of the down-market domestic women's titles *Prima* and *Best,* and many industry observers had predicted that IPC (with its stable of women's weeklies) would consolidate its interests and buy Bertelsmann out (Hodgson, 2000a: 10). However, as media buyer Paul Thomas, a senior partner at Mindshare observed, the purchase made sense for National Magazines: 'It's partly economies of scale – the more paper you buy, the better prices you get. It's also about digital assets, leveraging more brands into a digital medium, and it offers more of a one-stop shop for advertisers' (Thomas quoted in Hodgson, 2000a: 10).

IPC remained the leading magazine publisher in the UK throughout the 1990s, but its magazine portfolio saw diminishing sales (averaging 10 per cent in total between 1996 and 1998). In the mid-1990s IPC made an attempt to rethink and relaunch some weekly and glossy women's titles with low circulations. By the late 1990s, company strategy had moved from relaunching titles to closing them (Max-Lino and Poissonnier, 1999: 198). In 2000, IPC announced that it had decided to focus on the maintenance of its women's weekly portfolio, and to promote only a small portfolio of glossy women's titles (*Marie Claire* being the leading contender) (Seymour Marketing, 2000a: 4).

Throughout the 1990s, EMAP continued to diversify its business outside of consumer magazine publishing, stating a corporate objective 'to create one of the world's most highly rated media businesses' (Max-Lino and Poissonnier, 1999: 175). Operating a trilogy of media businesses – consumer magazines, radio and TV – EMAP proved opportunistic in their efforts at developing on-line and e-commerce. They also made significant acquisitions of media companies in the US, Australia and France, and acquired the UK lifestyle magazine publisher, Wagadon, from its 40 per cent shareholding company, Condé Nast (Crawford, 1999). Wagadon, publisher of titles including *Arena* and *The Face*, complemented EMAP's consumer magazine portfolio. In addition, it was hoped that EMAP would be able to access more magazine markets overseas by building on Wagadon's success with some foreign readerships (Max-Lino and Poissonnier, 1999: 172).

During the 1990s, EMAP competed strongly for a significant portion of the glossy women's lifestyle magazine market, even though *Elle* and *New Woman* (both acquired by EMAP in the late 1980s) were struggling to remain buoyant (Seymour Marketing, 2000a: 5). As part of their strategy of expansion, EMAP launched *Minx* in 1996 (for women in their late teens and twenties) and *Red* in 1998 (a magazine for 'women in their 30s who think younger') (Pratley, 1997). EMAP also employed its glossy women's magazine titles as vehicles for promoting their new media activities (including on-line publishing), offering, for example, free CD-ROMs with details of, and links to, other EMAP media on the covers of some of their titles (Max-Lino and Poissonnier, 1999: 173).

Advertisers, advertorials and women's magazines

Whilst magazine publishers expanded, concentrated, integrated and diversified during this period, so did other media businesses in Western Europe (see Weymouth and Lamizet, 1996: 18). This provided the advertising industry with an increasingly wide range of media options to choose from, and contributed to the fragility of the business of glossy women's magazine publishing. For advertisers keen to display their wares in print form, for example, many middle-class women could now be targeted through British newspapers that had introduced attractive (and often glossy) style, fashion and media sections. Supermarkets such as Sainsbury, and stores such as Marks and Spencer had also begun to produce out-sourced 'customer' magazines that vied for similar readerships. Indeed, advertisers were also offered a wider range of non-magazine, new media opportunities, and many of these claimed that they were vehicles for reaching young, middle-class women. Commercial satellite and cable broadcasting, for example, offered ranges of new niche channels. The Internet too opened up new, finely targeted advertising opportunities.

Not easily outdone, women's magazine publishers were increasingly innovative in developing new ways of adding value to their titles in the minds of advertisers (Bunting, 1997: 50). Many publishers with diverse media interests set up 'mini-media agencies' which used their teams in PR, marketing, advertising and editorial to offer media buyers 'total marketing solutions' (Stuart, 1997: 14). EMAP, for example, gave advertisers the possibility of strategically purchasing advertising space across their magazine, radio and television interests. IPC offered a similar facility, promoting their media agency, 'Southbank Solutions', as a 'creative think tank' of account managers (Stuart, 1997: 15).

One of the most successful techniques for attracting advertisers to women's magazines was the 'advertorial'. 'Advertorials' incorporated the advertised product into magazine editorial with the hopes that the sales pitch would be read as the objective comment of a 'trusted friend'. Advertorials had traditionally been viewed as 'tacky' and associated with 'the cowboy end of the publishing business' (Reid, 1992: 17). By the mid-1990s, however, magazine publishers were taking substantial portions of their advertising revenues from magazine advertorial services (Reid, 1992: 17). Indeed, the 'Big Four' took the advertorial sides of their businesses very seriously. Condé Nast, for example, offered advertisers the services of an in-house copywriter, house photographer and stylist for each title, and National Magazines a centralized advertorial promotions department of thirty staff (Purdom, 1996: 9).

Magazine advertorials became increasingly creative throughout the 1990s. Popular advertorial techniques included the celebrity interview, in which the celebrity would make continual reference to a product or product line. Food companies sponsored magazine recipe pages where their product could become the key ingredient. Travel sections in magazines were sponsored by particular travel companies, which would cover the expenses of the travel journalist in return for company recommendation in the final piece. Magazine publishers also offered advertisers the possibility of whole advertorial supplements, sometimes accompanied by product samples, banded to the covers or inserted within their publications. These supplements were found to have advantages for magazine publishers too, as they gave magazines a more sizeable appearance and achieved greater sales on the news stands (Stewart and Laird, 1994: 57).

Within the advertising trade press there were some doubts expressed about magazine publishers' claims for the effectiveness of these new methods. Media buyers for perfume and financial products, in particular, complained about 'clutter', claiming that the quantity of advertising within a magazine could make it difficult for their product to stand out against the rest. On the whole, however, these complaints were greeted unsympathetically by the magazine industry, who argued that 'clutter' was simply 'an all-purpose stick that media buyers can use to beat up the owners' when campaigns did not perform well (Mills, 1996: 2).

'The sweet sell of sex-cess': 'New Woman' glossies in the 1990s

From the mid-1990s onwards, most of the 'New Woman' magazines discussed in previous chapters of this book attempted to up-date their images of young middle-class femininity by altering their editorial mixes. Whilst fashion and beauty remained significant components within these titles, all increased their editorial focus on 'celebrity culture'. The women's glossies offered interviews and cover shoots with Hollywood film stars, popular singers and 'super-models', such as Gwyneth Paltrow, Geri Halliwell (The Spice Girls), and Courtney Cox (*Friends*) (Rumbelow, 1999: 11). Some also used celebrities as 'guest editors' for single issues. *Marie Claire*, in particular, was keen on 'guest editorships', even producing issues edited by Joanna Lumley and Jennifer Saunders (or 'Patsy' and 'Edina') of *Absolutely Fabulous*, and Joan Collins. The rule of thumb here appeared to be that the chosen celebrity should be (sometimes ironically) indicative of the lifestyle 'attitude' of the magazine itself, embodying the dispositions and aspirations of the 'ideal' reader. By definition, the celebrity was also a woman with a profession, who had distinguished herself through her individualism, often her 'desirable' visage and physique, and her success (see Marshall, 1997: x).[1]

In an American context, James Autry has observed the increase of what he terms 'celebrity journalism' within all forms of media, including fashion, news and sport of this period. Magazines in recent years, he argues, have been particu-larly driven by 'celebrity' as it has proved to be a sure-fire way of improving sales in recessionary conditions (Autry, 1998: 341–2). Whilst dwindling circulations probably contributed to the movement of the British women's glossies into 'celebrity journalism', another significant factor was undoubtedly the growing sales for weekly celebrity magazines, including *Hello!* (a British version of the successful Spanish magazine *Hola!*), *OK!*, *Here!* and *Now!*, *Hello!* and *Here!* were regularly achieving circulation figures of just under 500,000 weekly copies by 1996, figures that the glossies could not afford to ignore.

To the concern of the glossy women's titles, the celebrity weeklies were not only popular with readers, but also popular with advertisers. *Hello!* was the most successful in this respect, with over 80 per cent of the total advertising business in the celebrity weekly market. Advertisers were also impressed with the demographics of the celebrity weekly readerships and their high ABC1 market penetration. According to the NRS, over 50 per cent of *Hello!*'s readers, for example, were in ABC1 socio-economic groups, and nearly 80 per cent were women under the age of forty-four (NRS, 1997). Unsurprisingly, therefore, more than half of *Hello!*'s advertisements were for luxury products, including Estée Lauder, Guerlain and L'Oreal (*Marketing*, 1996: 27).[2]

The 'celebrity' focus of the glossies was not the only significant change in their editorial mix during the 1990s, and there was also an increased emphasis (sometimes tangentially linked to celebrities) on women's sexual confidence and independence. As plastic-wrapped sex-related supplements on (hetero)-sexual positions became commonplace in many women's magazines of this period, along with salacious stories on 'pornography in the suburbs' (*Company*, December 1994) and 'couples who go to prostitutes' (*Cosmopolitan*, April 1996), the sales of some of these magazines achieved some stability – and in some cases grew. This in itself generated a vast amount of media commentary about 'commercialism versus ethics' in the magazine industry, and about the relationships between magazine content and the lives of young women.[3]

Media commentators' responses to magazine representations of femininity were often remarkably reminiscent of the 'mass-culture thesis', first proposed by Adorno and Horkheimer (1947). Editorial content discussing sexual confidence and independence, it was widely insisted, was simply a 'cynical camouflage for building circulation' and a pandering to the lowest common denominator, or a 'dumbing down' (Braithwaite, 1994: 157). Stephen Cook (1992: 27) from the *Guardian* was one of the first journalists to call the motives of magazine editors into question, asking whether there could be anything more than a commercial justification for sex-oriented editorial mixes. Indeed, he found support for his 'dumbing down' thesis from David Durman, editor of the weekly *Woman* magazine ('where a picture of a penis would lose him his job overnight') who censured other titles for using sex as a 'marketing tool'. Durman also implied that magazine editors were acting against their better judgements in doing so, equating the attention that such content received with 'going topless the first time on holiday. You may not really want to but everyone else does it and when you do it doesn't seem so bad' (Cook, 1992: 27).

Whilst Cook might question the motives of women's magazine editors and the impact of commercialism on magazine content, other media commentators concerned themselves with the relationships between these sexualized representations of young femininities and young women's lives. These debates reached a peak with the publication of a condemnatory report on women's magazines – *The British Woman Today* (Anderson and Mosbacher, 1997). Produced by leading academics and journalists for a right-wing independent think-tank – the Social Affairs Unit (SAU) – contributors were unanimous that the content of contemporary women's magazines was morally reprehensible, offering 'a depressing portrait of the modern British woman' (Anderson and Mosbacher, 1997: 18). If magazine images of femininity were correct, the report claimed, Britain was in a state of moral decline.

The SAU's publication resulted in the pursuit of many women's magazine editors by the British press. Marie O'Riordan, editor of *Elle*, for example, was asked to justify her editorial decisions to a journalist from *The Times*. The SAU, she argued, had not understood the function of women's magazines in the lives of their readers. *Elle* was not bought by young women for a 'reality check', she claimed, but for 'fantasy and escapism' (O'Riordan interviewed in Gaudoin, 1997: 19). In the same article, Jane Procter of *Tatler* agreed, stating that *Tatler* was a satirical title about 'being incredibly rich, and consuming, and having lots of fun' (Procter interviewed in Gaudoin, 1997: 19). Procter also pointed out that *Tatler* was not a magazine for academics, who maybe had 'never learnt to view life with a sense of humour' (Procter interviewed in Gaudoin, 1997: 19). Jackie Highe (*Bella*), Fiona McIntosh (*Company*) and Mandi Norwood (*Cosmopolitan*) also justified their editorial decisions by arguing that circulation statistics and reader correspondence ensured that they were 'in touch' with women's lives. Critics needed to wake up to the 'real world', they argued, and realize that women's magazines were 'not for them' (McIntosh interviewed in Gaudoin, 1997: 19).

Although the advertising trade press certainly kept an eye on the shifting content of glossy women's titles, it tended to be less condemnatory about new representations of femininity than the broadsheets. This is not surprising, as for advertisers the abilities of women's magazines to reach highly targeted, high-income audiences were more important concerns than the moralities of young women. That is not to say, however, that advertisers were not bothered at all about magazine content, as they are often attracted to particular magazines because of the loyalty and trust they inspire in readers, and the possible 'halo effects' (see Johnson and Prijatel, 1998: 26). Advertisers, therefore, looked for evidence of credibility (as opposed to morality) in the editorial mix, and for evidence of reader commitment to the title in terms of NRS and ABC figures.

There is no doubt that the women's magazines that were accused by media commentators of 'dumbing down' in the mid-1990s (e.g. *Cosmopolitan*,

Company, She and *New Woman*) continued to achieve respectable circulation figures in increasingly difficult market circumstances. Rumours did abound in the advertising industry that *Company* had developed a 'magical' sales formula relating circulation figures to the number of times in which the word 'sex' appeared on cover lines (Mistry, 1992: 1). Magazine publishers, however, claimed that circulations had not been maintained purely through more sexualized editorial mixes. They pointed, for example, to their development and promotions for 'sale or return' which had increased the availability of their titles in newsagents. They also remarked on innovation in advertorials, and gimmicks such as loyalty cards which had 'added value' to women's magazines in the minds of their readers (Mistry, 1992: 1). Others pointed to the cultural intermediary expertise of a new band of magazine editors, who had responded to the needs of their readers through 'escapist', 'funny', 'lighthearted and witty' features, which were sometimes about sex (Mistry, 1992: 1).

She, Cosmopolitan and *Company* only witnessed slight falls in their ABC figures between 1991 and 1997. Given the recessionary economic conditions of much of this decade, coupled with the proliferation of new media products for women, this must be regarded as an achievement. Indeed, *New Woman* saw a rise to ABC figures of 250,240 during this period, an increase of 5 per cent. *Elle* also underwent a circulation increase to 210,067, a percentage growth of 10.4 (source: ABC). The most successful increase in circulation figures in this decade was, undoubtedly, *Marie Claire*. In Chapter 6 I showed how *Marie Claire* had been launched in 1988 as a 'me-too' for *Elle*. During the 1990s, however, the 'me-too' relationship was somewhat reversed. By 1997 *Marie Claire* was leaving its lifestyle competitor far behind, reaching ABC figures of 435,006, an increase of almost 92 per cent since 1991 (source: ABC). Indeed there were months during this decade when *Marie Claire* performed better than *Cosmopolitan* which had, for many years, been the highest achiever in the glossy women's title stakes.

Broadsheet media commentators tended to argue that *Marie Claire*'s dramatic circulation figures were purely a result of a more 'sex-focused' and shamelessly commercial editorial mix, and they pointed as an example to *Marie Claire*'s 'tabloid-esque' features such as 'When three lovers sleep together', 'What do you look like naked?' and 'Secrets of a millionaire prostitute' (*Marie Claire*, December 1990). *Marie Claire*'s publisher, Heather Love, however, did not agree, and she suggested that such criticisms were misguided: 'The basic blueprint of the magazine has remained the same since its launch', Love claimed:

> It's just that we have been much emulated by other women's magazines that have parodied the style and misunderstood the sex content. There's a world of difference between features about sex and sexy features. The market has changed rather than us.
>
> (Love quoted in O'Brien, 1996: 16)

Magazines for 'sassy lassies'

It is interesting to consider the shifts in glossy women's magazine representations of femininity in terms of other developments in popular culture of the 1990s. More sexually confident and independent feminine scripts appeared, for example, in Channel 4's controversial *The Girlie Show* (broadcast in 1996), novels such as Helen Fielding's *Bridget Jones's Diary* (1996), popular music's All Saints and The Spice Girls, and advertisements such as TBWA's campaigns for Playtex Wonderbra ('Or are you just pleased to see me?' and 'Hello Boys!').[4] Jackson *et al.* (2001: 1) have also observed that more '"laddish" forms of masculinity, associated with drinking, sport and sex' also emerged in popular cultural forms including: 'Nick Hornby's *Fever Pitch* (1992) . . . the situation comedies *Men Behaving Badly* and *Game On*, the sports quiz *They Think It's All Over* and chat shows like *Fantasy Football*' (Jackson *et al.*, 2001: 2).

Sean Nixon (1996: 203) has also pointed out that 'laddish' scripts began to appear in men's magazine publishing from 1990 onwards. Indeed, all of the major men's magazine publishers identified the 'lad' as a profitable commercial lifestyle image, producing highly successful titles including EMAP's *FHM* (first published in 1992), IPC's *Loaded* (first published 1994), National Magazines' *Esquire* (1991) and Dennis Publishing's *Maxim* (1995).[5] The 'lad', then, offered the more independent and sexually confident representations of femininity an equally irreverent male counterpart, broadly defined by his penchant for 'drinking to excess, adopting a predatory attitude towards women and a fear of commitment' (Jackson *et al.*, 2001).

The new 'lad' scripts in men's magazines proved extremely popular with target groups of young men. They were, however, also attractive to the target readerships of glossy women's magazines, and NRS figures suggested that many read 'lad' titles on a regular basis (Craig, 1998: 26; Mackenzie, 1998: 59). EMAP was the first publisher to respond to this market information, launching *Minx* in August 1996, which offered a woman dubbed the 'ladette' a glossy magazine of her own (Hodgson, 2000b: 4; McCann, 1996: 16; Spriggs, 1997: 14). *Minx* was positioned in the market as a direct competitor to National Magazines' *Company*, aiming to reach a core audience of eighteen to twenty-four-year-old women, described apprehensively by an EMAP executive as 'assertive, rather scary women' (*Campaign*, 1996: 32).

It was observed by media commentators that *Minx*'s editor, Toni Rogers, was at least ten years older than her 'Kookai-wearing, Sea Breeze-drinking' target readers (Izatt, 1996: 29). Rogers, however, legitimated her status as a 'cultural intermediary' by pointing not only to her previous success as editor of the teen title *J17*, but also to her belief that her target readers had lifestyle dispositions like hers. Rogers therefore informed the doubters at *PR Week* that she enjoyed 'shooting off on weekends' in her boyfriend's camper van, eating out and occasional clubbing (Izatt, 1996: 29). The ideal *Minx* reader

Figure 9 Cover of *Minx*, October 1996 (courtesy of EMAP).

would be very much the same: 'cool but stylish' (Izatt, 1996: 29). *Minx* would also, Rogers declared, offer readers something different from other magazines on the market – an optimistic 'celebration of life'. Taking a swipe at *Company*'s editorial, Rogers attempted to describe *Minx*'s alternative mix for advertisers, albeit in rather vague terms: 'We will certainly not be offering a cut-price therapy centre. The layout and the look will be clean . . . the writing will be spirited' (Rogers quoted in Izatt, 1996: 29).

The 'spirit' in *Minx* seemed to come from its sexually confident and independent representations of femininity, which generated much media debate. Some commentators were appalled at the crudity of its editorial tone, and even feminist commentator Germaine Greer (1999: 25) wailed that the *Minx* girl would learn that 'the only life worth living is a life totally out of control, disrupted by debt, disordered eating, drunkenness, drugs and casual sex'. In the *Independent*, an anonymous magazine editor alleged that *Minx* was lowering the tone of magazine journalism, claiming that even its fashion pages were 'about T-shirts to pull boys in, that show off your tits' (cited in McCann, 1997: 5).[6] Others were more complimentary about *Minx*'s editorial mix, Sheryl Garratt (1996: T15) in the *Guardian*, for example, welcoming the *Minx* generation who could:

> read the word fuck without fainting. They have sex not just for love or even pleasure but sometimes out of pity or to get revenge. They enjoy a problem page with its tongue in its cheek.
>
> (Garratt, 1996: T15)

NRS data for 1997 indicated that *Minx* was attracting readers with profiles roughly in its stated target group. Eighty-five per cent of *Minx*'s readers were aged between fifteen and twenty-four, and the majority of them were in the ABC1 social grades (NRS, 1997). Fourteen per cent of *Minx*'s readers were also thought to be readers of the 'lad's' magazine *Loaded* (NRS, 1997). At first, *Minx* seemed to be successful in attracting readers from *Company* magazine as had originally been intended, and *Company* even blamed it for falling sales in 1997. *Minx*'s circulation figures, however, were below par (Cook, 1997: S11). EMAP's projected circulation for *Minx* was 200,000, but in ABC figures it never came close, and sometimes only just reached the 150,000 mark (Hodgson, 2000b: 4). In 2000, EMAP finally took the decision to close the title.

Many media publications produced 'obituaries' for *Minx*. Some media commentators suggested that the title had been stymied by the launch of direct competitors such as Attic Futura's *B* (1999) which achieved circulation figures well over the 200,000 mark (source: ABC). Other media analysts argued that *Minx* lacked 'brand identity' with its target advertisers and readers, who 'never quite understood that *Minx* wasn't a teenage magazine' (Hodgson, 2000b: 4). 'Rude' and 'lewd' editorial mixes might work for the teenage market, it was argued, but for the twenty-something market, 'a degree of gravitas' was expected (Hodgson, 2000b: 4).

The most interesting analysis of *Minx*'s demise, however, came from an anonymous former *Minx* staff member who was interviewed for the *Guardian* (Hodgson, 2000b: 4). *Minx*'s downfall, she argued, was not due to its representations of feisty femininities, but to the conflicts between advertisers and editors. Whilst 'trying to make a success of going for a naughty niche', the imperative to attract advertisers meant *Minx* never had 'the balls to really go for it' (Hodgson, 2000b: 4). On a number of occasions, the interviewee claimed, editorial staff at *Minx* had been told by the marketing department 'not to do this or that so as not to upset the people from Chanel' (Hodgson, 2000b: 4). An article on female ejaculation was a casualty of this: 'I took it to show the editor of the time and she was absolutely terrified . . . She told me to go away and de-quim it a bit' (quoted in Hodgson, 2000b: 4).

This example points to the tensions that can occur between a magazine's marketing department – who attempt to sell space to advertisers – and the creative and editorial teams. Magazine editors 'walk a fine line' when they attempt to balance the needs of the different stakeholders in their titles, and sometimes this is almost impossible to do. In many of the commercially successful women's magazines discussed in this book, we have seen how the potential contradictions of advertiser–editorial–reader relationships were managed. In *Minx*'s case, however, there was serious conflict, as the advertising department feared a backlash from advertisers regarding its lifestyle address. Whilst magazine editors may employ the rhetoric of the 'cultural intermediary' to legitimate their roles and their editorial decisions, they cannot choose to go it alone if advertisers object to their vision. When publishers believe editors to have over-stepped the mark, they are swiftly replaced and magazines re-pitched. If the commercial premise becomes entirely unviable, publishers may simply cut their losses and close the magazine.[7]

It is difficult to assess how 'in tune' women's magazine publishers actually were with the lives of target groups of young, middle-class women in that latter part of the 1990s. The rhetorics of female sexual confidence and independence promoted by magazines such as *Minx*, *Cosmopolitan* and *Marie Claire* during this period certainly continue to resonate with Pierre Bourdieu (1984) and Mike Featherstone's accounts (1991) of 'new middle-class' calls for 'pleasure as a duty', 'self-expression' 'bodily expression' and 'natural sexuality'. As I observed in Chapter 7, however, claims for the *actual* existence of similar 'new middle-class' lifestyles and aspirations in late twentieth-century Britain are impossible to corroborate, as are claims for the adoption of these lifestyles by the readers of glossy women's magazines.

If there is little agreement about the actuality of a 'new middle class' in late twentieth-century Britain, the works of some cultural commentators suggest that new representations of femininity in women's magazines were indicative of real transformations in gender relations. Imelda Whelehan (2000: 52), for example, has argued that gender relations of the 1990s underwent 'some kind of quake', whilst Angela McRobbie (1997: 159) has attested to a shifting 'semi-structure of feeling' in the consciousness and experiences of the young.[8] Some sociologists have, however, expressed their doubts about whether a sea-change in gender relations really occurred, suggesting instead that this is entirely a media fiction. From empirical research, Sara Delamont (2001) and Janet Holland *et al.* (1998), for example, have argued that considerable differences of opinion about male power and female autonomy still existed between young men and women. According to these studies, whilst the lives of young men and women in the 1990s were, in many respects, significantly different from those experienced by previous generations, young men still exercised forms of masculinity predicated upon the 'exercise of power over women' (Holland *et al.*, 1998: 10). Young women also, it is argued, continued to live their feminine identities 'in relation to a male audience – measuring themselves through the gaze of the "male-in-the-head"' (Holland *et al.*, 1998: 11). For Delamont (2001: 55) this evidence suggests that whilst there had been *material* shifts in the lives of young men and women over a period of fifty years, there were strong indications that practices for negotiating hegemonic heterosexual identities had altered little.

It is clear, even from this brief discussion, that there is much disagreement and conflict amongst sociologists about the nature of gender relationships in the 1990s. It is not, however, my concern here to pursue evidence of social and economic shifts that might (or might not) have contributed to changes in relations between young men and women, or to map the impact of any shifts directly onto magazine representations. Certainly the glossy women's monthlies of this decade offered new images of gender relations in their editorial mixes and – in a commercial sense – these were reasonably successful in reaching young readers. Indeed, the commercial success of these magazines indicates that these constructions of femininity around sexual confidence and independence had some resonance with the real lives of young women. The actual nature of this resonance, however, is more difficult to explain and it is far too simplistic to suggest that such representations were 'popular' because young women actually lived lives that were like them.

What I want to consider, however, are the commercial purposes that the magazine business's claims for the emergence of new sexual, confident and independent femininities served. As I argued in Chapter 7, the 'lifestyle' orientations of women's magazines can be understood as the magazine publisher's attempts to differentiate their titles, in the eyes of both advertisers and readers, from other magazines on the market. In the mid-1990s, the need was to distance their lifestyle address not only from the mass-market magazines of the post-war period, but also from the now dated rhetoric of the 'New Woman' titles of the late 1980s. Editorial mixes with an emphasis on female sexual confidence and independence can therefore be understood as means of continuing to publicize the ability of the magazine industry to 'map' femininities, and to develop appropriate modes of address for young women. Furthermore, the new lifestyle rhetorics can be seen to have offered the readers of women's magazines new ways to understand and redefine themselves in the world. Women's magazines, therefore, attempted to encourage readers to develop a belief in (and thus legitimate) the *idea* that a new, transformative era of gender relations had been reached.[9] Whether it had been reached in reality, however, is open to question.

Women's magazines and the grown-up woman

In the late 1990s some publishers attempted to break from an editorial mix focused around sexual confidence and independence, and to generate advertiser and reader interest through new lifestyle images of contemporary femininity. The lifestyles of the 'ideal' readers were offered in a new generation of women's magazines, and they were all similarly defined as 'thinking', 'grown-up' and 'middle youth'. The general suggestion was that these magazines were aiming at women with a more 'serious' approach to life than the readers of other glossies. Furthermore, they also pointed to an ambition for core readerships of middle-class women in their late twenties upwards, who were thought to be abandoning the existing glossy titles.

The notion of this 'older' readership as a discrete market group suggests that publishers were hoping to attract those women who were ex-readers of the successful magazines of the late 1980s, such as *Elle* and *Marie Claire*. This was undoubtedly a shrewd move, as marketers had a good track record of 'speaking to' this target readership. The aspiration to reach an 'older' magazine readership, however, had a stronger foundation than just cultural intermediary 'savvy'. Indeed, indications of shifting demographics in Britain during this period pointed to an ageing society, marked by a population bulge of thirty-five to fifty-five-year-old 'baby boomers' who would begin to retire by 2010 (Central Statistical Office, 1995: 17). A report by the market researchers, Mintel, also observed that women born since the 1960s were having fewer children, and developing a distinctive set of 'pre-family' lifestyle attitudes as a consequence (Mintel, 1996: 13) One of the significant differences between these younger women and their 'baby boomer' mothers, Mintel claimed, was that almost a fifth of women born since the 1960s would remain childless through choice (Mintel, 1996: 13). This was, according to the report, because younger women gained a sense of self-achievement through their careers and work. Because of their career ambitions, younger women also reversed the patterns created by their 'baby boomer' parents, and migrated from the countryside to the big cities as they got older. Mintel predicted that women born since the 1960s would marry later (if at all), and would choose to have smaller families (Mintel, 1996: 13). According to Mintel (1996: 13), therefore, women without children were going to be a significant group of consumers for the British economy of the twenty-first century, advancing into the professions (and professional salaries) at an unprecedented rate.

The first efforts to launch a monthly glossy for the woman in her late twenties and thirties came from small, independent magazine publishers. *The Passion*, launched in May 1997 by the Passion Publishing Collective was a quarterly targeted at 'thinking women' between the ages of thirty and fifty. Describing itself in publicity as a 'Words, Music and Art' magazine, *The Passion*'s gimmick was to offer a free music CD attached to the cover of every issue. *The Passion* was unconventional in many ways, as it was not promoted to advertisers through the trade press at all. Editor Rose Rouse had a background in style and music journalism, and therefore relied on interviews with broadsheet newspapers as promotion. In interviews, Rouse described *The Passion* as a title for 'women like me, who haven't lost their edge, spirit or sense of adventure' (Rouse quoted in Roffey, 1997: M7). Indeed, *The Passion* was certainly popular with broadsheet journalists, receiving a short rave review in the *Independent* applauding the 'raw graphics, badass style-mag look and liberal scattering of Notting Hillbilly names and credits' (Roffey, 1997: M7). *The Passion* failed, however, to spark with advertisers or to achieve significant sales, and it was ignominiously extinguished after issue 2.

The downfall of *The Passion* was swiftly followed by the announcement of a launch for 'grown-up' women by Wagadon. Wagadon had produced the iconic eighties style magazine *The Face*, and the successful men's magazine *Arena*. *Frank* was therefore initially regarded with some interest by the advertising trade press who welcomed the high-fashion title free from 'horoscopes, letters and sensationalized sex stories' (Griffiths, 1997: 62). In publicity the editor of *Frank*, Tina Gaudoin, described her brief as to focus upon: 'the attitude and sensibility of the 15–40 mindset, rather than the age group itself. It will neither patronise nor preach. It will not shrink from highlighting hypocrisy or celebrating success where it is due' (Griffiths, 1997: 62). *Frank* was to be a title for women who had enjoyed, but since abandoned, the glossy launches of the late 1980s. 'My generation has grown up with women's magazines, and now we've outgrown them', Gaudoin stated confidently, '[t]he magazines haven't grown with us. A lot of women don't feel there's a magazine that's speaking their voice' (Gaudoin quoted in Viner, 1997: T7).

The launch issue of *Frank* appeared on newsagents' shelves in September 1997 and sold 140,000 copies. Some advertisers were very positive about it, describing it as 'different', 'hard going' and 'laugh out loud' (Murphy, 1997: 51), and suggesting that Wagadon 'couldn't have timed it better' (Conway quoted in Reid, 1997: 49). Alasdair Reed of *Campaign* said it was wonderful to see a non-domestic glossy for 'older' women, and remarked that 'it's certainly clear from *Frank* that most conventional conceptions of "older" are inadequate' (Reid, 1997: 49). Within months, however, *Frank* was in financial trouble due to a failure to attract appropriate readers, and consequently advertisers. By May 1998, *Frank*'s circulation was too low even to be included in the ABC figures, but sales were reputed to be at around 40,000 (Reid, 1999: 31). After attempts at breathing some life into the title with new editors and some extra PR, Wagadon closed *Frank* in May 1999 (Shelton, 1998: 8).

It is difficult to assess to what extent the rapid demises of *The Passion* and *Frank* were due to miscalculations about the lifestyles, tastes and aspirations of their 'target' markets. Wagadon was certainly criticized by advertisers and marketers for being more interested in 'hunches' than actual readership profile. In a newspaper obituary for the magazine, one media buyer even claimed to have:

called their advertising department to get a profile of who their readers are, [but] they couldn't supply one – which might be where the problem is. Who are they writing for? They could do with some research to find their niche, and then expand on it.

(Meacham quoted in Hughes, 1998: 19)

But in considering the reasons behind these market failures, it is also important to note that both *The Passion* and *Frank* were launched on shoe-string budgets. These restricted their abilities to commission readership

Figure 10 Cover of *Frank*, November 1997 (courtesy of Wagadon).

research on their own behalf, as well as their promotional funds. As we have seen, *The Passion* relied entirely on newspaper coverage to generate interest amongst both readers and advertisers. On the other hand, *Frank* depended on the Wagadon reputation for producing successful style magazines, and limited its promotional activities to a small amount of PR and an off-beat, low-cost, small-scale poster campaign.[10] Coupled with unusual and distinctive editorials and layouts, it is probably unsurprising that high-spending advertisers (i.e. large fragrance and fashion houses) reduced their financial risks by staying away (Shelton, 1998: 8). Target readers also failed to part with money for magazines that they had hardly, if at all, seen or heard mention of and which seemed 'unconventional'. Indeed, if potential readers did browse the magazine shelves for *The Passion* or *Frank* (and the fact that many women in their twenties and thirties were thought to have given up on most women's magazines available makes this unlikely), they were faced with products that were less substantial in volume than the other glossies due to a lack of advertising, advertorial supplements, etc.

'Seeing *Red*: magazines for the 'middle youth' market

Despite the failure of *The Passion* and *Frank* to reach advertisers and readers, publishers did not give up attempting to target markets of women in their late twenties and thirties. A more commercially successful attempt to break with the standard editorial mix was seen with EMAP Elan's *Red*. Following some extensive market research, EMAP Elan defined *Red*'s target reader as 'middle youth', determined:

> not so much by her age as her wage – and her relentlessly youthful attitude. She is happy to go to the pub with her friends (as long as there's somewhere to sit down), go clubbing until the early hours and settle down for the night with a cookery book. She also wants a magazine which is not fixated on sex.
>
> (Beenstock, 1998: 41)

Editor Kathryn Brown, previously of the teen title *Sugar*, promoted her new magazine – and cultural intermediary expertise – by describing herself as *Red*'s 'ideal' reader through and through:

> A lot of women love women's magazines but are feeling disenfranchised . . . there is a whole new generation of women in their thirties who still have a very youthful attitude but broad interests like gardening and food. It's such a pleasure to edit because I feel I am this woman.
>
> (Brown quoted in O'Rorke, 1997: 4)

Figure 11 Cover of *Red*, March 1998 (courtesy of EMAP).

Within the advertising trade press, the announcement of *Red*'s launch was widely discussed. In *Campaign* (1997b: 71), Richard Britton of CIA Media-network, for example, declared that he would be grateful for *Red* because there had 'been nothing of major consequence going on in the glossies' market since the early 80s and early 90s'. Others were more unsure about *Red*'s lifestyle proposition, suggesting that *Red* sounded like 'a Jack of all trades and a master of none' (*Campaign*, 1997b: 71). Style commentator, Peter York, also expressed some doubts about the commercial logic of *Red*'s target reader, describing her as 'the kind of woman who'd say she needs a new magazine like a fish needs a bicycle' (York, 1998: 20).

Responses by advertisers after *Red*'s launch in 1998 were diverse. In *Marketing*, Jackie Almeida (director of CIA Media Network) said that whilst she had initially spent some time trying to identify the *raison d'être* of the title, she felt that the finished result was 'deliberately bold'. *Red*'s editors, Almeida cautioned however, would need to 'remain focused on its audience and . . . not compromise its agenda' (Almeida, 1998: 61). Broadsheet newspapers were less complimentary, Nicci Gerard of the *Observer* saying that she 'felt a bit dejected' on reading the magazine, and that *Red*'s exuberance for life made her feel 'oddly tired' (Gerard, 1998: 64). Maggie Brown of *The Times* was more cutting, declaring:

> I would have thought the kind of reader *Red* wants to attract does not need to be told in such an irritating way how she spends her time. This is one of the most unoriginal and boring new magazines that I have ever read.
>
> (Brown, 1998: 65)

Despite Brown's reservations, a second PR push and a marketing campaign (including stylish cover mounts of sunglasses cases, CDs and scented candles) resulted in circulation figures of around 180,000 within months, which were acceptable to EMAP Elan (Brown, 1999: 8). NRS statistics suggested that 66 per cent of *Red*'s readers were in the ABC1 category, although only 49 per cent fitted *Red*'s core age group (NRS, 1999).

For some magazine publishers, the modest success of *Red* demonstrated that there was space for a glossy, non-domestic title for women in their late twenties and thirties. Indeed, whilst IPC's domestic title, *Good Housekeeping*, was reported to be attempting to reorient around this target group as a means of building circulation, *Red* was also spawning a number of 'me-too's. These included Parkhill Publishing's *Aura*, which defined its target market as 'grown-up', and IPC's ill-fated relaunch of the legendary 1960s title *Nova* (for 'ageless women'), which also swiftly closed (Craik, 2000: 10). Not to be deterred, the publishing arm of the BBC, BBC Worldwide, also tried its luck with *Eve*, which proved to be a moderately successful title that addressed women 'who have outgrown the existing range of younger glossies and are looking for a more intelligent, contemporary, thought provoking and wide ranging read' (*The Grocer*, 2000: 24).

If a market for glossy women's magazines exists amongst women in their late twenties and thirties at all, it is certainly a hard one for publishers to crack. Advertisers have been notoriously reticent about targeting this lifestyle group, and it is widely known that they are 'flatly unenthusiastic about reaching older consumers' (Reid, 2000: 16). Other media, including television, have also attempted to capitalize on targeting 'older' audiences of women. It has been advertisers, however, who have allegedly remained wedded to an ideation of a 'mythical female' who is all 'fashion, make-up and cellulite-free' (Flack, 2000: 50).

Market researchers have argued that one of the problems with targeting women in their late twenties and thirties as a market group is that they are much more fragmented and inconsistent in lifestyle and aspiration than women in their teens and early twenties. Whilst publishers believe that magazines for women in their twenties can afford to generalize about the lifestyles of their readers – by building on 'firsts' (e.g. first job, first serious relationship, etc.), for example – the lives of women in their thirties upwards are understood to be more diverse. Indeed, they could be 'single, divorced, no kids, massive disposable income; or be married with four kids and lumbered with a huge mortgage' (James quoted in Flack, 2000: 50; see also Reid, 2000: 16).

Another reason why target markets of middle-class women in their late twenties and thirties are so difficult for publishers and advertisers to grasp may be their attitudes towards the consumer cultures that advertisers and publishers promote. A report by Demos (an independent left-wing think-tank) in 1997 called *Tomorrow's Women* has suggested that women in their late twenties and thirties will never make up particularly profitable target markets (Wilkinson *et al.*, 1997). Basing its report on a range of demographic and psychographic shifts, *Tomorrow's Women* argues that whilst the 1990s witnessed the birth of a 'new breed' of 'professional women' in their twenties and thirties, these women are sophisticated and cynical about consumerism.

According to Demos, the 1990s witnessed the formation of a number of identifiable 'lifestyle' groups made up of middle-class women in their late twenties and thirties. Offering nicknames for them all, Demos identified the 'Networking Naomis' and 'New Age Angelas', for example, as the leaders of trends towards ethical consumerism and investing. 'Naomi' and 'Angela' were, therefore, 'green' and 'organic' consumers, who would attempt to weaken 'current distribution and retailing networks . . . dominated by large branded retailers' by using 'local, personalised and co-operative distribution services' (Wilkinson *et al.*, 1997: 62–86). They also refused to equate affluence with extravagance, suggesting that they would not be particularly lucrative target markets for businesses that hoped to persuade them to part with their cash. If Demos is correct, the future may not be that fruitful for 'middle-youth'-style magazine titles. Publishers may well have to consider setting their sights on other target groups – or even on much lower revenues from advertising and sales.

Postscript

The turn of the century saw the launch announcements of two new glossy titles that attempted to differentiate themselves from other magazines on the market without targeting core markets of women in their 'middle youth'. *In Style* and *Glamour*, published by Time Warner and Condé Nast respectively, promised to change the face of the glossy women's magazine market. Both titles were already successful brands abroad. The UK local edition of *In Style*, however, was targeted at ABC1 and C2 women, between the ages of eighteen and thirty-four, who were already readers of celebrity weeklies. Its editorial mix thus offered 'a starry mix of fashion, beauty and interiors' (Arlidge, 2000: 7). *Glamour*, with its unusual A5 format, hoped that young women would view it as 'a portable companion' of 'dip-in dip-out, on-the-hop reading, alongside longer, meatier pieces' (Arlidge, 2000: 7). Time Warner and Condé Nast put millions of pounds into special offers and promotions which, they hoped, would deliver them substantial shares of the women's magazine market. Media analysts were reported to be saying that the glossy magazine market was at its most competitive in decades. The mere thought of *In Style* and *Glamour* as competition reputedly made other publishers jittery about launching new titles for women, and worried about how they were going to maintain circulations on existing ones (Arlidge, 2000: 7).

Attempts to set foot in the contemporary UK glossy women's magazine market are certainly commercially risky. While the quantity of glossy women's magazines steadily grows, the total numbers *reading* monthly women's magazines are in a state of gradual decline. Whilst the problem for me commenting about current trends is that they will already have altered by the time this is read, it does seem safe to predict that the new titles that will be successful will be ones that – like *In Style* and *Glamour* – are backed by the financial clout of the larger publishing houses.

To add to publishers' concerns, advertising revenues in the UK have begun to fall. This follows the descent of such revenues in the US, and suggests an uncertain future for some magazine titles (Robins, 2001: 5). Whilst a 'pistols at dawn' mentality is currently prevalent amongst publishers, and they continue to develop new marketing and promotional strategies, some reverberation is inevitable. It is unlikely, however, that publishers will seek to pull out of the women's magazine business altogether. As Terry Mansfield of National Magazines has observed, Britain might currently be 'the toughest market in the world' for women's magazine publishing, but the financial rewards for those who develop successful brands, however, are too significant to ignore (Mansfield cited in Robins, 2001: 5).

CONCLUSIONS

This exploration of the business of glossy women's magazine publishing in the late-twentieth century has critically considered the relations between magazine production, advertising and marketing. Since the early 1980s, the organizational forms of these businesses, and the relationships between them, have been marked by change. The working practices and forms of knowledge produced by these industries have also altered. As I have shown here, these were prominent factors in the development of new glossy women's magazines of this period, and in the formation of new representations of young, middle-class femininities.

Whilst the relationships between magazine producers, advertisers and marketers have been important in this account, so too have the relationships between these industries and forms of feminine culture outside of them. I hope I have demonstrated how the commercial imperatives of these industries, combined with shifts in their established organizational forms and practices, generated a desire to understand cultures of femininity 'on the ground'. Publishers, marketers and advertisers produced new forms of knowledge about women consumers, and attempted to theorize the links between women's individuality and patterns of lifestyle and consumption.

One way in which publishers sought to understand young women was through developing and employing qualitative forms of 'lifestyle' market research. This assembled increasingly fragmented pictures of 'ideal' target markets, and could be used to construct more 'innovative' methods of addressing women. Magazine editors, in particular, had the job of promoting to advertisers their potential as 'cultural intermediaries', who were 'in touch' with the lifestyles of their target market groups because they were – quite literally – part of them. This, it was hoped, would encourage sceptical media buyers to believe in the existence of the feminine lifestyle formations of a 'New Woman' developed by magazine publishers, and to purchase advertising space as a vehicle for 'reaching' young women.

The stories of the glossy women's magazines I have considered here highlight the anxieties of publishers and advertisers about how to target young, middle-class women in the late twentieth century. New glossy women's magazines entered and left the market during this period, and whilst some were commercially successful, others lost fortunes. Whilst publishers of the profitable titles liked to claim that they had capacities for both mapping and interpreting the lives of young women, the rocky circulation figures – and sometimes closures – of these magazines suggest that the only certainty about the 'New Woman' was that she was unknowable. Publishers also had to juggle their desire to 'speak to readers' with their imperative for advertising revenues, and sometimes, as I have shown, tensions arose. Thus, the lifestyle rhetorics that women's magazines adopted during this period were not simply innovative ways of 'speaking' to women, but ways of addressing women without estranging advertisers.

I do not wish to argue that the commercially successful 'New Woman' or 'middle-youth' titles offered truisms about 'real' middle-class femininities in late twentieth-century Britain. Even if the imperative for advertising revenues had been absent from the picture of magazine publishing, to suggest that 'realistic' representations of femininity can explain commercial success (and failures) is far too neat an interpretation. If we want to 'grasp' the dynamics of the business of women's magazines, we need to interpret its depictions of women's lives and interests as functional, commercial 'motifs'. That is, the magazine industry's depictions of femininity are attempts to unify the perceived complexities of young women's lives around coherent, commercially viable, configurations of 'woman' that will appeal to advertisers and readers alike.

In the story told here, I have tried to show how the lifestyles of young, middle-class women of the late twentieth century were imaged by the business of women's magazines in several, sometimes contradictory, ways. Those that were commercially successful, I have argued, resonate with a rhetoric of an expressive and liberated 'new middle-class' lifestyle that has been described by Bourdieu (1984), Featherstone (1991) and others. The use of a language of a 'new middle-class' functioned for the magazine industry as a means of distancing new titles from the 'old-fashioned-ness' of traditional mass-market women's magazines. It is, indeed, possible to suggest that these formulations of feminine lifestyles actually generated a belief in the existence and expansion of this 'new middle-class' fraction and lifestyles both within the magazine and advertising industries, and amongst some readers themselves. This is not to say, however, that these lifestyles were actually adopted (at least in the forms that practitioners imagined) by young women's magazine readers. Indeed, as studies of women's magazine readers have shown (e.g. Hermes, 1995), magazines do not resonate with the lives of young women in ways that we can easily predict.

At the start of this book, I discussed my original intention to carry out an ethnographic study of the women's magazine industry. It therefore seems pertinent here to reflect upon the research methods I eventually employed for this study, and their possible consequences for this account of the business of women's magazines. There are clear limitations to the methodological approaches that I have employed, but I hope to have shown that much can be learnt about glossy women's magazines from this inquiry. As I argued in Chapter 1, there has been very little scholarly research on the practices, expertise and production of knowledge carried out by the women's magazine industry in the UK. This study provides, therefore, a route into understanding how 'women' have been 'made sense of' by magazine producers, and has offered an analysis of how industry professionals attempt to generate identification between women's magazines and their target groups of readers. What this account suggests is that the women's magazine industry places a much greater emphasis upon 'understanding' the lifestyles, lives and aspirations of some groups of women than previous media scholars have acknowledged. The late twentieth-century business of women's magazines that I have represented here was one that was very concerned with 'tracking' and interpreting the lifestyles and dispositions of young, middle-class women. It was also one that promoted the abilities of its practitioners – especially its editors – to be successful 'cultural intermediaries' in the hopes of making lucrative advertising deals. The proof, it was claimed, lay in high levels of sales and in NRS evidence of target market penetration.

Whilst we can learn much about the women's magazine industry from this analysis, it is important to emphasize the partiality of this account. The way I have chosen to 'understand' the women's magazine industry in the late twentieth century has largely been through versions that were offered in the advertising, marketing and magazine trade press. These cannot be viewed, therefore, as transparent descriptions of 'what went on'. The trade press consists, in effect, of 'business-to-business' titles. This means that we need to be aware that they are commercially driven publications that are concerned with promoting their activities to those in their own and related industries. The account that I have constructed here, therefore, will have played down the importance of some of the practices described, whilst according others too much significance. Other important practices and events will, no doubt, have been omitted. Activities that will have been detailed in the trade press, however, might not have been deemed significant for discussion by magazine practitioners in a fieldwork or interview situation. Thus, an ethnographic method would also have led to absences that are visible in this study.[1]

The methodological procedures of this study have also meant that I have been unable to provide an account of the *informal* practices and activities of magazine practitioners and advertisers, and that I have not considered their impact upon women's magazine production. In an ethnographic study, issues that might have been foregrounded are the general cultural knowledges and cultural capital of magazine producers, and their impact upon women's magazine production. Ethnographic methodologies might also have shed greater light on the cultural preferences and tastes of people employed in the variety of occupations discussed. These might have influenced the visual and linguistic languages that they drew upon in the magazine texts.

Also absent from this study is empirical analysis of the workplace cultures developed within the women's magazine industry. Whilst I have investigated formal management practices, accounts of more informal dynamics of magazine workplaces are lacking. Drawing upon a variety of descriptions of the 'new middle class', however, I have made suggestions about how some of these 'cultural intermediaries' may have imagined themselves as members of a 'new class fraction'. The non-ethnographic nature of this study, however, has meant that I have not been able to investigate other identity scripts that the magazine workplace might have sanctioned. I have not, therefore, directed this account towards questions of gender, 'race' and sexuality in the magazine publishing workplace, which undoubtedly had an impact upon the conduct of business. An examination of such factors might well have offered up a more complicated picture of the organizational cultures of the contemporary women's magazine industry, and there is still much work to do in this area. Considerations of temporality in relation to this study would, however, make it difficult to discuss the impact of such scripts on women's magazine production in the late twentieth century unless a methodology derived from oral history was used.

Where does this conclusion leave us in terms of understanding the relationship of femininity to the cultural industries? My broader aim here has been to redirect academic debate about media texts for women towards the dimensions of production. In doing so, however, it has not been my intention to resurrect a form of crass economic reductionism of the kind elaborated in some neo-Marxist studies of the political economy of the media. Production, as I have demonstrated, should be understood as a fundamentally important site within the circuit of culture. We should, however, resist the temptation to view it as either pre-eminently determining or as possessing sovereign autonomy. Production cannot be considered in isolation, and is inextricably bound up with the meaning-making processes that exist in the realms of cultural circulation and consumption.

A more general aim of this study has also been to develop a framework in which the relationship between the economic and the cultural can be productively reconceptualized. As Paul du Gay (1997b: 2) has argued, culture is a crucial element within equations that lead to economic success. This necessitates a framework of analysis in which 'culture' and 'economy' are conceived not as separate spheres, but as 'mutually constitutive' (1997b: 2). Economic practices, processes of production and systems of organization depend upon meaning for their effective operation and are thus cultural phenomena that operate through language and representation (du Gay, 1997b: 4). 'Culture' itself is also increasingly important in the sphere of the economic as a means of generating meanings and associations for 'cultural goods' that will induce desire amongst the consumers of products. Furthermore, 'culture' has also become a key component of the internal life of business organizations which seek greater commercial success by reconstructing organizational cultures around the figure of the 'customer' (du Gay, 1997b: 4).

Notions of 'cultural economy' should have, in my view, important repercussions for feminist media studies, generating questions which textually based modes of analysis find particular difficulty in addressing. As I argued in Chapter 1, textually based analyses of media products that have utilized neo-Marxist assumptions about structure and ideology have spoken of the practices of media practitioners as an 'effect' of such structures. Thus, as Angela McRobbie has observed (1996a), concrete descriptions of the 'ideological' and 'economic' practices of cultural producers have been largely absent from accounts of forms of media consumed by women. The activities of media professionals who, as McRobbie argues (1996a), are frequently highly educated young women, have consequently been understood as 'mechanical'. Thus they are forms of activity that are seen to reflect and parallel the inequalities present in the social structure and which ultimately contribute to the maintenance of women's oppression.

In contrast, however, the concept of 'cultural economy' draws attention to the day-to-day practices of both media professionals and consumers. For feminist studies of the media its value is that it allows space for, and accounts for, varying degrees and modes of agency amongst those who participate in both production *and* consumption. Angela McRobbie (1996a: 179) has argued that this indicates that production is 'a world of strongly articulated cultural values, tastes and commitment' and is not linear, causal or mechanical. In Bourdieu's terms (1984), it is a world that, like that of consumption, produces perceptions, classifications and dispositions that can be applied both advantageously and innovatively by its participants.

The methodological approaches of this study suggest the productive possibilities for future studies of cultural production. They also raise issues of approach for further studies of women's magazines. Studies of the magazine texts themselves, for example, have focused upon the structures of textual meaning in women's magazines. They have not, however, explored the ways in which that meaning is structured through processes of magazine production. Practices of textual production have been assumed in such studies to be coherent and smooth. A study that went beyond the text to the publishers, advertisers and design professionals of the industry might indicate how magazine texts themselves are viewed as sites of multiple, uneven and sometimes conflictual practices. Ethnographic studies of readers too could benefit from situating the magazines more fully within the cultural circuit. This study has examined the ways in which the reader can become a space of projection for magazine professionals. An ethnographic analysis attentive to the entirety of the cultural circuit could examine how the same commercial maps of femininities are consumed by women readers. This would problematize and explore the ways in which discourses of commercial femininity are employed, manipulated, capitalized upon and/or played out by their consumers.

Access to the culture industries may be a problem for future feminist academic research in this field. However, the methodological approach of this study has also been intended to offer a starting point for research into new and emergent culture industries more generally. While the main focus of this book has been on the distinctiveness of the women's magazine industry in late twentieth-century Britain, I have also been attentive to the ways in which developments in this industry interacted with the practices of other culture industries, such as fashion journalism and creative advertising. I have, for instance, considered the ways in which the women's magazine industry and the advertising profession both shifted towards multiskilled, flexible and increasingly freelance workforces during this period. I have also detailed the ways in which both businesses attempted to embody the concept of 'lifestyle' within their organizational cultures as well as in their specific products. Comparative analyses of other British culture industries of this period – for example, television or popular music – might reveal similar patterns of transformation. This would facilitate a more extensive understanding of trajectories of change within the culture industries. This broader model of shifts in the economic organization of business practice is likely to highlight ways in which the development of women's magazines during the 1980s and 1990s was both distinctive and unique. As well as capturing elements of particularity, a broader analysis of patterns of 'cultural economy' will provide for a more thorough-going understanding of the nature of the culture industries in contemporary society. Issues of business practice, knowledge and organization will therefore be recognized as important for understandings of culture, as well as for studies of the economy.

NOTES

1 UNDERSTANDING WOMEN'S MAGAZINES

1 Winship also employs this method in other articles published during this period (see Winship, 1978; 1980; 1981; 1983a; 1983b; and 1984). She makes a notable shift in her work on *Best* magazine (Winship, 1991), where she engages with approaches that envisage the magazine reader as 'active in meaning-making'. Nevertheless, while she acknowledges that conceptions of the active reader may be appropriate for analyses of magazine reading during the 1980s (a period that witnessed a disruption of dominant ideologies of femininity), she contends that during the 1950s 'available discourse registers did not offer alternative ideologies' to their readers that would allow such reflexivity (Winship, 1991: 138).

2 My survey does not include the extensive literature that focuses specifically on magazines aimed at teenage girls and young women. There exist, however, a number of particularly interesting textual analyses of these titles, which argue that such magazines can operate as counter-hegemonic spaces. See Budgeon and Currie (1995); Currie (1999); McRobbie (1991a; 1991b; 1996a); and Winship (1985).

3 Prior to the publication of *Women's Worlds* (Ballaster *et al.*, 1991), Elizabeth Frazer (1987) conducted one of the first reader-centred studies, focusing on young women reading the teenage publication, *Jackie*.

4 For an interesting critique of Hermes's findings see Ulla Outtrup and Birgitte Ramsø Thomsen's unpublished (1994) study of women reading *Cosmopolitan*.

5 It is difficult to say exactly why production-oriented research seems to be absent from feminist studies of women's magazines. Angela McRobbie (1997: 173) suggests that practical factors may be significant. She argues that issues of textuality and representation (and their associated methods of structuralist and poststructuralist analysis) have been relatively easily transferable within an increasingly international academic feminist context. In contrast, the 'transferability' of discussions of the specificities of institutional context, policy, employment practice and discrimination has been more problematic. Structuralism and poststructuralism, therefore, 'travelled further and faster than their culturalist counterparts' which were more concerned with the specificities of localized situations (McRobbie, 1997: 173).

6 For a more detailed consideration of these debates on research method, see McRobbie's (1996b) discussion of the philosophical underpinnings of cultural studies research.

7 For valuable studies of media organizations and practices see Cottle (1993; 1995); Elliott (1972); Ericson *et al.* (1987); Fishman (1980); Hetherington (1985); Schudson (1991); Shoemaker and Reese (1991); Sigal (1973); Tuchman (1978); and Tunstall (1964; 1971; 1983; 1993).

8 Participant observation is the principal method employed in ethnographic study. Although the terms 'ethnography' and 'participant observation' are often used interchangeably, ethnography also makes use of other relevant methods (for example, 'life-histories') for in-depth studies of human groups and societies. For further discussion see Cottle (1995).

9 Discussion of similar problems encountered in researching media organizations and practices can be found in Altheide (1976: 200); Giddens (1989: 669); and Schlesinger (1989: 347).

2 POST-FORDISM, POST-FEMINISM AND THE 'NEW WOMAN' IN LATE TWENTIETH-CENTURY BRITAIN

1 For a more detailed discussion of these deficiencies in narratives of post-Fordist change, see McDowell (1992: 181–92).

2 For various accounts of strategies that resolved the 'crisis' of Fordism, see Aglietta (1979); Hirst and Zeitlin (1997); Lash and Urry (1987); Lipietz (1987); Murray (1989); and Piore and Sabel (1986).

3 Amin (1994a: 18) has argued that there is a third key approach, that of *'après-fordisme'* This 'after-Fordist' stance argues that post-Fordism presents an over-optimistic interpretation of economic change. Instead, *'après-fordisme'* stresses the negative consequences of the new economic era.

4 For an account of the controversies about British industrial decline in this period see Lowe (1984).

5 McDowell (1992: 182) cites Piore and Sabel (1984) as key proponents of this 'emancipatory' thesis.

6 According to Walby (1997: 67), over half of women workers are to be found in the temporary, part-time workforce compared to only a quarter of working men.

7 Macdonald is one of many commentators who have attacked the consumer and lifestyle culture of this period for its appropriation of 'quasi-feminist' ideas. See also Cameron (2000); Talbot (2000); and Winship (2000).

8 Cronin (2000) argues that women's participation in consumerism is not simply a matter of being able (or unable) to purchase consumer products. She argues that consumer citizenship also involves the recognition by advertisers and marketers of the individual as a 'consumer'. Here, Cronin observes the ways in which advertising and marketing industries operate by targeting and generating financially viable segmented market groups. Through their campaigns, she argues, they generate imaginary subject positions that can be occupied by their potential consumers. The 'masculine' work environment of the advertising industry, however, means that not only do advertisements exclude a large number of subject positions through their visual imagery, but that they also address women in ways that subordinate women (see Cronin, 2000).

9 For another popular 'post-feminist' critique of the beauty myth see Orbach (1993).

3 THE EMPIRES STRIKE BACK: FROM FORDISM TO POST-FORDISM IN THE BRITISH MAGAZINE INDUSTRY

1 An account of the development of the internal organization of the British newspaper industry can be found in Bromley (1996: 235–6).

2 During the 1970s, some British magazine publishers even turned to printers on the continent. This was due to the declining British availability of photogravure printing, then the major type of printing used for colour magazines.

3 Driver and Gillespie (1993a: 58) observe that in the early 1990s London accounted for between 40 per cent and 60 per cent of sales for British style monthlies such as *The Face* and *i-D*. For trade weeklies like *Campaign* the figures were even higher, London accounting for 80 per cent of sales.

4 As Johnson and Prijatel (1998: 5–7) explain, the principle of 'niche' magazine publishing is to aim a title at a market segment fairly well defined in terms of its demographics and 'lifestyle orientation'. As such, the magazine editorial attempts to correspond closely with the perceived values, attitudes and tastes of the target readership.

5 IPC remained the leading magazine publisher in Britain throughout the 1980s and 1990s, though the 1990s saw a steady decline in the circulation of the company's magazines, the slide averaging 10 per cent between 1996 and 1998. Against this backdrop, IPC underwent significant internal reorganization. In 1998, a management buyout (supported by the private equity group, Cinven) put IPC in debt and plans for a stock market flotation – later abandoned in preference of a trade sale of the company – prompted a phase of internal restructuring, with the creation of a new set of five subsidiary companies focused on specific market segments. IPC's radical restructuring was designed to halt the circulation slide, build advertising revenues and strengthen the company's magazine portfolio (Max-Lino and Poissonnier, 1999: 198).

6 In 1999 EMAP also acquired Wagadon, a British publisher specializing in the men's fashion market, after disagreements about Wagadon's future prompted Condé Nast to sell their 40 per cent interest in the company (Crawford, 1999). Wagadon's titles were thought to complement EMAP's consumer magazine portfolio, but the purchase also facilitated EMAP's access to overseas markets where Wagadon's titles such as *The Face* were notably successful (Max-Lino and Poissonnier, 1999: 172).

7 More generally, Murray (1989) has argued that the computerization of retailing represented the catalyst for the rise of post-Fordist production processes and business structures in Britain. From the 1950s, British retailers' adoption of computer technology allowed a more effective co-ordination between demand forecasts and supply orders which, in turn, transformed the distribution system within manufacturing industries.

8 Bromley (1996) provides an interesting account of similar shifts in the newspaper industry during the same period. Unlike magazine journalists, Bromley notes that news journalists offered more resistance to changes in their working conditions, possibly as a result of their high investment in an ethos of 'professionalism' that placed a premium on such qualities as 'objectivity' and 'public service'.

4 WHO'S THAT GIRL?: ADVERTISING, MARKET RESEARCH AND THE FEMALE CONSUMER IN THE 1980S

1 In 1958, an article in *The Director* estimated that no fewer than 43 per cent of the twenty million women in Britain read *Woman* magazine. Given the scale of these figures, businesses scrambled into the medium, women's magazines soon accounting for a substantial share of the £27 million annual expenditure on magazine advertising (Elliott, 1962: 210).

2 The arguments forwarded by Theodore Levitt in his article 'The globalization of marketing' were especially influential in this respect. See Levitt (1988: 92–102).

3 There also exist numerous other official systems of socio-economic classification – for example, the Official Classification of Occupations; the General Household Survey; the National Food Survey of the Ministry of Agriculture, Fisheries, and

Food; the Family Expenditure Survey of the Department of Employment; and EC Socio-Economic Classifications (see Chisnall, 1992: 84–9).

4 For more detailed accounts of the rise of qualitative market research in the UK during the 1970s see May (1978), Szybillo (1976) and Wells (1974).

5 The shift in media buying practices was related to a breakdown of the professional 'recognition' system in British advertising during the early 1970s as a consequence of growing competition from 'media independents'. See Brierley (1995: 66) and Nevett (1982: 196).

6 Edwards (1997), Mort (1996) and Nixon (1996) all offer accounts of the emergence of new representations of masculinity within the commercial cultures of 1980s Britain.

7 Women between the ages of twenty-five and forty-four (the major childbearing group) increased their economic activity by 13.5 per cent between 1971 and 1984. Averaged across all age groups, however, the increase was only 5.1 per cent. See Bradley (1992: 36).

5 SERIOUSLY GLAMOROUS OR GLAMOROUSLY SERIOUS?: WORKING OUT THE 'WORKING WOMAN'

1 The data produced by the NRS, however, does not satisfy all market researchers, and many are critical of its findings because socio-economic groups defined by the head of household are 'imperfect measures of the propensity of consumers to purchase certain products' (Chisnall, 1992: 220). A 1987 report from the Technical and Development Committee of the Market Research Society (MRS), for example, maintained that the NRS's classification of respondents by the occupation of the head of household was fundamentally flawed. The MRS report argued that those people categorized by someone else's occupation (for example, women) often demonstrated their annoyance about this by providing the NRS with inaccurate responses (Chisnall, 1992: 222). The MRS also observed that students and the short-term unemployed tended to be relegated by the NRS to socio-economic category E, although their consumption patterns were likely to be significantly different from other members of this group. Moreover, new techno-logical industries had also emerged, and many new occupations were increasingly difficult to classify in simple A to E terms. All of these factors, the Market Research Society concluded, made NRS data highly unreliable.

2 Studies carried out on behalf of publishing groups during the 1980s include Magazine Marketplace Group (1984, 1985, 1986). Other media monitoring services included MEAL (Media Expenditure Analysis Limited), Magazine Monitor/Brand Monitor, IMS MediaLog, The Media Register, The Auditor, and Media Audits (cited in Barrell and Braithwaite, 1988: 119–20).

3 Bill Osgerby (2001) has observed that whilst this discriminating approach to advertising may have been new to the UK magazine industry, Hugh Heffner's American men's magazine, *Playboy*, had taken a highly selective approach to advertising as early as the 1950s and 1960s.

4 For an interesting account of *Honey*'s original launch see Janice Winship (1987: 42–5).

5 Perfect-bound magazines have a book-like binding. The edges of the pages are glued and a cover is attached. The title of the magazine, the issue number, etc., can be printed on the spine. It is usually a more expensive method of binding than the saddle-stitched method, which holds the magazine together with staples in the middle (see Johnson and Prijatel, 1998: 261–3).

6 Audrey Slaughter was already well known in the industry for her role as editor on

magazines for the 'independent woman', having been a successful editor of *Honey* until the late 1960s (Winship, 1987: 62).

6 'WHAT WOMEN WANT UNDER THE COVERS': NEW MARKETS AND THE 'NEW WOMAN' IN THE 1980S

1 Hachette had prior experience of working in partnership with News International, using them to safeguard the entry of *Elle* into the American magazine market in 1983 (Hafstrand, 1995: 3; Usherwood, 1997: 181).

2 Murdoch soon sold half of his stake in *Elle* to Hachette, and subsequently both his share in *Elle* and *New Woman* to EMAP. EMAP later entered discussions with Hachette, and purchased *Elle* from them in full (Braithwaite, 1994: 148).

3 An advertorial is a style of advertising section that has proliferated in magazine publishing since the 1980s. Products 'borrow' the credibility of the magazine title by presenting their advertising message in a style that closely reflects the title's editorial. Fearing that if 'enough advertisers are allowed to borrow the credibility of the medium, then the medium won't have the credibility to borrow', the Periodical Publishers Association (PPA) drew up guidelines in 1992 for this area, to ensure that an advertorial 'free-for-all' did not develop (Dear, 1992: 7).

4 By early 1993, however, *Marie Claire* was more of a threat to *Cosmopolitan*, demonstrating a 40 per cent year-on-year increase in sales *(Marketing*, 1993: viii).

5 For a more detailed analysis of the response to *Company* during this period see Gough-Yates (2000).

7 '*MARIE CLAIRE – C'EST MOI!*': MAGAZINE EDITORS, CULTURAL INTERMEDIARIES AND THE 'NEW MIDDLE CLASS'

1 Indeed, many industry commentators later used Bailey's unorthodox demeanour as a means of ridicule, likening her to 'Jimmy Nail in a fright wig'! (Feay, 1996). (Jimmy Nail was a popular actor of the 1980s, coming to prominence in the BBC-TV series *Auf Wiedersehen Pet* as Oz, a builder from Newcastle-upon-Tyne. By the mid-1980s he was also a well-known solo vocalist, with a number of hit singles entering the British pop charts.)

2 The term 'cultural intermediaries' was introduced to international sociological debate by Bourdieu in *Distinction* (1984: 359). Other sociologists have also argued for the growth of similar segments in the contemporary middle class. Scott Lash and John Urry (1994: 222), for example, suggest that the 'advanced-services middle class' are a 'critical mass' in society, operating both as 'symbol-processing producers and as consumers of processed symbols'. Kristin Ross (1995) has also observed the presence of the *jeune cadre*, who achieved social prominence in France from the 1960s onwards. Describing them as 'ideologically homeless', Ross draws a picture of a social group with 'expansionist ideas, new attitudes towards consumption, and a universal belief in the desirability of growth' (Ross, 1995: 171).

3 David Hesmondhalgh (2002: 54) has argued that Mike Featherstone's (1991) use of the term 'cultural intermediaries' is based upon a misunderstanding of Bourdieu (1984). Hesmondhalgh argues that Bourdieu intended the term 'cultural intermediary' to describe a particular 'new petite bourgeois' profession of cultural commentary in the media. Featherstone, however, equates the entire new petit bourgeoisie with the cultural intermediaries, when they are only a small subset of that class. Indeed, Hesmondhalgh argues, subsequent writers have

inherited this confusion, including Sean Nixon (1997a). Hesmondhalgh (2002: 53) ultimately suggests that the term 'cultural intermediaries' has become confusing because of its wide range of uses, and prefers to replace it with 'creative managers' and/or 'creative practitioners'. Whilst I accept Hesmondhalgh's observations, I have continued to use the term 'cultural intermediaries' as it is defined and expanded upon by Featherstone and Nixon, which acknowledges the impact of their work on this study. I am therefore using the term to refer generally to those media practitioners who produce symbols and texts – and more loosely than Bourdieu originally intended.

4 Whilst such criticisms of Bourdieu's work are common, Leslie McCall (1992) and Toril Moi (1991) have both maintained that his ideas have useful applicability for feminist cultural and social analysis.

5 What is also interesting in this respect are McDowell's discussions with American women working for both American and British financiers during this period. These interviews indicate that a distinctly different work ethos existed amongst American financiers in the 1980s, and that American women financiers got by through being 'really butch, really pushy and aggressive, and that sort of thing' (quoted in McDowell, 1997: 121). A British employee of a US bank also stressed the differences in workplace culture, describing her bank as 'terribly Darwinian . . . chuck people in and see who comes out on top' (McDowell, 1997: 120). Such interviews do not tell us anything about the consumer practices of these women, or whether they read women's magazines. They do suggest, however, why a popular magazine formula based on women's attitudes to work (e.g. *Working Woman*) would not translate easily for British women laying claim to a 'new middle-class' work-as-'fun' ethic and a 'feminine' professional identity.

8 DESPERATELY TWEAKING SUSAN: THE BUSINESS OF WOMEN'S MAGAZINES IN THE 1990S

1 Janice Winship (2000) offers an interesting discussion of the relationships between feminist politics and the culture of celebrity in her work on feminism and billboard advertising in the 1990s.

2 Cultural commentator Judith Williamson (1991: 29) has argued that *Hello!*'s appeal for readers resides not just in the celebrity system, but also in the way in which the magazine is predicated on the idea that meaning resides in the way things – particularly people – look. *Hello!*'s driving logic is for revelation, promising to provide readers with snapshot glimpses of 'the reality' of the emotional and personal lives of the celebrity. This provides *Hello!* with an almost inexplicable fascination for readers, Williamson asserts, as they scour the pages for a glimmer of the 'spirit' of the individual, a chink in the facade of the celebrity's public face (Williamson, 1991: 29).

3 See Gough-Yates (2000) for a more detailed analysis of this.

4 See Janice Winship (2000) and Myra Macdonald (1995) for analyses of such advertising campaigns in the context of 1990s femininities.

5 By 1999, the men's lifestyle magazine sector was estimated to have a £61 million retail sales value close to that of the women's lifestyle sector (Seymour Marketing, 2000b: 6).

6 *Minx* reached the height of controversy after it published an article on drugs in the January 1999 issue that recommended to readers an Ecstasy-type narcotic, BOD, available for purchase over the Internet. *Minx* described BOD as 'hip', suggesting that readers 'check it out' for its offer of eight to sixteen hours of 'inner strength, good humour and contentedness' (*Minx*, January 1999). Although the magazine

pointed out the side effects of the drug, as well as its illegality, the *Daily Telegraph* was (characteristically) appalled, obtaining a condemnatory statement about the magazine from Keith Hallawell, Britain's anti-drugs co-ordinator. *Minx* staff responded fierily that the newspaper had taken the article out of context and out of all proportion. The article on drugs was meant to be 'tongue in cheek', a fact the broadsheet journalists had failed to notice: 'Our readers are adults who can make up their own minds', a spokesperson for *Minx* announced. 'If they want to take drugs they will' (quoted in Pook, 1999: 3).

7 Jackson *et al.* (2001: 59–62) offer an interesting account of the relationships between commercial imperatives and editorial freedoms in the British men's magazine industry of this period.

8 McRobbie (1996a) and Whelehan (2000) strongly disagree about whether these sexualized feminine scripts are productive for feminist politics. Whelehan (2000: 37–57) deplores the way in which young women 'remain blissfully unaware of the social and political critiques offered by second wave feminism' arguing that symbols of female empowerment in contemporary society are 'pure patriarchal recuperation'. McRobbie, however, is more positive, suggesting that such a view ignores the 'political effectivity of young women' and that older generation feminists need to encourage rather than ridicule young women who attempt to 'develop their own language for dealing with sexual inequality' (McRobbie, 1996a: 160).

9 A similar conclusion is reached about the so-called 'crisis of masculinity' in Jackson *et al.*'s (2001) account of men's magazines of this era.

10 *Frank*'s advertising campaign focused around a ninety-six-sheet poster distributed worldwide, featuring a still of a model's legs from a fashion shoot, accompanied by the slogan: '*Frank*. Another women's magazine. The last thing you need' (*Campaign*, 1997a: 55).

CONCLUSIONS

1 See Alasuutari for an in-depth discussion of the relationships between research data and narrativity (1995: 70–84).

BIBLIOGRAPHY

Adams, C. and Laurikietis, R. 1977. *The Gender Trap: Messages and Images*, London: Virago.

Adorno, T. and Horkheimer, M. 1947. 'The culture industry: enlightenment as mass deception', from *Dialectic of Enlightenment* [1947], reprinted in During 1993.

Aglietta, M. 1979. *A Theory of Capitalist Regulation: The US Experience*, London: Verso.

Alasuutari, P. 1995. *Researching Culture: Qualitative Method and Cultural Studies*, London: Sage.

Allen, D., Rush, R.R. and Kaufman, S. J., eds, 1996. *Women Transforming Communications: Global Intersections*, London: Sage.

Allen, J. 1992. 'Post-industrialism and post-Fordism', in Hall, Held and McGrew 1992.

Almeida, J. 1998. 'Media choice: *Red* magazine', *Marketing*, 22 January, 61.

Altheide, D. L. 1976. *Creating Reality – How TV News Distorts Events*, Thousand Oaks, CA: Sage.

Althusser, L. 1970. 'Ideology and ideological state apparatuses: notes towards an investigation', in Beechey and Donald 1985.

Amin, A. 1994a. 'Models, fantasies and phantoms of transition', in Amin 1994b.

Amin, A., ed., 1994b. *Post-Fordism: A Reader*, Oxford: Blackwell.

Anderson, B., ed., 1976. *Advances in Consumer Research*, vol. 3, 447–8.

Anderson, D. and Mosbacher, M., eds, 1997. *The British Woman Today: A Qualitative Survey of the Images in Women's Magazines*, London: The Social Affairs Unit.

Anderson, M., Bechofer, F. and Gershuny, J., eds, 1994. *The Social and Political Economy of the Household*, Oxford: Oxford University Press.

Andrews, M. and Talbot, M., eds, 2000. *All the World and Her Husband: Women in Twentieth-Century Consumer Culture*, London: Cassell.

Arlidge, J. 2000. 'Glossies go to war as editors launch battle for women', *Observer*, 12 November.

Armstrong, S. 1998. 'Bucking the women's trend', *PR Week*, 5 June.

Atkinson, L. 1989. 'Cosmopolitan Mr Kippin', *Media Week*, 1 September, 20.

Audit Bureau of Circulations 1999. 'ABC and the consumer press: an overview', http://www.abc.org.uk/, accessed 1999.

Autry, J. A. 1998. 'The evolving magazine: influence of celebrity journalism', in Johnson and Prijatel, 1998.

Avery, R. K. and Eason, D., eds, 1991. *Critical Perspectives on Media and Society*, New York: Guilford Press.

Bagguley, P. 1991. 'Post-Fordism and enterprise culture', in Keat and Abercrombie 1991.

Baker, M. J. 1984. *Macmillan Dictionary of Marketing and Advertising*, London and Basingstoke: Macmillan Press.

Ballaster, R., Beetham, M., Frazer, E. and Hebron, S. 1991. *Women's Worlds: Ideology, Femininity, and the Women's Magazine*, London: Macmillan.

Barrell, J. and Braithwaite, B. 1988. *The Business of Women's Magazines: The Agonies and Ecstasies*, London: Associated Business Press.

Baxter, M. 1990. *Women in Advertising: Findings and Recommendations of a Study Commissioned by the Institute of Practitioners in Advertising*, London: Institute of Practitioners in Advertising.

BCCCS Women's Studies Group, eds, 1978. *Women Take Issue*, London: Hutchinson.

Beechey, V. 1982. 'The sexual division of labour and the labour process: a critical assessment of Braverman', in Wood 1982.

Beechey, V. and Donald, J., eds, 1985. *Subjectivity and Social Relations*, Milton Keynes: The Open University.

Beenstock, S. 1998. 'Campaigns: making the most of middle youth: media launch', *PR Week*, 6 February.

Benton, R. 1987. 'Work, consumption, and the joyless consumer', in Firat, Dholakia and Bagozzi 1987.

Berry, D., ed., 2000. *Ethics and Media Culture: Practices and Representations*, Oxford: Focal Press.

Blackett, D. 1990. 'So you're barcoded? – that's just the starting point', *Magazine News*, April, 13.

Bland, H. 1989. 'Distributors – the vital link with the readers', *Magazine News*, October, 19.

Blix, J. 1992. 'A place to resist: reevaluating women's magazines', *Journal of Communication Inquiry*, vol. 16, no. 1, Winter, 56–71.

Bocock, R. 1992. 'Consumption and lifestyles', in Bocock and Thompson 1992.

Bocock, R. 1993. *Consumption*, London: Routledge.

Bocock, R. and Thompson, K., eds, 1992. *Social and Cultural Forms of Modernity*, Cambridge/Milton Keynes: Polity Press/The Open University.

Bouchard, D., ed., 1977. *Language, Counter-Memory, Practice: Selected Essays and Interviews*, trans. Bouchard, D. and Simon, S., Oxford: Blackwell.

Bourdieu, P. 1984 [1979]. *Distinction: A Social Critique of the Judgement of Taste*, trans. Nice, R., London: Routledge.

Boyd-Barrett, O. 1995. 'The analysis of media occupations and professionals', in Boyd-Barrett and Newbold 1995.

Boyd-Barrett, O. and Newbold, C., eds, 1995. *Approaches to Media: A Reader*, London: Arnold.

Bradley, H. 1992. 'Changing social divisions: class, gender and race', in Bocock and Thompson 1992.

Braithwaite, B. 1989. 'The eagle has landed', *Media Week*, 8 December, 28–9.

Braithwaite, B. 1994. *Women's Magazines: The First 300 Years*, London: Peter Owen.

Braithwaite, B. 1998. 'Magazines: the bulging bookstalls', in Briggs and Cobley 1998.

Brampton, S. and Parsons, T. 1985. 'Stamp out Sloanes', *Elle*, November, 14–16.

Brierley, S. 1995. *The Advertising Handbook*, London: Routledge.

Briggs, A. and Cobley, P. 1998. *The Media: An Introduction*, Harlow: Longman.

Bromley, M. 1996. 'Markets, management and the media', in CMCR 1996a.

Brooks, A. 1997. *Postfeminisms: Feminism, Cultural Theory and Cultural Forms*, London: Routledge.

Brooks, T. 1983. 'Magazines set to halt sales slide', *Campaign*, 26 August.

Brooks, T. 1986. '*Elle* storms the market', *Media Week*, 29 August, 6.

Brooks, T. 1988. 'The survival of the fittest', *Media Week*, 8 April, 29–30.

Brown, M. 1998. '*Red*: or will it be unread?', *The Times*, 16 January, 65.

Budgeon, S. and Currie, Dawn H. 1995. 'From feminism to postfeminism: women's liberation in fashion magazines', *Women's Studies International Forum*, vol. 18, no. 2, 173–86.

Bunting, H. 1997. *European Consumer Magazine Publishing: Facing the Electronic Challenge*, London: *Financial Times* Management Report.

Burchill, J. 1986. 'Why "housewife" is now a dirty word in adland', *Campaign*, 16 May, 40–1.

Butler, J. 1993. *Bodies that Matter*, London: Routledge.

Cameron, D. 2000. *Good to Talk? Living and Working in a Communication Culture*, London: Sage.

Campaign 1983a. 'Axe falls on *Honey* editor as sales slide', *Campaign*, 16 September.

Campaign 1983b. 'IPC out to lure big spenders away from TV', *Campaign*, 5 August.

Campaign 1983c. 'New title launch hit as backer pulls out', *Campaign*, 12 August, 7.

Campaign 1984. 'IPC breakaway signs two for publishing role', *Campaign*, 1 June.

Campaign 1986a. 'Cadbury signs editor for *Working Woman*', *Campaign*, 23 May, 6.

Campaign 1986b. 'Cadbury pulls out of *Working Woman* rescue', *Campaign*, 5 September, 6.

Campaign 1987a. '*Cosmopolitan* set on expansion trail', *Campaign*, 16 October, 29.

Campaign 1987b. 'Jenner set to spearhead new *She* look', *Campaign*, 20 February, 2.

Campaign 1987c. 'Staff join creditors as *Working Woman* folds', *Campaign*, 9 January, 6.

Campaign 1988a. '*Company* aims at 200,000 circulation', *Campaign*, 12 February, 24.

Campaign 1988b. '*Cosmo* slams *S. Times* "hype"', *Campaign*, 15 July, 21.

Campaign 1988c. '*New Woman* leads among summer titles', *Campaign*, 14 October, 26.

Campaign 1988d. 'UK set for Murdoch monthly', *Campaign*, 15 January, 20.

Campaign 1989. '*New Woman* and *Prima* sales cheer glum publishers', *Campaign*, 21 April, 25.

Campaign 1990. 'Nat Mags' first TV launch for revamped *She*', *Campaign*, 19 January, 20.

Campaign 1996. 'Emap Elan names *New Woman*'s boss as *Minx* publisher', *Campaign*, 23 August, 32.

Campaign 1997a. 'Wagadon uses legs theme in poster for first issue of *Frank*', 5 September, 55.

Campaign 1997b. 'Emap Elan unveils *Red* in bid to shake up women's market', 7 November, 71.

Campbell-Lyons, P. 1983. 'Why the women's press fails,' *Campaign*, 28 January, 35.

Carr, J., Prescott, M. and Turner, J. 1983. *The UK Market for Women's Monthly*

Magazines, Centre for Business Research in Association with Manchester Business School: University of Manchester, March.

Central Statistical Office 1995. *Social Trends*, London: HMSO.

Chisnall, P. 1992. *Marketing Research*, 4th edn, Maidenhead: McGraw-Hill.

CMCR 1995. 'Mass Communication Research Methods', MA in Mass Communications, Leicester: Leicester University.

CMCR 1996a. 'Module Seven', MA in Mass Communications, Unit 41, Leicester: Leicester University.

CMCR 1996b. 'Module Five', MA in Mass Communications, Unit 26b, Leicester: Leicester University.

CMCR 1997. 'Module Six', MA in Mass Communications, Unit 41, Leicester: Leicester University.

Coles, J. 1995. 'Mistress of the universe', *Guardian*, 31 July, 14.

Colwell, J. 1990. 'Qualitative market research: a conceptual analysis and review of practitioner criteria', *Journal of the Market Research Society*, vol. 32, no.1, January, 13–36.

Cook, R. 1997. 'Sector profiles', *Campaign*, 11 April, Section 11.

Cook, S. 1992. 'Sweet sell of sexcess', *Guardian*, 27 June, 27.

Cooper, A. 1984. '*Working Woman* meets a cool reception among the ABs', *Campaign*, 21 September, 15.

Cottle, S. 1993. 'Behind the headlines: the sociology of news', in O'Donnell 1993.

Cottle, S. 1995. 'Participant observation: researching news production', in CMCR 1995.

Cova, B., Rad-Serecht, F. and Weil, M. 1993. '*Elle* goes European – the internationalization of *Elle* magazine', in Halliburton and Hünerberg 1993.

Coyle, F. J. 1991. 'Wholesalers' procedure has been "revolutionised"', *Magazine News: Periodicals Barcoding Association Special Supplement*, January, iii.

Craig, O. 1998. 'Men on top', *Sunday Telegraph*, 7 June, 26.

Craik, L. 2000. 'Back to the future', *Guardian*, 28 April, 10.

Crawford, A. 1999. 'Emap buys *Face* publisher Wagadon', *Marketing*, 8 July.

Creedon, P. J., ed., 1993. *Women in Mass Communication*, London: Sage.

Cronin, A. M. 2000. *Advertising and Consumer Citizenship: Gender, Images and Rights*, London: Routledge.

Cuff, E. C. and Payne, G. C. F., eds, 1981. *Perspectives in Sociology*, London: George Allen and Unwin.

Cullen, T. 1984. 'The medium that took over from television?', *Campaign*, 30 March, 63–4.

Cumberpatch, F. 1988a. 'The establishment fights back', *Media Week*, 11 November, 25–9.

Cumberpatch, F. 1988b. '*Marie Claire* – c'est moi!', *Media Week*, 5 August, 22–3.

Curran, J. and Seaton, J. 1991. *Power without Responsibility: The Press and Broadcasting in Britain*, 4th edn, London: Routledge.

Curran, J., Morley, D. and Walkerdine, V., eds, 1996. *Cultural Studies and Communications*, London: Arnold.

Currie, D. 1983. 'World capitalism in recession', in Hall and Jacques 1983.

Currie, D. H. 1999. *Girl Talk: Adolescent Magazines and their Readers*, Toronto: University of Toronto Press.

D'Arcy, K. 1982. 'Making a case for the press', *Marketing*, 2 December, 39–42.

Davie, L. 1988. 'The new girls' networks', *Media Week*, 3 June, 22.

Davis, A. 1995. *Magazine Journalism Today*, Oxford: Focal Press.

Dear, P. 1992. 'Magazines' credibility', *Magazine News*, September, 7.

Delamont, S. 2001. *Changing Women, Unchanged Men? Sociological Perspectives on Gender in a Post-Industrial Society*, Buckingham: The Open University.

Diamond, J. 1990. 'The world according to *Cosmo*', *Sunday Times*, 4 March.

Dichter, E. 1960. *The Strategy of Desire*, London and New York: Boardman and Company.

Dignam, B. 1989. 'Get barcoded by Christmas', *Magazine News Special Supplement*, 17 October, i.

Direct Marketing Association (US) 1997. *Trade Association Report; Time Series*, no. 305, 1 December, New York: Direct Marketing Association.

Driver, S. and Gillespie, A. 1992, 'The diffusion of digital technologies in magazine print publishing: organizational change and strategic choices', *Journal of Information Technology*, no. 7, 149–59.

Driver, S. and Gillespie, A. 1993a. 'Information and communication technologies and the geography of magazine print publishing', *Regional Studies*, vol. 27, no. 1, 53–64.

Driver, S. and Gillespie, A. 1993b. 'Structural change in the cultural industries: British magazine publishing in the 1980s', *Media, Culture and Society*, vol. 15, 183–201.

du Gay, P. 1996. *Consumption and Identity at Work*, London: Sage.

du Gay, P. 1997a. 'Organizing identity: making up people at work', in du Gay 1997b.

du Gay, P., ed., 1997b. *Production of Culture/Cultures of Production*, Milton Keynes/London: The Open University/Sage.

du Gay, P. and Pryke, M., eds, 2002. *Cultural Economy: Cultural Analysis and Commercial Life*, London: Sage.

Durden, J. 1988. '*New Woman*'s comfy old hat', *Media Week*, 22 July, 30.

Durham, G. 1996. 'The taming of the shrew: women's magazines and the regulation of desire', *Journal of Communication Inquiry*, vol. 20, no. 1, 19–31.

During, S. 1993. *The Cultural Studies Reader*, London: Routledge.

Edgell, S., Hetherington, K. and Warde, A., eds, 1996. *Consumption Matters: The Production and Experience of Consumption*, Oxford: Blackwell.

Edwards, M. 1986. 'What's so special about working women?', *Media Week*, 4 July, 17.

Edwards, T. 1997. *Men in the Mirror: Men's Fashion, Masculinity and Consumer Society*, London: Cassell.

Elliott, B. B. 1962. *A History of English Advertising*, London: Business Publications/Batsford.

Elliott, P. 1972. *The Making of a Television Series – A Case Study in the Production of Culture*, London: Constable.

Entwistle, J. 1997. '"Power dressing" and the construction of the career woman', in Nava, Blake, MacRury and Richards 1997.

Entwistle, J. 2000. *The Fashioned Body: Fashion, Dress and Modern Social Theory*, Cambridge: Polity Press.

Ericson, R. V., Baraneck, P., and Chan, J. B. L. 1987. *Visualizing Deviance*, Toronto: Toronto University Press.

Eyre, R. 1985. 'Ads that reach women', *Campaign*, 28 June, 37–41.

Faludi, S. 1992. *Backlash: The Undeclared War Against Women*, London: Chatto and Windus.

Featherstone, M. 1991. *Consumer Culture and Postmodernism*, London: Sage.

Feay, S. 1996. 'Profile: Glenda Bailey', *Independent on Sunday*, 21 January.

Ferber, R., ed., 1974. *Handbook of Marketing Research*, New York: McGraw-Hill.

Ferguson, M. 1983. *Forever Feminine: Women's Magazines and the Cult of Femininity*, London: Heinemann.

Ferguson, M. and Golding, P., eds, 1997. *Cultural Studies in Question*, London: Sage.

Finley, M. 1983. 'Magazine marketing: why the in-fighting had to stop', *Campaign*, 31 March.

Firat, A. F., Dholakia, N. and Bagozzi, R. P., eds, 1987. *Philosophical and Radical Thought in Marketing*, Lexington, MA/Toronto: Lexington Books.

Fishman, J. 1980. *Manufacturing News*. Austin, TX: University of Texas Press.

Flack, J. 2000. 'Golden oldies', *Marketing Week*, 9 March, 50.

Formations Editorial Collective, eds, 1984. *Formations of Nation and People*, London: Routledge and Kegan Paul.

Foucault, M. 1977a. 'Nietzsche, genealogy, history', in Bouchard 1977.

Foucault, M. 1977b. *Discipline and Punish*, London: Tavistock.

Foucault, M. 1980. *The History of Sexuality,* vol. I: *An Introduction*, New York: Vintage Books.

Fraser, A. 1989. 'IPC Big Four face crisis as women's press explodes', *Campaign*, 24 February, 18–19.

Frazer, E. 1987. 'Teenage girls reading *Jackie*', *Media, Culture and Society*, vol. 9, 407–25.

Friedan, B. 1963. *The Feminine Mystique*, Harmondsworth: Penguin.

Gall, G. 1998. 'The changing relations of production: union derecognition in the UK magazine industry', *Industrial Relations Journal*, vol. 29, no. 2, June, 151–62.

Garratt, S. 1996. 'And not to be outdone, *Loaded*'s little sister takes a bow', *Guardian*, 9 September, T15.

Garrett, A. 1988. 'Arc assault chases PR on *New Woman*', *Campaign*, 15 July, 8.

Garth, A. 1988. 'Thomson sale gives Reed a Trojan horse for the supermarkets', *Campaign*, 18 March, 37.

Gaudoin, T. 1997. 'Nothing but sex, clothes and boyfriends?', *The Times*, 24 November.

Gerard, N. 1998. 'Thirty, love?', *Observer*, 18 January, 8.

Gerrie, A. 1987. 'How gossip and style have become buzzwords for today's glossy titles', *Campaign*, 24 April, 42–5.

Gershuny, J., Godwin, M. and Jones, S. 1994. 'The domestic labour revolution: a process of lagged adaptation', in Anderson, Bechofer and Gershuny 1994.

Giddens, A. 1989. *Sociology*. Cambridge: Polity Press.

Glazer, N. 1980. 'Overworking the working woman: the double day in a mass magazine', *Women's Studies International Quarterly*, vol. 3, no. 1, 79–93.

GLC Women's Committee 1984a. Free bulletin no. 16, May.

GLC Women's Committee 1984b. Free bulletin no. 17, June.

Goldthorpe, J., Lockwood, D., Bechhofer, F. and Platt, J. 1968–9. *The Affluent Worker: Industrial Attitudes and Behaviour*, Cambridge: Cambridge University Press.

Gough-Yates, A. 2000. '"Sweet sell of sexcess": the production of young women's magazines and readerships in the 1990s', in Berry 2000.

Gramsci, A. 1971. *Selection from Prison Notebooks*, trans. Quintin Hoare and Geoffrey Nowell-Smith, London: Lawrence and Wishart.

Greer, G. 1999. 'The whole woman: Greer on girl power', *Daily Telegraph*, 25 February, 25.

Griffiths, A. 1997. '"Serious maverick" aims to buck magazine trend', *Campaign*, 22 August, 62.

The Grocer 2000. 'BBC bites into women's mags with tempting *Eve*', *The Grocer*, 24 June, 24.

Hafstrand, H. 1995. 'Consumer magazines in transition: a study of approaches to internationalization', *Journal of Media Economics*, vol. 8, 1–12.

Hall, S. 1989. 'The meaning of New Times', in Hall and Jacques 1989.

Hall, S. and Jacques, M., eds, 1983. *The Politics of Thatcherism*, London: Lawrence and Wishart.

Hall, S. and Jacques, M., eds, 1989. *New Times: The Changing Face of Politics in the 1990s*, London: Lawrence and Wishart.

Hall, S., Held, D. and McGrew, T., eds, 1992. *Modernity and its Futures*, Milton Keynes/Cambridge: The Open University/Polity Press.

Halliburton, C. and Hünerberg, R. 1993. *European Marketing: Readings and Cases*, Wokingham: Addison-Wesley.

Hammersley, M. and Atkinson, P. 1995. *Ethnography: Principles in Practice*, London: Routledge.

Hast, A., ed., 1991. *International Directory of Company Histories*, vol. IV, Chicago, IL and London: St James Press.

Hayes, M. 1994. *The New Right in Britain: An Introduction to Theory and Practice*, London: Pluto Press.

Hebdige, D. 1988a. 'The bottom line on planet one: squaring up to *The Face*', in Hebdige 1988b.

Hebdige, D. 1988b. *Hiding in the Light: On Images and Things*, London: Comedia/Routledge.

Hebron, S. 1983. '*Jackie* and *Woman's Own*: ideological work and the social construction of gender identity', unpublished BA (Hons) dissertation, Department of Communication Studies: Sheffield City Polytechnic.

Hekman, S. 1990. *Gender and Knowledge: Elements of a Postmodern Feminism*, Polity Press: Cambridge.

Helland, K. 1996a. 'News production, news construction', in CMCR 1996a.

Helland, K. 1996b. 'Methodological approaches in the study of media organisations and production', in CMCR 1996b.

Hennion, A. and Méadel, C., 1993. 'In the laboratories of desire: advertising as an intermediary between products and consumers', *Reseaux: The French Journal of Communication*, vol. 1, no. 2, 171–92.

Hermes, J. 1993. 'Media, meaning and everyday life', *Cultural Studies*, vol. 7, no. 3, October, 493–506.

Hermes, J. 1995. *Reading Women's Magazines: An Analysis of Everyday Media Use*, Cambridge: Polity Press.

Hermes, J. 1997. 'The "ethnographic turn": the histories and politics of the new audience research', in CMCR 1997.

Hesmondhalgh, D. 2002. *The Cultural Industries*, London: Sage.

Hetherington, A. 1985. *News, Newspapers and Television*, London: Macmillan.

172

Hirsch, M. and Keller, E. F., eds, 1990. *Conflicts in Feminism*, London: Routledge.

Hirst, P. Q. and Zeitlin, J. 1997. *Governing Flexibility : Flexible Specialisation, Industrial Districts and Economic Governance,* London: Routledge.

Hobson, J. 1961. *The Selection of Advertising Media*, 4th edn, London: Business Publications Ltd.

Hodgson, J. 2000a. 'Dawn raid in Magland', *Guardian*, 24 July, 10.

Hodgson, J. 2000b. 'A missed opportunity', *Guardian*, 3 July, 4.

Hodson, V. 1985. 'The "lost" women of advertising', *Campaign*, 22 March, 77–9.

Holland, J., Ramazonoglu, C., Sharpe, S. and Thomson, R. 1998. *The Male in the Head*, London: Tufnell Press.

Hopkirk, J. 1988. 'Are you getting what you want from your women's magazine?', *Campaign*, 16 September, 22–4.

Howard, F. 1989. 'Moving in', *Campaign*, 25 August, 48–50.

Hughes, S. 1998. 'Pitch: an advertising agency and a PR firm fight it out to revive the ailing women's magazine *Frank*', *Independent*, 9 June, 19.

Hutton, W. 1996. 'The stakeholder society', in Marquand and Seldon 1996.

Illouz, E. 1991. 'Reason within passion: love in women's magazines', *Critical Studies in Mass Communication*, vol. 8, no. 3, September, 231–48.

Izatt, J. 1996. 'Profile: flirting with female experience', *PR Week*, 29 August, 29.

Jackson, P., Lowe, M., Miller, D. and Mort, F., eds, 2000. *Commercial Cultures: Economies, Practices, Spaces*, Oxford: Berg.

Jackson, P., Stevenson, N. and Brooks, K. 2001. *Making Sense of Men's Magazines*, Cambridge: Polity Press.

Jeal, N. 1992. 'Today we have naming of parts', *Observer*, 31 May, 52.

Jhally, S. 1990. *The Codes of Advertising: Fetishism and the Political Economy of Meaning in the Consumer Society*, London: Routledge.

Jivani, A. 1986. '*Working Woman*: on the brink of closure', *Campaign*, 14 March, 6.

Johnson, R. 1986/7 'What is cultural studies anyway?', *Social Text*, vol. 16, 38–40, reprinted in Storey 1997.

Johnson, S. 1993. 'Magazines: women's employment and status in the magazine industry', in Creedon 1993.

Johnson, S. and Prijatel, P. 1998. *The Magazine From Cover to Cover: Inside a Dynamic Industry*, Chicago, IL: NTC Publishing Group.

Jordan and Sons 1990. *Britain's Newspaper and Magazine Industry*, Bristol: Jordan and Sons.

Keat, R. and Abercrombie, N., eds, 1991. *Enterprise Culture*, London: Routledge.

Kepos, P., ed., 1993. *International Directory of Company Histories*, vol. 7, Detroit, MI: St James Press.

King, J. and Stott, M. 1977. *This is Your Life?,* London: Virago.

Kronlund, S. 1991. 'Hachette', in Hast 1991.

Labovitch, C. 1985. 'Selling mags to those who sell the mags', *Media Week*, 22 March, 26–8.

Lash, S. and Urry, J. 1987. *The End of Organized Capitalism*, Cambridge: Polity Press.

Lash, S. and Urry, J. 1994. *Economies of Signs and Space*, London: Sage.

Leadbeater, C. 1989. 'Power to the person', in Hall and Jacques 1989.

Lee, C. 1985. *Magazine Publishing in the UK*, London: *Financial Times* Business Information.

Leman, J. 1980. 'The advice of a real friend': codes of intimacy and oppression in

Women's Magazines 1937–1955', *Women's Studies International Quarterly*, vol. 3, no. 1, 63–78.

Levitt, T. 1988. 'The globalization of marketing', *Harvard Business Review* May/June, 92–102.

Lind, H. and Wisson, P. 1984. 'Housewives: the end of a myth', *Campaign*, 5 October, 71–3.

Lipietz, A. 1987. *Mirages and Miracles: The Crises of Global Fordism*, London: Verso.

Lockwood, D. 1966. *The Blackcoated Worker*, London: Unwin University Books.

Longhurst, B. and Savage, M. 1996. 'Social class, consumption and the influence of Bourdieu: some critical issues', in Edgell, Hetherington and Warde 1996.

Lowe, N. 1984. *Mastering Modern British History*, London: Macmillan.

Lury, C. 1996. *Consumer Culture*, Cambridge: Polity Press.

Lury, C. and Warde, A. 1997. 'Investments in the imaginary consumer: conjectures regarding power, knowledge and advertising', in Nava, Blake, MacRury and Richards 1997.

Macdonald, M. 1995. *Representing Women: Myths of Femininity in the Popular Media*, London: Arnold.

Mackenzie, S. 1998. 'It's a man's world', *Marketing Week*, 26 February, 59–60.

Magazine Marketplace Group 1984. *Media Involvement Study*, London: Magazine Marketplace Group.

Magazine Marketplace Group 1985. *Multiplying the Media Effect*. London: Magazine Marketplace Group.

Magazine Marketplace Group 1986. *The MPX Readership Study*, London: Magazine Marketplace Group.

Magazine News 1989a. 'The whoosh factor', *Magazine News*, August, 10.

Magazine News 1989b. 'Wholesale revolution by code', *Magazine News*, May, 9.

Marketing 1993. 'National Magazines follows a branded philosophy', *Marketing*, 25 February, viii.

Marketing 1996. 'Media watch: celebrity titles', *Marketing*, 12 December, 27.

Marketing Week 1995. 'Which route for women's mags?', *Marketing Week*, 25 August, 5.

Marketing Week 1997. 'Say Hello! to a successful mag', *Marketing Week*, 28 February, 36.

Marquand, D. and Seldon, A., eds, 1996. *The Ideas that Shaped Post-War Britain*, London: Fontana.

Marshall, P. D., 1997. *Celebrity and Power: Fame in Contemporary Culture*, Minneapolis, MN: University of Minnesota Press.

Marwick, A. 1990. *British Society Since 1945*, 2nd edn, Harmondsworth: Penguin.

Mason, T. 1983. 'The Divorcynics: women that the ad world forgot?', *Campaign*, 4 March, 40–4.

Max-Lino, R. and Poissonnier, C. 1999. *European Consumer Magazines*, Leatherhead, Surrey: Pira International.

May, J. 1978. 'Qualitative advertising research – a review of the role of the researcher', *Journal of the Market Research Society*, vol. 4, no. 20, 203–18.

Mayes, R. 1988. '*New Woman*: not new enough, say agencies', *Media Week*, 15 July, 2.

McCall, L. 1992. 'Does Gender *fit*? Bourdieu, feminism and conceptions of social order', *Theory and Society*, vol. 21, 837–67.

McCann, P. 1996. 'EMAP prepares launch for *Minx*', *Marketing Week*, 26 July, 15.

McCann, P. 1997. '"B" is for beautiful', *Independent*, 5 May, 5.

McCracken, E. 1993. *Decoding Women's Magazines: From* Mademoiselle *to* Ms., London: Macmillan.

McDonald, C. and King, S. 1996. *Sampling the Universe: The Growth, Development and Influence of Market Research in Britain Since 1945*, Henley on Thames: NTC/ The Market Research Society.

Macdonald, M. 1995. *Representing Women: Myths of Femininity in the Popular Media* London: Arnold.

McDowell, L. 1992. 'Gender divisions in a post-Fordist era: new contradictions or the same old story?', in McDowell and Pringle 1992.

McDowell, L. 1997. *Capital Culture: Gender at Work in the City*, Oxford: Blackwell.

McDowell, L. and Pringle, R. 1992. *Defining Women: Social Institutions and Gender Divisions*, Cambridge: Polity Press.

McKay, R. 1983a. 'IPC boosts spend in *Options* revival plan', *Campaign*, 19 August.

McKay, R. 1983b. '*Options*: The desperate search for a true identity', *Campaign*, 16 September.

McKay, R. 1984. 'Slaughter's plans to capture the working AB woman', *Campaign*, 16 March, 34.

McKay, R. 1987. 'Will Britain launch against the invaders?', *Media Week*, 8 May, 25.

McKee, V. 1987. 'UK's lesson in launches', *Campaign*, 23 October, 34–6.

McRobbie, A. 1991a. '*Jackie* magazine: romantic individualism and the teenage girl', in McRobbie 1991c.

McRobbie, A. 1991b. '*Jackie* and *Just Seventeen*: girls' comics and magazines in the 1980s', in McRobbie 1991c.

McRobbie, A. 1991c. *Feminism and Youth Culture: From* Jackie *to* Just Seventeen, London: Macmillan.

McRobbie, A. 1996a. '*More!*: new sexualities in girls' and women's magazines', in Curran, Morley and Walkerdine 1996.

McRobbie, A. 1996b. 'All the world's a stage, screen or magazine: when culture is the logic of late capitalism', *Media, Culture and Society*, vol. 18, no. 2, 335–42.

McRobbie, A. 1997. 'The Es and the anti-Es: new questions for feminism and cultural studies', in Ferguson and Golding 1997.

McRobbie, A. 1998. *British Fashion Design: Rag Trade or Image Industry?*, London: Routledge.

Media Week 1987. 'Miss *Cosmo*, Miss who?', *Media Week*, 9 October, 22–3.

Media Week 1988. '*Marie Claire* £2m push', *Media Week*, 18 August, 4.

Meffert, H. and Bolz, J. 1993. 'Standardization of marketing in Europe', in Halliburton and Hünerberg 1993.

Miller Freeman Information Services 1988. *Benn's Media*, Tonbridge, Kent: Miller Freeman PLC.

Mills, D. 1996. 'Often, advertising clutter looks, well, rather uncluttered', *Campaign*, 9 August, 2.

Mintel 1996. *Pre-Family Lifestyles*, London: Mintel.

Mistry, T. 1992. 'How we beat the slump', *Campaign*, 28 August, 1.

Moi, T. 1991. 'Appropriating Bourdieu: feminist theory and Pierre Bourdieu's sociology of culture', *New Literary History*, vol. 22, 1017–49.

Molloy, J. T. 1980. *Women: Dress for Success*, New York: Peter H. Wyden.

Mort, F. 1989. 'The politics of consumption', in Hall and Jacques 1989.

Mort, F. 1996. *Cultures of Consumption: Masculinities and Social Space in Late Twentieth-Century Britain*, London: Routledge.

Mort, F. 1997. 'Paths to mass consumption: Britain and the USA since 1945', in Nava, Blake, MacRury and Richards 1997.

Mort, F. 2000. 'The commercial domain: advertising and the cultural management of demand', in Jackson, Lowe, Miller and Mort 2000.

Mower, S. 1985. '*Elle* puts the faintheart out of fashion', *Guardian*, 7 October, 13.

Murphy, I. 1997. '*Frank*: an expert's view', *Campaign,* 19 September, 52.

Murray, G. 1997. 'Agonize, don't organize: a critique of postfeminism', *Current Sociology*, April, vol. 45, no. 2, 37–48.

Murray, R. 1989. 'Fordism and post-Fordism', in Hall and Jacques 1989.

Myers, K. 1986. *Understains: The Sense and Seduction of Advertising*, London: Comedia.

Nathanson, P. 1988a. 'August launch set for UK *Marie Claire*', *Campaign*, 19 February, 23.

Nathanson, P. 1988b. 'Relationships to be *New Woman*'s USP', *Campaign*, 29 April, 24.

Nava, M., Blake, A., MacRury, I. and Richards, B., eds, 1997. *Buy this Book: Studies in Advertising and Consumption*, London: Routledge.

Nevett, T. R. 1982. *Advertising in Britain: A History*, London: Heinemann.

New, K. 1983. 'The mystery of magazines', *Campaign*, 14 October.

Nicholls, J. and Moan, P. 1982. '"What offends one of us won't offend the next chap": the Advertising Standards Authority's line on sexism', in Rowe 1982.

Nixon, S. 1996. *Hard Looks: Masculinities, Spectatorship and Contemporary Consumption*, London: UCL Press.

Nixon, S. 1997a. 'Circulating culture', in du Gay 1997b.

Nixon, S. 1997b. 'Advertising executives as modern men: masculinity and the UK advertising industry in the 1980s', in Nava *et al.* 1997.

Nixon, S. 1999. 'The cult of creativity: gender and creative identities in the UK advertising industry', paper presented at the 'Living in a Material World' conference, Coventry University, June 25–7.

Norton, F. E. 1993. 'IPC Magazines Limited', in Kepos 1993.

NRS 1989. *National Readership Survey 1989: Tables Relating to January–December 1989*, London: JICNARS.

NRS 1992. *National Readership Survey: Latest Estimates of Average Issue Readership for Periods to December 1992*, London: JICNARS.

NRS 1997. *National Readership Survey: Latest Estimates of Average Issue Readership for Periods to December 1997*, London: JICNARS.

NRS 1999. *National Readership Survey: Latest Estimates of Average Issue Readership for Periods to December 1999*, London: JICNARS.

Nuttall, G. 1983. 'Keeping an eye on roles', *Marketing*, 4 August, 22–5.

O'Brien, L. 1996. 'New woman at the frontier of the sex war', *Independent*, 9 April, 16.

O'Donnell, M., ed., 1993. *New Introductory Readings in Sociology*. Walton-on-Thames: Thomas Nelson.

O'Kelly, L. 1991. 'Sexy but never salacious', *Independent*, 18 September.

O'Malley, D. 1987. 'How to captivate a modern woman', *Campaign*, 8 May, 54–5.

O'Reilly, D. 1983. 'The new faces of Eve', *Marketing*, 26 May, 29–38.

O'Rorke, I. 1997. 'Well *Red*', *Guardian*, 3 November, 4.

Oates, Caroline. 1999. 'Designing women's magazines', paper presented at the 'Design Culture' conference, Sheffield Hallam University and the European Academy of Design, 30 March–1 April.

Orbach, S. 1993. *Hunger Strike: The Anorexic's Struggle as Metaphor of our Age*, Harmondsworth: Penguin.

Osgerby, B. 2001. *Playboys in Paradise: Masculinity, Youth and Leisure-style in Modern America*, Oxford: Berg.

Outtrup, U. and Thomsen, B. R. 1994. 'Mixed messages – mixed feelings: women reading *Cosmopolitan*', unpublished MA dissertation, Denmark: Department of Languages and Culture, Roskilde Universitetscenter.

Payne, V. 1986. '*Working Woman* can exploit a market gap', *Campaign*, 16 May, 12.

Penn World Tables, Mark 5.6 (1950–1992), http://www.nber.org/pwt56.html, accessed 1999.

Piore, M. J. and Sabel, C. F. 1984. *The Second Industrial Divide: Possibilities for Prosperity*, New York: Basic Books.

Polan, B. 1986. 'The alchemy transforming Brampton's mettle into gold for *Elle*', *Campaign*, 19 September, 64.

Political and Economic Planning 1980. 'Sampling surveys – part two', *PEP Report*, vol. 16, no. 314, June, London: Political and Economic Planning.

Pollert, A. 1988. 'Dismantling flexibility', *Capital and Class*, vol. 34, 42–75.

Pook, S. 1999. 'Teenagers' magazine "backs" drug', *Daily Telegraph*, 25 January, 3.

Pratley, N. 1997. 'Emap and *FHM* lads outgun *Loaded*', *Electronic Telegraph*, 18 November.

Price, D. 1997. 'Surveyors and surveyed: photography out and about', in Wells 1997.

Purdom, N. 1996. 'Advertorials: securing write of way from editors', *PR Week*, 3 May, 9.

Ramazanoglu, C., ed., 1993. *Up Against Foucault: Explorations of Some Tensions Between Foucault and Feminism*, London: Routledge.

Rand, A. 1991. 'Analysis of data enables retailers to make decisions affecting their profitability', *Magazine News: Periodicals Barcoding Association Special Supplement*, iv.

Randall, G. 1993. *Principles of Marketing*, London: Routledge.

Rawsthorn, A. 1984. 'What Katy did wrong', *Marketing*, 9 February, 28–31.

Rawsthorn, A. 1985. 'Birth of a stylish UK cousin for the French trendsetter', *Campaign*, 4 October, 34.

Reed, B. S. 1996. 'Women at Hearst magazines: a case study of women in magazine publishing', in Allen, Rush and Kaufman 1996.

Reid, A. 1992. 'Will advertorial formats outlive the recession?', *Campaign*, October, 17.

Reid, A. 1997. 'Spotlight on: Women's magazines: how *Frank* could change the focus of women's magazines', *Campaign*, 19 September, 49.

Reid, A. 1999. 'Cutbacks at *Frank* bode ill for glossy market's small players', *Campaign*, 21 May.

Reid, A. 2000. 'Media spotlight on: Women's magazines', *Marketing*, 3 March, 16.

Restall, C. 1985. 'A breakthrough in the study of women', *Campaign*, 22 November, 26–8.

Richmond, S. 1989. 'What odds on a National winner?', *Campaign*, 18 August.

Robins, J. 2001. 'Mags facing tough times slap on the gloss', *Independent on Sunday*, 15 April, 5.

Robins, K. 1997. 'What in the world's going on?,' in du Gay 1997b.

Roffey, M. 1997. 'For women who get off on rocking, rolling, thinking, grooving and, come to that . . . juggling', *Independent*, 20 October, M7.

Ross, K. 1995. *Fast Cars, Clean Bodies: Decolonization and the Reordering of French Culture*, London: MIT Press.

Rowe, M., ed., 1982. *Spare Rib Reader: 100 Issues of Women's Liberation*, Harmondsworth, Penguin.

Rowthorn, B. 1983. 'The past strikes back', in Hall and Jacques 1983.

Royal Commission on the Press 1977. *Periodicals and the Alternative Press*, London: HMSO.

Rumbelow, H. 1999. 'Supermodels are sent under cover', *The Times*, 6 February, 11.

Sarler, C. 1983. 'How a brash young upstart beat IPC to the bookstalls', *Campaign*, 28 October.

Savage, M., Barlow, J., Dickens, P. and Fielding, T. 1992. *Property, Bureaucracy and Culture: Middle Class Formation in Contemporary Britain*, London: Routledge.

Schlesinger, P. 1989. *Putting 'Reality' Together*, London: Methuen.

Schudson, M. 1991. 'The new validation of popular culture', in Avery and Eason 1991.

Scorah, K. 1990. 'How women's ads are skin deep', *Campaign*, 25 May, 14.

Scott, J. W. 1990. 'Deconstructing equality-versus-difference: or, the uses of poststructuralist theory for feminism', in Hirsch and Keller 1990.

Scott, V. 1989. 'Battle stations', *Campaign*, 24 November, 61–2.

Seymour Marketing Department 2000a. *The Women's Lifestyle/Fashion Sector: Market Sector Report*, London: Periodical Publishers Association.

Seymour Marketing Department 2000b. *The Men's Lifestyle Sector: Market Sector Report*, London: Periodical Publishers Association.

Seymour-Ure, C. 1991. *The British Press and Broadcasting Since 1945*, Oxford: Blackwell.

Shelton, E. 1998. 'Hard to be perfectly *Frank*', *Observer*, 9 May, Business Page 8.

Shoemaker, P. J. and Reese, S. D. 1991. *Mediating the Message*, New York and London: Longman.

Sigal, L. V. 1973. *Reporters and Officials*, Lexington, MA: Lexington Books.

Sked, A. and Cook, C. 1990. *Post-War Britain: A Political History*, 2nd edn. Harmondsworth: Penguin.

Skeggs, B. 1997. *Formations of Class and Gender*, London: Sage.

Slaughter, A. 1984. 'Birth of a new breed of woman', *Campaign*, 5 October, 77–8.

Slaughter, A. 1988. 'A new breed of read?', *The Times*, 23 May, 21.

Spriggs, D. 1997. 'Soap box: using male jokes to reach women is just laughable', *Marketing*, 11 September, 14.

Steiner, L. 1991. 'Oppositional decoding as an act of resistance', in Avery and Eason 1991.

Stephenson, H. and Mory, J. 1990. *Journalism Training in Europe*, Paris: EJTA.

Stewart, C. and Laird, J. 1994. *The European Media Industry: Fragmentation and Convergence in Broadcasting and Publishing*, London: Financial Times.

Storey, J., ed., 1997. *What is Cultural Studies?: A Reader*, London: Arnold.

Stuart, L. 1997. 'EMAP bypasses the media shops', *Marketing Week*, 4 December, 14–15.

Syedain, H. 1992. 'Female touch works in the recession', *Marketing*, 27 February, 21.

Szybillo, G. 1976. 'What administrators should know about the group interview', in Anderson 1976.

Talbot, M. 2000. 'Strange bedfellows: feminism in advertising', in Andrews and Talbot 2000.

Teather, D. 2000. 'IPC flotation abandoned in favour of sale', *Guardian*, 1 May, 18.

Tuchman, G. 1978. *Making News – A Study in the Construction of Reality*, New York: Free Press.

Tuchman, G., Kaplan Daniels. A. and Bénet, J., eds, 1978. *Hearth and Home: Images of Women in the Mass Media*, Oxford: Oxford University Press.

Tunstall, J. 1964. *The Advertising Man in London Advertising Agencies*, London: Chapman and Hall.

Tunstall, J. 1971. *Journalists at Work: Specialist Correspondents: Their News Organizations, News Sources, and Competitor Colleagues*, London: Constable.

Tunstall, J. 1983. *The Media in Britain*, London: Constable.

Tunstall, J. 1993. *Television Producers*, London: Routledge.

US Department of State 1995. *United Kingdom Country Commercial Guide*, Washington, DC: Office of the Co-ordinator for Business Affairs, June.

Usherwood, B. 1997. 'Transnational publishing: the case of *Elle Decoration*', in Nava, Blake, MacRury and Richards 1997.

Viner, K. 1997. 'Glossies for grown-ups', *Guardian*, 21 August, T7.

Walby, S. 1997. *Gender Transformations*, London and New York: Routledge.

Wallsgrove, R. 1982. 'Pornography: between the devil and the true blue Whitehouse', in Rowe 1982.

Wells, L., ed., 1997. *Photography: A Critical Introduction*, London: Routledge.

Wells, W. 1974. 'Group interviewing', in Ferber 1974.

Weymouth, A. and Lamizet, B., eds, 1996. *Markets and Myths: Forces for Change in the Media of Western Europe*, London: Longman.

Whelehan, I. 2000. *Overloaded: Popular Culture and the Future of Feminism*, London, The Women's Press.

Wilkinson, H., Howard, M., with Gregory, S., Hayes, H. and Young, R. 1997. *Tomorrow's Women*, London: Demos.

Williamson, J. 1978. *Decoding Advertisements: Advertising, Ideology and Symbolic Expression*, London: Marion Boyars.

Williamson, J. 1991. 'Second sight: Hello! and what have we here?', *Guardian*, 12 September, 29.

Winship, J. 1978. 'A woman's world: *Woman* – an ideology of femininity', in BCCCS Women's Studies Group 1978.

Winship, J. 1980. 'Advertising in women's magazines, 1956–74', stencilled paper, Centre for Contemporary Cultural Studies, Birmingham: University of Birmingham.

Winship, J. 1981. 'Woman becomes an "individual": femininity and consumption in women's magazines, 1954–1969', stencilled paper, Centre for Contemporary Cultural Studies, Birmingham: University of Birmingham.

Winship, J. 1983a. 'Femininity and women's magazines', in *The Changing Experience of Women*, U221, Milton Keynes: The Open University.

Winship, J. 1983b. '"*Options* – for the way you want to live now", or a magazine for superwoman', *Theory, Culture and Society*, vol. 1, no. 3, 44–65.

Winship, J. 1984. 'Nation before family: *Woman* the national home weekly, 1945–1963', in Formations Editorial Collective 1984.

Winship, J. 1985. '"A girl needs to get streetwise": magazines for the 1980s', *Feminist Review*, no. 21, Winter, 24–46.

Winship, J. 1987. *Inside Women's Magazines*, London and New York: Pandora.

Winship, J. 1991. 'The impossibility of *Best*: enterprise meets domesticity in the practical women's magazines of the 1980s', *Cultural Studies*, vol. 5, no. 2, 131–56.

Winship, J. 2000. 'Women outdoors: advertising, controversy and disputing feminism in the 1990s', *International Journal of Cultural Studies*, vol. 3, no. 1, 27–55.

Wolf, N. 1991. *The Beauty Myth*, London: Vintage.

Wolk, S. 1980. 'Women gain new ad image', *Marketing*, 25 June, 27–30.

Wood, S., ed., 1982. *The Degradation of Work?*, London: Hutchinson.

Yates, K. 1988. 'The pan-European magazine', *Campaign*, 25 September, 7–9.

York, P. 1998. 'Black and white and *Red* all over', *Independent*, 8 March, 20.

York, P. and Barr, A. 1982. *The Official Sloane Ranger Handbook: The First Guide to What Really Matters in Life*, London: Ebury.

INDEX